The Business Internet and Intranets

THE BUSINESS INTERNET AND INTRANETS

A MANAGER'S GUIDE TO KEY TERMS AND CONCEPTS

PETER KEEN, WALID MOUGAYAR, AND TRACY TORREGROSSA

Harvard Business School Press
Boston, Massachusetts

02 01 00 99 98   5 4 3 2 1

Library of Congress Cataloging-in-Publication Data

Keen, Peter G.W.
    The business internet and intranets : a manager's guide to key
    terms and concepts / Peter G.W. Keen, Walid Mougayar, and Tracy
    Torregrossa.
        p.   cm.
    Includes bibliographical references and index.
ISBN 0-87584-820-6. — ISBN 0-87584-840-0 (pbk.)
    1. Industrial management—Computer network resources.
    2. Business enterprises—Communication systems.   3. Internet
    (Computer network)   4. Information networks.   I. Mougayar,
    Walid, 1959–   .   II. Torregrossa, Tracy 1966–   .   III. Title.
HD30.37.K44   1998
004.67'8'024658—dc21   97-28848
                                                                    CIP

The paper used in this publication meets the requirements of the
American National Standard for Permanence of Paper for Printed
Library Materials Z39.49-1984

For my family—Raymonde, Antoine, Sam, and Fred—who is the source of my happiness.

W.M.

To my ever-supportive and fun circle of family and friends, with a special thanks and affection to Jennifer Hunter, without whom I'd be lost (and so would my tickets, laptop, passport, and diary).

P.G.W.K.

To my very special friends Peter and Sherry Keen for literally everything, but most importantly for believing in me; to the most wonderful, loving family for their never-ending encouragement; and to Tom and Kenja for their unconditional support and love.

T.A.T.

Contents

Preface

This book is a business guide to technology. But it's also a technology guide to business. The Internet is a territory that should be viewed from both perspectives—as both an end point and a beginning for managers. It's the end point of the forty year movement of information technology, computers, and telecommunications from the periphery to the center of business focus. The proliferation of personal computers in business today has put information technology in the offices and in the hands of most business people. Already, the Internet has made information technology a huge part of traditional business—in the supply chain, the sales channel, and customer contact, and at the fingertips of potentially anyone, anywhere, anytime.

This pervasiveness makes the Internet a beginning point for business managers. This is the first time in the history of information technology (IT) that business managers have to incorporate IT into their thinking and planning. We're just beginning the early stages of an entirely new style of business and competition. No one can predict its pace or the impacts it may have; it's somewhat like the legendary line in the Sam Goldwyn movie, "Men of the Middle Ages, we're about to begin the Hundred Years War." Managers of the information age, we're about to begin—

what? We aren't exactly sure, but we know that the Internet means business "not as usual." But it definitely means business.

The Business Internet is the fifth in the series of management guides that I have authored or co-authored and that have been published by Harvard Business School Press. My goal for all five has been to help managers use information technology as a business resource. In many ways, this one has been the most difficult of the five to write. From a technology perspective, it involves a new language, new concepts, and, alas, mind-numbing and tongue-tangling new jargon. Much of this jargon and other information is irrelevant to business managers, in that knowing it doesn't in any way help them make more effective plans and decisions about exploiting their own Internet and intranet opportunities. But, as was true with the development of personal computers, there are some key concepts and terms that will migrate into the everyday language of business managers. Vocabulary that arose with the development of PC technology—words such as Windows, hard disk, e-mail, and operating system—is part of everyday language for most people. Helping managers build an equivalent language and understanding of the Internet is difficult because the explosion of new Internet technology and the rate at which it is being introduced into everyday use is occurring much more rapidly than was true with PCs—by the month, rather than by the year.

Nowhere is this more evident than in the massive new industry that is being generated as a direct result of the Internet. It is so volatile and so full of hype that it's impossible to provide a stable guide. Similarly, the young age of the business focus on the Internet makes it hard to identify clear patterns and trends.

These factors have made this management guide a challenge to write. To overcome this challenge, we have tried to focus on the basics. This, perhaps, may have made us somewhat conservative in our assessments and interpretations. On the other hand, it may make our book intensely realistic. No manager needs any more Internet hype, whether about technology or business. Any book that is based on Internet hype will be outdated in months. One grounded in sound analysis and an explanation of basic terms, trends, and impacts will be valid for years, even though the landscape of business, technology, and the Net industry will change in ways, directions, and degrees no one can precisely forecast.

We hope you'll find this to be a guide to the Internet territory that will help you navigate your own or your firm's business path. It's based on a very wide variety of sources and experiences: our individual work with and in companies, an almost non-stop monitoring and review of companies' experiences, and a constant gathering and sifting of examples from current media sources. Above all, this book is based on the answers we discover as we continually ask ourselves the most important question of all—what does this mean for managers?

Peter G.W. Keen

Introduction

We wrote *The Business Internet and Intranets* with the goal that every manager who reads it, browses through it, or uses it for reference will come away feeling that she or he now understands what the Internet is and what it means for *business*. We aim to provide our readers with a good sense of the key technical terms and their *business* relevance, illustrated with apt and vivid examples of the Internet's *business* use and impact. Our readers, we hope, will be convinced that the picture we present is hype-free, reliable, and useful and that we do not push any personal positions or predictions about the Internet.

We designed this Internet business traveler's guide foremost to differentiate between the Internet and the Business Internet. We believe that one of the main reasons managers find it so hard to make sense of the Net is that too often they view it as *the* Internet rather than as a set of diverse constituent spaces. *The* Net is a set of addresses—somebody@somewhere.something. The Business Internet is a space of *relationships* among an ever-growing directory of Internet users.

Having an Internet address makes you a member of a global electronic population; you're "on" the Net. That is equivalent to saying that, because you have a name, a home, and a vote, you are a citizen of the United States. Such membership doesn't say anything about you as an *individual,* different from other individuals. As a citizen you live in many spaces: family, education, work, politics, religion, commerce, and so on. The business space in your life is not the same as, say, the religious space. The institutions you deal with in business and in religion are obviously very different in goals, priorities, values, implicit and explicit contracts, memberships, traditions, and so on. You likely have different priorities and modes of operation yourself, say in your job space as opposed to your leisure space. The same is true with the Internet; as a business space, it differs in character and relationships from a leisure space. In designing business relationships for the Net, many other spaces must, of course, be respected, just as in designing business relationships within communities and neighborhoods.

Our management guide abstracts from the Internet universe —for that is what it has become, a self-contained and ever-expanding electronic universe—to focus specifically on the Business Internet space. Each of the Internet's many spaces opens up entirely new dynamics of relationships. Success in these relationships rests on understanding the nature of and what drives the particular space you focus on. The only common feature across Internet communities is means of access: Anyone with a standard personal computer, a modem that can access an Internet node, and a registered Internet address can enter the relationship space. Internet spaces are independent of location and time zone. The Internet is always open for business, and Sydney is as close as New York or London. The cost of entering the space is very low; in many instances it costs the user nothing. This presents a very different situation from earlier technologies of connection, which tended to have high entry fees. Accessibility opens opportunities for broader relationships across the entire Internet physical space.

Selecting, designing, building, and sustaining relationships is the challenge and opportunity of the Business Internet. We have drawn this conclusion after reviewing hundreds of companies' experiences, both successes and failures, in forging and following Internet strategies. It's not enough to get "on" the Internet: The Internet's population of thirty, forty, or fifty million is not homogeneous. Mere simultaneous presence on the Net will not lead these millions to respond to a firm's offers. The companies that have been most successful in Internet commerce are those that have used its technology to create a combination of three types of relationship.

- *Transaction:* Electronic ordering of goods and services and electronic payments, a market that many firms see as a digital gold mine but one in which relatively few have as yet made money.

- *Information:* Electronic catalogs, news, ads, demonstrations, product updates, company data, contact lists, videos; information ranging from static displays of text to the full range of dynamic multimedia.

- *Interaction:* Electronic links between company and customer, ranging from passive one-way communication by electronic mail to two-way flows of messages to participation (providing feedback to the company about products, design, and so on, to which the firm actively responds) to collaboration.

The common thread among firms experiencing Internet success is that they attend to all of the three parts of the relationship space—Transaction, Information, and Interaction—rather than try to move forward along just one. They create a relationship cube rather than a sliver. (See the illustration in Figure 1.)

Companies taking a sliver approach to the Internet meet with less success than do those building a cube. Firms that base their Internet strategies on exploiting the transaction dimension, for example, via Internet shopping malls, catalogs, and so on, have found the results disappointing. Trying to base a relationship on transactions alone may be self-defeating; potential customers may simply use one of the many Internet search engines (software that can almost instantly locate all or most Web sites containing a given

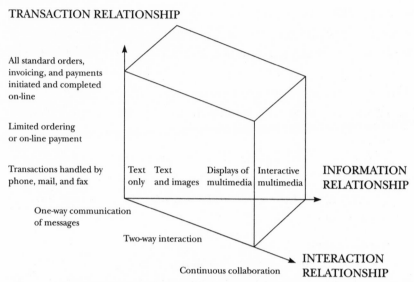

TRANSACTION RELATIONSHIP

Figure 1   The Relationship Cube: Transactions with Rich Information Access and Collaborative Interaction

word or subject) to get a list of firms offering a product and then order from the one with the lowest price. A transaction relationship is basically a commodity relationship. You can find out your competitors' prices. They monitor yours. They try to match your deal and vice versa. Figure 2 illustrates this sliver.

Further, despite claims that the Internet is fundamentally an information cornucopia, many companies have found that the information relationship, too, cannot by itself generate business for them. Their Web pages may get many hits each day, but these don't translate into orders for the goods and services offered. In some instances, this lack of connection results when the information page requires customers to pick up the phone or switch to a transaction page containing complex electronic forms. Many potential customers don't bother with the phone and browse elsewhere.

The Interaction approach obviously builds relationships, but the firm must determine the goal of such relationships. Just

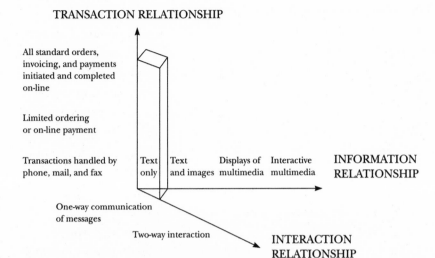

TRANSACTION RELATIONSHIP

All standard orders, invoicing, and payments initiated and completed on-line

Limited ordering or on-line payment

Transactions handled by phone, mail, and fax

Text only | Text and images | Displays of multimedia | Interactive multimedia

INFORMATION RELATIONSHIP

One-way communication of messages

Two-way interaction

INTERACTION RELATIONSHIP

Continuous collaboration

Figure 2 A Relationship Sliver: Impersonal Transactions with Limited Information Access and No Interaction

opening up lines of communication may or may not build value for both parties. The following two examples show how encouraging interaction can lead to negative rather than positive business impacts.

Volvo used to have a feedback area on its Web site that invited people to offer opinions and comments. The company quickly discontinued it. Dissatisfied customers were leaving complaints about their cars and about the poor service they received from their dealers or from Volvo itself. The messages often ended with the query "What are you going to do about it?" According to Volvo's lawyers, such messages might be *legally* interpreted under many states' "lemon" laws as formal notification of problems. If Volvo accepted the messages, as its very invitation that customers send electronic mail via its Web site implied it would, Volvo would need to catalog, file, and respond to the complaints under those laws. The lawyers' advice was not to accept any complaints—which meant not reading any of the mail. Once read, Volvo couldn't "unread" it, but would have to treat it as a complaint. Now the site provides a feature headed "For More Information" that does not include space for comments.

In a second example, one large retailer used a company called CareerMosaic to put information about job openings on the Net. It expected to get resumes, which it did, but it also received many electronic mail complaints from customers asking how they could get refunds or return goods. Internet analyst Jim Sterne summarized the lesson: "CareerMosaic dutifully forwarded these missives to the merchant. If you have a Web site, people will use it for customer service even if you don't want them to."[1]

Each dimension of the Internet business relationship space has many components, the handling of which will affect customer satisfaction. A few of these are listed here:

- *Transaction:* Reliability, security, guarantees, payment mechanism, availability of goods, cost.
- *Information:* Relevance, responsiveness, privacy, support.
- *Interaction:* Ease of access, promptness of reply, perceived honesty, openness.

While none of these are unfamiliar to relationships in any business environment, locating the relationship in Internet space adds to the customary people element involved in their realization—attitude, expectation, and emotion—technical elements unique to the Net, such as software design, service access, computer operating systems, and software and hardware capabilities. In addition, in face-to-face transactions and ones handled by phone or mail, people feel comfortable, on the basis of their experience, familiarity with the organization and/or process, and laws of consumer protection. Today, only a fraction of consumers have comparable experience, familiarity, and a sense of safety on the Net. The relationship has to be built, almost from scratch.

Building an Internet Web site should be viewed as the means to the end of building people relationships, not as a technical end in itself. But both elements must mesh. Designing relationships requires careful attention to the targeted customer as well as to the technology. Both have to be kept in balance, and they must be allowed to interact with each other. A key issue for any company aiming to sell goods and services over the Internet, for instance, is security, a complex technical issue. Without evidence that the firm uses the best technical tools to encrypt (code) credit card information, most people will not feel safe giving their card number over the Net, a complex emotional issue. But even when assured of total security, users may or may not respond to the firm's offers. The lack of response may reflect technical weaknesses in the design and operation of the site; for example, it may strike users as too slow to download, awkward to navigate, or cluttered with irritating and distracting "eye candy." More often, though, the failure to reach consumers reflects a misunderstanding about the Internet's inhabitants: Internet demographics differ significantly from those of the wider population, to the extent that what works, say, in a store may be a dud on the Net.

The Demographics of the Internet

One reason for the wide gap between companies' expectations of massive revenues from the Internet and the embarrassingly small orders they report is the demographics of the Total Internet—our phrase for the total community of somebodies@somewhere.something. As many commentators note, firms shouldn't be surprised that in the last few years the main traffic by far on the Internet has been pornography and that on-line consumer shopping has to date been little more than a dribble: Until recently, around 70 percent of Internet users were male students, technical professionals, and researchers, many of them in the adolescent nerd category. Women account for about 70 percent of all U.S. shopping, but they account for only around 30 percent of the Internet potential customer base. These figures are changing but, as explained below in the glossary entry "Demographics," Internet survey data and estimates are highly volatile and largely unreliable, mainly due to the rapid growth and change of the Net; the variable number of people, from one to thousands, who may be using a single Internet address; and the lack of any central organization to coordinate and manage the Internet. *Business Week* reported in 1997 that women constitute 41 percent of World Wide Web users.[2] But that figure applies only to the United States and only to the Web, admittedly two of the main subsets of the total Net. It does not indicate extent of use, which can range from the "netizen," who spends much of any given day surfing the Net, handling e-mail, joining in non-Web discussion groups, and frequenting sites they have "bookmarked," to the occasional user who happens upon sites by accident or while browsing the Net.

Companies have learned that just putting up an Internet transaction service or a few web information pages will not create customer relationships. They must, rather, learn about the person accessing the site. A whole mini-industry has grown up to track patterns of Web use and build profiles to help companies customize offerings. Many companies send "cookies" to users' hard disks when they access their Web sites—that is, small pieces of software capture information about the user and store it so that when the user next accesses the site, the system will know the person, any previous purchases, how they were paid for, and so on. The Web site software can then customize its ads and offers to particular customers, and the firm will, in some instances, sell the cookie data to other companies, with an effect similar to the junk mail that results when credit card companies and magazine publishers sell data about their customers.

Cookies are a small instance of the much broader issue of trust. Cookies are both a positive and negative element in relationship-building on the Business Internet: They are positive in that they can be used to enhance the Interaction relationship, but they are very negative in that they represent a covert invasion of privacy. If you occasionally surf the Net out of curiosity just to see what all the fuss over pornography is about (as probably 99.9 percent of Internet users have at some time), would you feel safe if you knew that without your being informed a cookie has recorded the pictures you downloaded and that the Web site can legally pass on that information to virtually anyone?

The Trust Economy

The Business Internet is not part of a growing information economy: It is part of an emerging trust economy. Looking back over the mainstream of business innovation over the past forty years, we see three very distinct phases in the evolution of the trust economy: the quality movement, customer service movement, and now the relationship movement. The most far-reaching opportunity for the Business Internet lies in accelerating this historical progress. The quality movement basically resulted from consumers' loss of trust in products. American companies fell behind Japanese firms—most prominently Toyota in car manufacturing and Sony in consumer electronics—that had explicitly and aggressively made quality their total commitment. Consumers picked the high-quality Japanese products over American ones, even when they had to pay premium prices. Often, however, they got both a better product *and* a better price. Total quality management was a sustained—if belated—campaign by U.S. companies to rebuild trust. Firms such as Motorola made quality their brand. Xerox, which had created the market for photocopiers but lost its commanding position to Japanese competitors, had to retool its entire business, using quality as the driver in design and manufacturing. Customers received unconditional guarantees: They could return a product without giving any reason. Xerox's message: "You can trust our product."

The customer service movement focused on building trust in the transaction. Retailers such as Wal-Mart overtook Sears, K-mart and other erstwhile leaders, using quality service—achieved through a combination of culture and attitude, technology used in inventory control and replenishment, pricing and guarantees of everyday low pricing—as a lever. Wal-Mart's message: "We make you feel welcome and comfortable" (Wal-Mart famously instituted a greeter in each of its stores); "We keep our promises" (advertised goods will be in stock); and "We offer consistent low prices" (an item sold for $10 on Thursday won't be marked down to $7.95 on Saturday).

Banks and insurance providers belatedly realized that they knew little about their customers and too often provided them service with a scowl. Having built their strategies mainly on products, they had little knowledge of customers. Bank branches were too often uninviting places with long lines to get at one's own money and intimidating approaches to loan officers' desks. Claims processors at insurance firms worked in back offices at lower pay than did front office sales, underwriting, and broking employees. But a comparison of the TV ads of the late 1970s versus the late 1980s shows a shift from "Bank at X for the best interest rate—we've been in business for a hundred years" to jingly tunes, smiling faces, and the claim "You have a friend at Bank Z." Some of this was window-dressing, but it signaled that customer service was taking center stage rather than being treated as an add-on to the really important stuff.

Hotels, airlines, and many other service firms starting making the customer the center of their business universes. Training programs focused on customer service as urgent, unconditional, and a core value. British Airway's turnaround from being known as Bloody Awful and "winning" awards as Britain's most hated company was strongly driven by its huge "Putting Customers First" training effort. Marriott made service its differentiator and staff training and incentives for service its competitive lever.

The service phase in the emergence of the trust economy coincided and intertwined with the shift of information technology—computers and telecommunications—from the back office, head office, and plant operations to just about every point of customer contact. In the product trust phase, IT was used mainly for operational applications, such as inventory management, company-supplier electronic links for ordering, engineering design, manufacturing process control, project management, and collection and analysis of data for statistical quality control. In the service phase, IT was used more and more to add customer convenience and to make it easy to deal with the firm: ATM machines on the corner, in the airport, and in the office building lobby; 1-800 phone numbers for customer information, placing orders, and getting account balances; online data bases for customer service agents to access and respond immediately to inquiries; and twenty-four hour telephone airline reservation service.

By the early 1990s, quality and service had increased very substantially across most industries (though cost and pricing pressures have recently led many airlines and retailers to cut back on staff and training, at the expense of service). Today, quality and service are taken for granted, with their absence rather than their presence arousing notice. We take it for granted that the ATM will be up or that we can return Christmas presents to stores. American cars are no longer likely to be lemons, and we can pick a leading maker's product almost at random and be confident it won't have warranty problems or the loose doors, incorrectly installed parts, and faulty electronics all too common in the 1970s. We know that Federal Express will deliver packages on time and that McDonald's will provide consistent product and service. (Even McDonald's can miss its mark, however. In a spring 1997 marketing promotion, the 100 million beanie babies it had ordered to give away with Happy Meals fell far short of demand; customers were even taking the beanie baby and leaving the food at the counters.) Confidence, safety, and reliability—the hallmarks of the product quality and customer service revolution—have set new levels of trust.

What happens when all competitors offer comparably high standards of product and service? Trust becomes the norm, not the exception, and it doesn't offer competitive differentiation. Television ads for the Infiniti line of cars offer an example. A tall, balding British actor, dressed all in black, highlights some minor feature of the black and white car shown in artistic shots and rambles on about the Infiniti ethos. What he really seems to be saying is "Look, the Infiniti's a fine car. So are the cars made by its competitors. They're all good value. You can trust them. So all I can do is hope this neat piece of video makes our car stand out in your mind."

Similarly, banks today can't do much to differentiate their products and services. They all have ATMs. They all match one another's special prices for car loans or cuts in mortgage interest rates. If you have a bad experience with a bank, you can quickly move your account to another one. You don't even need to go to the bank now for most services. Applications for car loans can be processed electronically in the auto dealer's office, with no advantage to the consumer in going to a bank. Sixty percent of all consumer loans are now held by the financial subsidiaries of General Motors and Ford. USAA, the insurance firm that has been the pacesetter in customer service and in the use of information technology over the last decade, can process and approve a car loan, fax the authorization, issue the insurance policy, and update police and department of motor vehicle agency records in as little as five minutes. Full-service banking is offered by security brokers and mutual fund providers; Fidelity Investments, for instance, can be your bank without having any bank branches.

In this situation, firms increasingly realized—a few years before the Internet took off as a low cost, easy-to-access, easy-to-use resource for anyone@anyplace.anything—that the new source of differentiation now lay in relationship-building. *The Internet adds a new technology base for this and adds momentum to a major business shift already well under way.* The following examples illustrate the range of relationship-building innovations.

- A shift from marketing to new customers to retaining existing ones; financial services estimate that increasing retention by 5 percent increases operating profits by 95 percent.
- Frequent flier or buyer programs and loyalty cards with the goal of rewarding customers for long-term

relationships rather than merely offering them a one-time deal.

- Customization; a common practice for many companies today of targeting products, information, and offers to individuals who have specific patterns of purchase, specific characteristics and demographics, and known interests. Customers are no longer considered anonymous statistics. *Mass customization* aims at combining economies of scale in manufacturing, distribution, and standardization—mass—with personalization in selling, service, and support—customization.

- Data mining; companies use credit card information, point of sale data, customer records, and anything else of pertinence in the firm's data "warehouses"—its mass of computer data bases—to understand the dynamics of customer behavior and to personalize and customize products and services.

- Interaction; firms are following another cliché, "get close to the customer," in every way they can. Private banking, the privilege of the ultra-rich in the 1970s, today is offered to the affluent: a single point of contact—a real person—handles all relationships with the bank, knows the customer as an individual, and responds to the customer's personal needs. When you phone firms such as Dell Computer and American Airlines, where the staff is friendly, courteous, knowledgeable, and well-informed, you interact with a person. When you handle the same transaction with some of their competitors, at which the staff is less well-trained and informed, you'll note and remember the difference.

Relationships rest on trust. The Internet has made new relationships possible—basically with anyone with a personal computer anywhere in the world who can make a local phone call. It can also block relationships; most consumers do not yet trust it for purchases. Trust and safety are now the two single most important issues for the growth of Internet commerce. Because it is so open and uncontrolled and because it enables relationships with people and entities who, literally, may be anywhere and anyone, security, privacy, the nature of contracting, and safety constrain consumer acceptance and hence business use of the Net. Many people, for instance, are unwilling to make credit card transactions on the World Wide Web, even though it's far more secure than giving their card number over the phone or handing it to a waiter who then disappears into another room. The Net may be secure, but its users don't feel safe.

Just about every commentator agrees that until consumers believe their credit cards are safe, the Internet will not take off as a base for mass market sales. Looked at from a technical perspective, the Internet is pretty safe. From a *relationship* perspective, however secure it may be, many users do not feel safe. This is further illustrated by the refusal by many Internet users to fill out electronic forms that ask them to identify themselves. A survey reported in February 1997 that a fifth of the respondents, all of whom use the Net regularly, either immediately leave a Web site that asks for their name, address, and phone number or lie when they answer the questions. Other surveys have reported that over half of all Web users display this behavior, indicating that most users, and 20 percent of the experts, don't trust the Web.

Trust is the currency of the Business Internet. It has many elements, such as contractual protection, privacy, security, and reliability of service (today, by far the weakest area of Internet performance). But of far more impact is confidence in and value from the relationship itself. Trust, of course, is important in all relationships, but it seems to be the essence of those in the Business Internet space, partly because it involves the risk of dealing with new situations via a new medium that is inherently unstructured, unmanaged, and unregulated. Outside the Internet, electronic relationships have always been very manageable. Contract law, regulation, consumer protection law, liability law, and industry practice ensure requisite trust, though, of course, the threat exists of fraud and of litigation when the trust systems break down. Electronic commerce in business-to-business relationships similarly has a well-defined trust boundary. Electronic data interchange—computer-to-computer handling of purchase orders, invoicing, inventory management, and distribution and related logistical functions—works through trading partner agreements. Electronic payment systems for funds transfers, letters of credit, and cash management move trillions of dollars per day through telecommunications networks with amazingly few court cases, errors, or newspaper headlines. Copyright laws are well-established for print, music, and film.

Almost every element of these trust mechanisms is either made invalid, suspect, unenforceable, or of limited applicability as the Internet expands in terms of geographic reach, number, and variety of users in many different countries constituting many different legal jurisdictions. The electronic relationship adds new risks compared with traditional customer-business equivalents, most obviously financial risk, such as credit card fraud, invasion of privacy, and the problem of doing business with a party that exists only as an Internet address. Most problems can be solved; however, some are mere worries. The estimated fraud in Internet commercial transactions, for example, is less than one dollar per thousand, just about half that for credit cards. But just about every survey shows that risk is uppermost in consumers' minds when they consider using the Internet for purchases or even filling out forms that ask for personal information.

Opening Up the Business Relationship Box

Despite the perception of risk, consumers are using the Web in growing numbers. They increasingly access companies' Web sites, and more and more companies see the Internet as a means of offering something of value. Problems with Internet security, un-

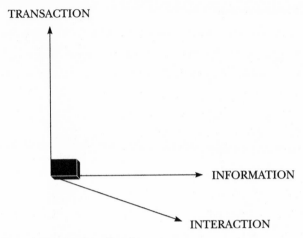

TRANSACTION

INFORMATION

INTERACTION

Figure 3 The Organization Box*

*The figure represents transactions conducted by mail, phone, and fax; the firm's systems can be accessed only internally. Information is limited to printed publications and interaction to traditional "channels."

reliability, and traffic overloads are offset by its ability to open up what we term the business relationship box. In the 1980s and even into the early 1990s, a small firm's information technology base tended to be a closed box, as illustrated in Figure 3.

In "box" organizations, as Figure 3 demonstrates, transactions that are processed electronically, such as orders, invoices and payments, are sent to the organization but not to the organization's information technology systems. Transactions may come in by mail, phone, or fax, and the information must be entered into the systems and output documents mailed to relevant parties.

Throughout the 1980s and 1990s, this organizational box has been opening more and more through increased use of electronic data interchange and payment systems. Transactions are handled directly through computer-to-computer links. *Electronic commerce* (EC) has emerged as an umbrella term for these developments. EC has grown at close to 20 percent a year for well over a decade, and its benefits have been substantial, to the degree that EDI (Electronic Data Interchange) and FEDI (Financial Electronic Data Interchange) are close to becoming essential requirements for well-run firms. It is difficult to see how any firm today could operate productively without reliable telephone systems, fax machines, and personal computers. Electronic commerce is close to being just as essential. Below are a few examples:

- *Automotive industry:* Processing and administrative costs per truck shipment have been cut from an average of $61 to $6 by eliminating paper documents and invoices, using instead EDI documents to match order to delivery.

- *Digital Equipment Corporation:* Procurement lead times dropped by 30 percent and inventory levels by 90 percent between 1987 and 1993, by using EDI for over $4 billion per year of procurement of materials, supplies, and services.

- *Thermo King:* Order costs were cut from $50 to $10 for twenty thousand spare parts items. "Hard" savings were achieved of $3.4 million in stocking costs and release of $4.9 million of cash from reduced inventory for a firm with $65 million sales.

- *General Electric:* Materials inventory was cut from 7 to 2.5 weeks supply and suppliers' inventory was reduced by half. Material lead times dropped from sixty to ten days and the cost of a purchase order from $52 to $12.

- *Pacific Bell:* Purchase cycle time was cut by thirteen days through the use of basic EDI, another seventeen days by adding advanced shipment electronic notices and bar coding, and yet another thirteen days by adding electronic funds transfers.

- *Grocery industry surveys:* Before EDI, almost 30 percent of supplier invoices were "in dispute" because of some processing error. With EDI, the figure is close to zero.

- *Texas Instruments:* EDI was linked to bar coding for tracking office supplies, freeing up 40,000 square feet of warehouse space worth close to a million dollars a year;

reducing inventory by $2 million and cycle time from three days to one; and cutting error rates from one in every twenty-five orders to one in ten thousand.

- *IBM, Fishkill, New York:* Savings included consolidation of 7700 orders per year to 970 for the same volume of goods; and reduction from 718 to 8 suppliers, with an average of 9 percent price cut in return for volumes, a 6 percent error rate for incoming shipments cut to close to zero, and 65 percent savings in inventory carrying costs.

- *EDI:* The EDI Group survey of 1,560 EDI users in the United States, conducted in 1994, showed error rates cut from 10 percent to 4 percent post-EDI, and cycle time reduced by an average 40 percent.

- *Car dealers:* A survey of one hundred dealers revealed that the time needed to process paper-based car loan applications was cut from one or two weeks to as little as one minute, with 25 percent of the applications requiring no human intervention.

EDI technology creates what may be termed the trading partner box, illustrated in Figure 4.

Despite all these benefits and despite its impressive growth rate, relatively few companies have implemented electronic commerce; most surveys conclude that around 150,000 of the more than ten million firms in the United States are EDI-enabled and that most banks can handle only simple funds transfers, not the full range of FEDI services. The main reasons for the slow adoption of electronic commerce have been the financial and organizational costs of investment. Limitations in the available technology have meant that while a firm can open up the organizational box to reach out into the space of customers, suppliers, and trading partners (such as banks, insurers, distributors, and so on), the parties had to implement specific types of telecommunications links, software, and, often, hardware. Costs of the technology base for the trading partner box have been declining, including

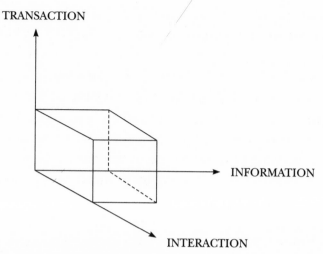

TRANSACTION

INFORMATION

INTERACTION

Figure 4   The Trading Partner Box*

*The figure represents online transactions for electronic interchange, but only with specific organizations using specific technology. Information includes online catalogs and databases, and interaction is via e-mail.

both the initial investment required and operating expenses, while reliability has been increasing, but both concerns still limit the number of EDI relationships possible. The following elements are some among the many needed by all parties in an electronic trading network.

- *Telecommunications:* Special-purpose networks are required to handle the transmission of large volumes of computer data quickly and efficiently; the standard phone system, designed for voice transmission only, is inadequate. Large companies invest in "private" high-speed leased lines. Value-added networks, resources shared by and linking companies within an industry, have become the workhorses of electronic data interchange. Internationally, the government-directed or government-owned telephone monopolies offer public data networks. No simple, low-cost, fast system exists for establishing the telecommunications capability needed for electronic data interchange. The technology and its costs improved dramatically in the early 1990s, driven by technical innovation and industry deregulation, but small companies still cannot easily and quickly link to large firms for electronic commerce transactions.

- *Software:* The software needed for EDI is inexpensive and widely available; it mainly handles the translation of, say, a purchase order from the format used by the sending firm to that of the receiving firm, via what amounts to electronic dictionaries that name, define, and transpose key terms in the message. Individual companies, however, must provide the software that sends and receives messages from the EDI translation software. Links are needed between systems and databases, a complex process even for firms with experience in electronic commerce and a nightmare for small and inexperienced ones.

- *Hardware:* Efficient electronic operations require many add-on hardware devices to manage traffic flow, security, and network control. This hardware—including servers, firewalls, hubs, routers, and so on—can turn a $3,000 personal computer into a $30,000 computer department.

- *Organizational procedures:* The need for training, support, business process analysis, and design as well as new audit and control procedures greatly increase when a company opens up its organizational relationship box. Electronic data interchange, despite being relatively simple technically, requires radical IT-centered organizational and process change that rarely comes easily.

- *Industry procedures:* EDI and FEDI rest on agreements on terms and procedures that permit the automatic, fast, reliable, easy translation from one company's data and document formats to another's. The pace of agreement, adoption, and standardization varies greatly across industries, as does the pace of development of the needed expertise.

The Internet is a natural extension of today's electronic commerce because it removes most of the above hurdles. Most obviously, it provides the telecommunications links between trading partners, without requiring large capital investments and at far smaller operating costs; this brings just about any company into the relationship space, right down to the smallest business. Second, when operating EDI via the Internet, the only *essential* hardware is a standard personal computer; in practice, much additional hardware is needed for large-scale electronic commerce operations, but it can be supplied by the service provider, including existing value-added networks, acting as the parties' Internet address or link.

The Internet reduces hardware and software costs for many business-to-business electronic commerce transactions, because all that is needed is a PC that can send an Internet-formatted message to the relevant Internet address, which provides the additional hardware and software needed for processing. The use of easy to learn and use browsers, such as Netscape Navigator and Microsoft Explorer, also reduces most of the need for training.

Use of the Internet thus opens up the trading partner box. Among the many advantages of the Total Internet space for electronic business commerce are the following:

- The Internet is unbounded. Obviously, the space is not infinite, but as yet its limits are unknown. It's fully practical for NASA to add an Internet link to a robot landed on the surface of Mars—see Mars@NASA.org. A camera, television set, car cellular phone, or even a coffee pot may be an Internet address. As more and more personal computers in foreign nations are able or permitted (many national governments try to control its use for political or religious reasons) to access the Net, any firm has the opportunity to extend its relationships by reaching out to them.

- The Internet is heterogeneous. It does not require that users have specific types of hardware or software. Without the Internet, it would be difficult, expensive, and often impossible in practice to link, for example, a Macintosh device to an electronic commerce resource built on the UNIX operating system. Internet access devices present no known restrictions or limitations in terms of geographic location, demographics of users, media type employed, tools used for access, or minimum and maximum size of user organization.

- The Internet is geography-independent in terms of cost. Today, the Internet is virtually free. Users are not charged by volume of messages; most ISPs (Internet Service Providers) and such online services as AOL have adopted a fixed price strategy of $10 to $30 per month for unlimited use. That will almost certainly change: It is likely, as the Internet becomes flooded with traffic to the point that it nears collapse, that usage rates will be set to optimize the flow of traffic at peak times, with a premium paid for priority and immediate service. (Pacific Bell, for example, the local phone company providing phone service in California, complains that local systems, designed for calls lasting an average of three minutes, cannot handle the huge new volumes of Internet traffic, with users online for an average twenty minutes or more.) What will not change, though, is what the *Economist* magazine calls "the death of distance" in telecommunications. New telephone technologies and falling rates and fixed pricing for long-distance are making telecommunications increasingly affordable around the world. Long distance phone rates have always been distance- and geography-dependent. Phoning

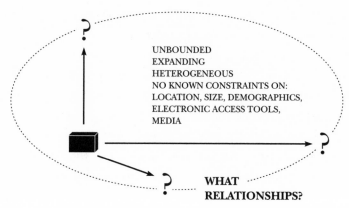

UNBOUNDED
EXPANDING
HETEROGENEOUS
NO KNOWN CONSTRAINTS ON:
LOCATION, SIZE, DEMOGRAPHICS,
ELECTRONIC ACCESS TOOLS,
MEDIA

WHAT
RELATIONSHIPS?

Figure 5   The Internet Space

between Boston and Los Angeles entailed a higher rate per minute than calling between Boston and New York. Calling London from Boston cost even more than phoning LA, even though the distance is roughly the same. We say "cost" rather than "costs" because the Internet, competition among telecommunications service providers, and accelerating innovations in telecommunications technology have led long distance phone companies to offer fixed cost prices—Sprint's 10 cent a minute rate advertised nationally on TV in late 1996 has been followed by MCI and AT&T offering deals for as little as 6 cents, regardless of distance. If Internet charges had been geography-dependent, we might be calling the Web the U.S.-Wide Web, not the World Wide Web.

Figure 5 shows the resulting opportunity: No organizational electronic relationship box and no trading partner relationship box—just an open space. The challenge and opportunity now for any firm will be to answer the question: With whom do you want to build an electronic relationship and how will you do it?

An essential caveat: The Internet extends, it cannot replace today's electronic commerce. Value-added networks, although more expensive, offer many features that today's Internet cannot match, including reliability, customer support and service, and software and security. For all the euphoria about the Net's promise, a highly credible body of expertise challenges the notion of its inevitable take-over of electronic commerce. One voice of caution belongs to Robert Metcalf, inventor of the Ethernet local area network "protocol" that is the telecommunications equivalent of the liberation of the personal computer from the mainframe in its liberation of communications from expensive wide area networks (spanning wide geographic distances). Metcalf played a major role in the evolution of the Internet and was for many years its enthusiastic advocate. Now, he's a pessimist, even forecasting the Net's collapse. Here is a summary of his concerns.

- *Investment:* The flurry of IPOs (initial public offerings) made several firms rich, most obviously Yahoo! and Netscape. Investors paid a premium for companies that have no earnings and that, in some cases, may never have any. Will this excess of enthusiasm generate a backlash, drying up new funds? The Internet needs large, continuing investment in services, support, and improved telecommunications, most of which must come from private investment.

- *Digital cash:* The cost of handling electronic payment transactions will turn out to be far higher than proponents of innovations such as digital cash (a new, widely accepted electronic currency) predict, making unlikely fulfillment of expectations that the Web will become a mass market for small purchases. Without low-cost electronic cash, micropayments of a few cents or less for items such as electronic newspapers or snippets of data will be impossible since handling the electronic payment will cost more than the initial purchase.

- *Advertising payoff:* Advertisers will not invest large sums on the Web until they see results and get reliable measures of audience size and audience response. They will be deterred by reports that most people don't even look at the ads that come up on their PC screens.

- *Phone companies:* Local telephone systems are already becoming overloaded with Internet traffic, and the hitherto monopolistic and monolithic behemoths will be slow and reluctant to add new capacity to meet demand.

- *Security:* In the future, well-publicized security breaches will be inevitable. The resulting furor will increase consumers' and companies' already high levels of concern about the Net's safety, and they will back off from trusting and using it.

- *Technical incompatibilities:* The Web's success was due to its ease of use and the standardization that allowed any computer to access any other and any browser to obtain any information. Technical innovations and market competition among firms such as Microsoft and Netscape threaten standardization. Each company aims to establish its own products as the standard, thus creating many incompatibilities, especially in multimedia.

- *Privacy:* Security breaches (such as theft of electronic mail and data) and misuse of information (such as tracking users' purchases or the political and sexually-centered discussion groups they join) will make the Web's openness in the future its weakest point, just as it is now its strongest.

- *Politics:* Many right wingers see the Net as a political and social issue demanding regulation, especially of pornography. Many radicals also see it in political terms, seeking to use it as a platform for espousing libertarian, antigovernment and antiauthority views. The public fight will increase and will affect the reputation and freedom of the Net.

These concerns originate with one of the people most knowledgeable about the Internet. Metcalf's public airing of his views is tinged with journalistic provocation, and most commentators discount his pessimism about the Web's future, especially his belief that it is close to collapsing. (Metcalf said he'd eat his words if the Web didn't collapse by 1997. He did eat them at an Internet conference in April 1997, but he stuck to his prediction.) But a 1996 report from Morgan Stanley weighing Metcalf's position summarizes the situation nicely: "Do we think that all these problems will appear? No. Will some? Yes. It's just tough to predict which and when, although the likeliest problems, we believe, will relate to security and capacity."[3]

The Internet as Relationship Space

The Internet contains many relationship spaces—for example, the Education, Entertainment, and Political Internets, to name just a few—all differing in terms of communities, priorities, values and interests, and the Internet tools and services they rely on. This makes it dangerous to generalize from one space to another or to assume, for instance, that explosive growth in the flow of information across the Education Internet means a corresponding increase in business purchases of goods and services. It's even more dangerous to assume that the sheer size of the physical Internet translates to market size and that growth in its use translates into business growth.

Firms basing their Business Internet strategies on what they see happening on the Total Internet are almost sure to make increasingly expensive mistakes because the specific, constituent relationship spaces differ so greatly. The Political Internet, for example, is driven by debate and information-sharing, with Internet Usenet discussion group forums as the main vehicle for this. Political groups from the extreme left to the extreme right demand freedom of expression on the Net and are largely very opposed to any idea of outside control over it. For the Business

Internet space, Usenet is of minimal interest and value, but security, and in many instances new regulations and laws for controlling transactions and payments, are as vital as they are antithetical to the users on the Political Internet.

The Education Internet similarly places a premium on access to information and open communication. Its community tolerates the many traffic jams on the Net that prevent access to particular servers at peak times, but it is very sensitive to cost, to the degree that most of its members will not pay even a few cents for information, because for them the Internet has for years been a source of free data to be browsed for and downloaded. By contrast, the Business Internet community must have reliable and immediate service, for which it is generally willing to pay a premium, and it is looking to sell some information as well as to give some away.

The Entertainment Internet focuses on multimedia, with very few financial transactions; for its community, multimedia tools are central, as are issues of cost, time demands, and quality in downloading music and video; they require massive bandwidth (the basic measure of telecommunications carrying capacity, measured in bits per second). Multimedia demands far more bandwidth than today's standard phone lines can provide. By contrast, most Business Internet transactions use low bandwidth, and to date the rule of thumb has been to minimize any multimedia traffic, such as video, that will slow down the interaction between company and customer.

The differences between Internet spaces are—not can be, but *are*—extreme. This is demonstrated by two unrelated concerns widely voiced in the mid-1990s. As a business manager, as a citizen, or as a parent, would you *at the very same time* (1) actively seek to preserve the legal rights of pedophiles to use the Internet to proselytize and contact children while being protected from government and police interference in doing so, and (2) equally actively object to any form of commercial advertising on the

Internet, to the extent of joining a worldwide venture to drive it off the Net? Almost certainly not. Yet, many people on the Internet are ready to organize as a community in support of their own values of, first, freedom for the Net from any form of censorship and, second, preservation of its non-commercial nature.

In 1996, a local prosecutor in Bavaria, Germany, ordered the national telecommunications company, Deutsche Telekom, and the U.S.–based online information service, CompuServe, to remove access to bulletin boards and discussion groups that contained sexual material. (Many CompuServe subscribers use it as a gateway to connect to the Internet.) The prosecutor was explicitly concerned with the protection of minors. CompuServe's solution was clumsy; the firm installed software that scanned the system looking for words such as *breast,* inadvertently censoring several women's discussion groups about breast cancer. In any case, within a few days, volunteers had set up more than two hundred mirror sites on the World Wide Web to provide copies of the censored material. (CompuServe's actions did not settle the matter. In April 1997, the Bavarian state prosecutor indicted the head of its German operations on charges of aiding the dissemination of child pornography and permitting access to games containing images, forbidden under German law, of Hitler and of Nazi swastikas.)

By contrast with this immediate response by netizens (Internet citizens) against a threat to free speech, when two lawyers in 1994 broadcast an electronic mail message across many of the Internet's UseNet discussion groups (a practice called "spamming") advertising their services, the mainstream Internet community was outraged. Again on a volunteer basis, people went to great lengths to organize a campaign of vilification against the pair, overloading their Internet access service provider's computer with so many abusive messages that it could not handle the overload and canceled the lawyers' subscription.

The Internet is highly differentiated. But it is also a space with a strong anti-business bias. The following quotation from Daniel

Burstein and David Kline, writing in their book *Road Warriors,* captures this quality well.

> *Free. Egalitarian. Decentralized. Ad hoc. Open and peer-to-peer. Experimental. Autonomous. Anarchic.* These words make up the lexicon of the cyberspace frontier, and it is remarkable how closely they parallel those which once described America's last frontier, the Old West of the nineteenth century. . . . Notice, however, how sharply these words contrast with the hard-headed vocabulary of business and commerce: *For profit. Hierarchical. Systematized. Planned. Proprietary. Pragmatic. Accountable. Organized and Reliable.* There is more than simple word play here. There appears, in fact, to be a core conflict of values between the basic nature of the Internet and the demands of organized, large-scale commerce. One side or the other must give.[4]

It seems more accurate to say that both sides must coexist. But businesses need to recognize that Internet business is not business on the Total Internet in terms of values, priorities, interests, or, above all, relationships.

The Size of the Business Internet Market

The Total Internet can be bewildering and elusive in its ever-expanding size, its rate of growth, the variety of its uses and users, the claims and hype advanced on its behalf, its technology, and the innovations it has made possible. Claims, opinions, and experts abound, but few guidelines exist for separating the reliable and informed from the fanciful and hopeful. Reliable information on Internet trends and usage is hard to find and usually out of date even as it is being collected. Just how little *basic* data we have is shown by figures from six studies published between February and July 1996, in which estimates of the number of Internet users in the United States vary by 600 percent.

- Morgan Stanley: eight million
- Computer Intelligence Infocorp: fifteen million
- Hoffman/Novak: seventeen million

- Louis Harris: twenty-nine million

- Intelliquest: thirty-five million

- Wirthin Worldwide: forty-two million

Adding to this confusion are two surveys that conclude that the Internet *worldwide* has either twenty-three or twenty-six million users.[5] If this were the case, U.S. usage would be either as low as 35 percent of the total or as high as 180 percent of the world total—clearly impossible conclusions. Combining the results of these surveys yields the graph in Figure 6.

Looking at the available data, we can provide our readers with an absolutely reliable forecast about the future of business on the Internet: *By 2000, it will be somewhere between zero and infinity.* That's hardly a helpful statement, but it is about all that businesses today have to go on when setting their Internet strategies. They can be assured that it will continue to grow; they know that few companies have yet found a way to make money through it, despite the

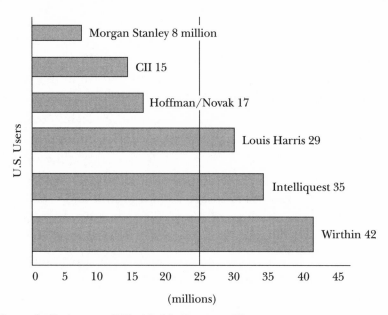

Figure 6 Estimate of Worldwide Internet Usage

Source: Adapted from CyberAtlas (www.cyberatlas.com/Market) and www.andromedia.com.

many promising avenues open for exploration; and they can assume that the Internet will almost surely *at some point* have as large and far-reaching an impact on everyday life as do the car, phone, and airplane today. The problem for business is how to plan for what can't be predicted. Firms must ask and answer the question "what will be this company's business model for an Internet strategy?" And they must do this knowing no more than that the Net is big and will get bigger. Welcome to the electronic China!

Table 1 below shows estimates from various surveys of Internet level activity from 1994 to 1996 (most 1996 figures were published in 1997). Using projected growth rates of 10, 20 and 50 percent per year, we've shown estimates for 2002 for a variety of goods and services. One survey, for example, estimated Web advertising revenues to be $63.5 million in 1995. If they grow 50 percent per year, they will reach just over $1 billion in 2002.

The actual growth rates are, of course, unknowable, but these figures are useful for reality-testing the compounded growth rates assumed in figures reported—by the week—in the press. Note that even at a 50 percent per year rate of increase, $300 to $350 million in 1995 electronic commerce sales grows to just $5 to $6 billion by 2002. Business strategists' willingness to accept forecasts that electronic commerce will amount to many hundreds of billions of dollars by 2002, rests on their belief in the likelihood of a sustained seven-year compounding that is several times larger than 50 percent.

The China Syndrome

From a business perspective, the Total Internet is rather like China: very large, very promising as a market, very diverse, and very hard to make sense of from a distance. And as with China, doing business on the Internet is not as easy as may at first appear. It isn't a matter of just getting "on" the Net or of putting up a World Wide Web site, any more than opening an office in Beijing means that a firm is really in business there. Companies require

Table 1   Internet Business Opportunities: Projected Growth Rates

Report	Figure Units	Date	Resulting 2002 figure at different compounded growth rates		
			10%	20%	50%
Average age of Internet user	32 years	1995	N/A	N/A	N/A
Average age of Internet user	35.5 years	1997	N/A	N/A	N/A
Average age of Internet user (FIND/SVP)	38.2 years	1997	N/A	N/A	N/A
Average number of sites visited	8 sites	1995	16	29	137
Average number of sites visited	20 sites	1997	32	50	152
Average time (weekly) on Internet	20 hours	1996	35	60	228
Hosts connected to the Internet (network Wizards)	12.8 million	1996	23	38	146
Hosts connected to the Internet (FR)	16.1 million	1997	26	40	122
Households using online financial services (CA)	9.2 million	1996	16	27	105
Households with Internet access (JC)	23.4 million	1996	41	70	267
Internet domains (CA)	612 thousand	1996	1084	1827	6971
Internet domains/commercial (CA)	548.6 thousand	1996	972	1638	6249
Internet population (Harris Poll)	35 million	1996	62	105	399
Internet population (Media Research Inc.)	27 million	1996	48	81	308
Internet population (Find/SVP) [Note:1Q1997data]	42.5 million	1997	68	106	323
Internet population—Men (Find/SVP)	23 million	1996	41	69	262
Internet population—Women(Find/SVP)	15 million	1996	27	45	171
Internet population—Women (AdAge)	9.45 million	1995	18	34	161
Internet population—Women (Internet World)	6.21 million	1995	12	22	106
Internet US adult users (Find/SVP)(Forecast)	75 million	1998	110	156	380
Online advertising revenue (US) (Simba)	538 $million	1997	866	1339	4085
Online advertising revenue (World) (JC) (Feb.'97)	1.1 $billion	1997	2	3	8
Online US advertising Expenditure	260 $million	1996	461	776	2962
Online financial revenue (1Q1997)(FR)	111 $billion	1997	179	276	843

many years of new thinking and new practices to learn to exploit the China opportunity while avoiding its pitfalls. The same will be true for business on the Internet. The size of the Internet market is not in any way a guarantor of business success, any more than China's 1.4 billion potential consumers translates to a guaranteed mass market of customers.

Reaching the market in both instances demands first, an understanding of the territory itself; second, identification and

Table 1   Internet Business Opportunities: Projected Growth Rates (*continued*)

Report	Figure Units	Date	Resulting 2002 figure at different compounded growth rates		
			10%	20%	50%
Revenue—Apparel (FR)	46 $million	1996	81	137	524
Revenue—Computer Products (FR)	140 $million	1996	248	418	1595
Revenue—Entertainment (FR)	85 $million	1996	151	254	968
Revenue—Food/drink (FR)	39 $million	1996	69	116	444
Revenue—Gifts/flowers (FR)	45 $million	1996	80	134	513
Revenue—Sex related (Economist)	52 $million	1997	84	129	395
Revenue—Sex related (Economist)	156 $million	1997	251	388	1185
Revenue—Travel (FR)	126 $million	1996	223	376	1435
Revenue—Travel (CA) [March 1997]	827 $million	1997	1332	2058	6280
Revenue—Other (FR)	37 $million	1996	66	110	421
Web advertising revenue (Nua.com)	63.5 $million	1995	124	228	1085
Web advertising revenue (FR)	37 $million	1995	72	133	632
Web advertising revenue (Nua.com)	171.5 $million	1996	304	512	1953
Web advertising revenue (1Q1997) (USA Today)	217 $million	1997	349	540	1648
Web shoppers (Computer Intelligence)	2.7 million	1996	5	8	31
Web shopping revenues (JC)	132 $million	1994	283	568	3383
Web shopping revenues (FR)	200 $million	1994	429	860	5126
Web sites reporting sales	57 %	1996	101	170	649
Web sites (commercial) (IDC)	45 thousand	1996	80	134	513
Web sites (avail. publically) (Ora.com)	500 thousand	1996	886	1493	5695
Web sites (Netcraft)	1.2 million	1997	2	3	9

Source: CyberAtlas (www.cyberatlas.com)
Note: CA = cyberatlas; JC = Jupiter Communications: IDC = International Data Center; and FR = Forrester Reports.

definition of the key concepts and terms needed to navigate that market; third, an understanding of the demographics of a very diverse population; and fourth, careful selection and design of the relationships a firm wants to build within those demographics. Then, and only then, can a firm design its specific offers—products, services, and information—and build its distribution and marketing systems. Firms that went into China thinking in the reverse order—offers first, understanding of the territory later—

for the most part failed. Evidence shows that many, even most, firms' Internet strategies repeat the same pattern. Recognizing the size of a target market does not constitute a business model for reaching it. Technology in itself does not create customer demand. Predicting a huge mass market for Internet electronic commerce—both the sale of goods and services and payment systems—does not in any way make it a reality.

Reason for optimism abounds, too, of course, and the optimists who focus on the current size and current growth rate of the Internet argue that every company simply must have a presence on it. They recognize that, to date, very few firms have made money on the Net, but they believe that Net profits are merely a matter of time and timing. They adopt the modern technological imperative—we are in the Information Age and on the Information Superhighway—and consider President Clinton's 1997 State of the Union exhortation to Congress that every school child have access to the Net equivalent to John Kennedy's goal of putting a man in space. They see a natural mass market emerging from the combination of a body of Internet users already numbering a probable forty million, and growing at double-digit rates every month, with the informationization of society.

Here again, our comparison of the Internet opportunity with China is useful. China has a population of around 1.4 billion people. When this previously closed country opened up in the 1980s and its doctrinaire socialism gave way to an idiosyncratic blend of state capitalism, entrepreneurship, ongoing government restriction, and first world–third world coexistence, firms saw it as a market to be rushed into. They had dreams of just, say, a quarter of a percent market share for their toothpaste, light bulbs, telephone switches, or bicycles, a share that would translate, however, into a massive revenue boost. They assumed that they could apply to China their established practices of business—marketing, distribution, contract negotiation, finance, and the like—just as they had for many decades applied them when entering other new foreign markets, such as Korea, Chile and Japan. Sure, many barriers would need to be overcome, and firms would need to be careful about cultural, social, and legal differences, but business is business—and, anyway, the sheer size of China and its pace of growth must mean success. It hasn't turned out that way. Building relationships is more complex than just "going into" China.

The Internet has to be made part of business thinking today, in the same way and for the same reason that China is: It can't be ignored. If managers are to make it part of their knowledge and business skill set, they will need an orientation to the Internet's key features, comparable to briefings about business practices in China, and using other firms' experiences, including the many failures, to enter successfully this new marketplace of more than a billion people.

Deciphering the Business Internet

A realistic business model for electronic commerce on the Internet must derive from an understanding of what we know today rather than on what some people think will happen sometime soon. None of the future-of-the-Net discussions and claims that are everywhere in print, on TV, and, of course, on the Internet itself will help managers develop a sound Business Internet strategy.

To use the Net as a business tool, managers need to factor it into their planning and competitive positioning *now* by taking one of three positions: (1) giving the Internet priority in developing innovations in customer service, products, and distribution; (2) making a few selective investments; or (3) trying only small-scale experiments until the evidence is in about whether the Net will offer the company real, secure business opportunities.

Many arguments can be made both for and against all three levels of commitment. But whatever the ultimate decision made, it should be the result of careful thought by business managers working in consultation with Internet professionals, familiar with the relevant technology, who can provide reliable assessments of what is practical now, likely to be practical soon, potentially practical at some point, and sheer hype and hope. The decision should not be made by default: Businesses cannot decide not to decide, opting to wait and see, nor should they take a leap of faith onto the Internet bandwagon in kneejerk response to the news, claims, and hype it inspires. The Internet destabilizes the status quo, rendering suspect if not inoperative many old—that is, dating back five years or more—assumptions about business, the role of technology in business relationships, the nature of markets, the means for controlling marketing and distribution channels, and consumer acceptance of electronic transactions impinging on their sense of privacy and personal security, to name just a few issues.

The Internet destabilizes itself, too. It changes by the month, in terms of its scale, users, uses, media, and effects on many areas of society. The Internet of 1998 bears little resemblance to that of 1995, which in turn is as different from that of 1992 as a butterfly is from a caterpillar. Change and the Internet go together. A firm's strategy for the Internet should be a strategy for taking charge of change by using its technology as a carefully planned business resource. But it is very easy for companies to view the Internet as a technical resource that will in itself generate business results. They then adopt a strategy of fast reaction, going with the Internet flow and waiting to see what results—Web pages are the in-thing, so let's have one. Internet radio, advertising, secure credit card transactions, virtual reality, network computers, push technology, agents. . . . At some point these will all generate business results, so let's not worry about the details—just get moving.

That approach may or may nor work, and since the Internet's next three years are likely to be as unpredictable as were the past three, this opportunism may be the best strategy many firms can come up with. The problem here, though, is that business managers become dependent on the widely-varying opinions and even preferences of technical professionals, whose enthusiasm for the Internet isn't necessarily coupled to an understanding of business dynamics. They naturally have an investment in the future as a massive improvement over the present and in technology as the path to that future—did you ever, for instance, hear someone in your firm's Information Systems department argue passionately in favor of leaving a business process unautomated or praise fountain pens as user-friendly tools for word "processing"? Listen to the voices at the extremes of Internet enthusiasm, and you will learn that newspapers and books represent the dead hand of the past, that consumer advertising will move rapidly off TV screens and magazines pages onto the Web, and, of course, that Internet electronic commerce will be an X hundred billion dollar market within the next two to three years.

Books, far from being an endangered species, are at the heart of one of the most widely-publicized Internet success stories— Amazon.com, which "stocks" over two million titles with no inventory and sells books over the Net using a brilliant combination of Transaction, Information, and Interaction. The non-paper Internet has spawned an industry of paper Internet magazines, and any large book store will have at least a shelf devoted to hefty Internet tomes. Internet advertising has not yet created large revenues for ad agencies; the largest advertising expenditures on the World Wide Web are made by Internet product and service providers, such as Netscape, Yahoo!, and Microsoft. And, of course, as yet no reliable evidence demonstrates a coming Internet mass consumer market.

Evidence does exist, however, for coming mass change. As noted above, the Internet is basically about change. It is already rapidly extending the scale and reach of personal computer use around the world—New Zealand's tourist agency, Playboy magazine online, and Amazon.com are all just a keystroke away. The Internet is changing government policies and priorities; who could have imagined ten years ago that the 1997 presidential State of the Union address would have as one of its highlights the goal of giving every school kid Internet access? (That may or may be either a practical or sensible idea, but by making it a national priority, Bill Clinton indicated his own sense of impending change.) The Internet is disturbing even the most traditional of businesses, to the extent that newspapers that fear the Internet's potential to erode their print franchise nonetheless feel compelled to offer electronic versions. The Internet is attracting the focused attention of governments in China, Singapore, Iran, and elsewhere, who see it as making subversive inroads against their control over free speech. The Internet has become a tool in such countries as Peru, Chile, Ukraine, and Estonia for fast-forwarding education and scientific communication. And, in business, the Internet concerns even the most entrenched players in such industries as banking, securities, and retailing, who fear that their traditional assumptions and practices may be undermined or invalidated. The Internet represents the possibility, the opportunity, and the threat of change.

This Book

For business managers to take charge of change, rather than react to it, they need an appropriate level of understanding of the Internet—appropriate to business planning, not to technical planning. Managers need to learn the vocabulary and concepts that will help them feel comfortable about the technology basics and able to discuss the relevant issues with technical experts. *The Business Internet and Intranets: A Manager's Guide to Key Terms and Concepts* offers managers a focused overview of the Internet from a business perspective. Its glossary of more than one hundred key terms, most with examples of their business application and impact, and its approximately twenty vignettes, short reviews of companies' *proven* business successes, present a comprehensive picture of current knowledge and best practice regarding the Business Internet. Business-relevant figures, comments, and mini-examples appear in marginal glosses, amplifying and complementing the discussions in the main text. These features—this introduction, the reference guide (the glossary), and the company snapshots (the vignettes)—combine to form a compact, easy to read, browsable introduction and guide to a crucial business issue.

Our book balances discussion of Internet technology and Internet business, because that is what managers have to do. Technology enables business. Business drives the choice and use of technology. Technical knowledge in itself provides no base for making business judgments, as is apparent from the many poorly-designed—from a business customer perspective—Web pages that get "hits" but no results. Equally, though, business knowledge in itself provides no base for planning a venture where business choices often have complex and expensive technical consequences. That careful planning and trade-offs are required for success is apparent from early claims that a Web site can be put up for a few thousand dollars; only later did most companies recognize that a fully operational site, one that can handle transactions and payments rather than merely displaying static information, can be very expensive. In December 1995, Forrester Research reported the costs of business Web sites as $304,000 per year for a promotional site, $1.3 million per year for a content site, and $3.4 million per year for a transaction site. Only a few months earlier, the *New York Times* had reported that the average Web-site start-up costs for a mid-sized company were just $2,500 for two to three pages of text plus an order form. Anyone with business knowledge alone would see the *Times* figure as so attractive that a firm would have nothing to lose by investing in a Web site. Anyone with technical knowledge would be thinking ahead to the costs of moving from a simple Web site to an operational system.

Apart from being vulnerable to cost surprises, business knowledge divorced from basic technical understanding may leave managers unaware of the key choices and trade-offs required to turn an Internet business idea into an Internet business capability. Internet security, telecommunications bandwidth, servers, browsers, etc. These technical issues become as much business variables as are the equally "technical" terms of finance, such as derivatives, depreciation schedules, swaps, and 401K plans. To be part of the finance planning dialogue, instead of the audience for a mono-logue by a banking expert, managers must know something about them. The same is true for the Internet dialogue.

The question is how little, not how much, must the business manager know about the Internet? Obviously, neither extreme—*only* technical knowledge or *only* business knowledge—will lead to successful business exploitation of the Internet. But equally no one—except, perhaps, Bill Gates—can be both an in-depth business expert and an in-depth technology expert. (Even Bill Gates originally missed out on the Internet, dismissing it for years as a tributary of the great information technology river, whose main flow was Ol' Man Windows.) Business people shouldn't and can't try to become Internet technology stars for the simple reason that the effort required would take time away from business. But they must become Internet-involved and Internet-comfortable.

No one on this planet knows where the Internet is headed. Obviously, the trends suggest that *at some point* it will become as integral to business as the telephone, that more and more goods will be sold through it, and that it will create many as yet unan-ticipated innovations that are likely to be as far-reaching as ATMs in banking or computerized airline-reservation systems. That's like saying that at some point China will become a mass consumer market and may even become a little bit democratic. Sure, it will and it may, but that's beside the point. China is part of global business *now,* presenting many opportunities and risks. It must be factored into most large firms' business thinking today, regardless of where it may be tomorrow.

The Internet, too, must be made part of business thinking today, in the same way and for the same reason that China is; it can't be ignored. For managers to make the Internet part of their own knowledge and business skill set, they need an orientation to its key features comparable to their briefings about business prac-tices in China, taking heed of the lessons to be gleaned from other firms' varied experiences, both the successes and the many failures. They'll need to understand some new terms and concepts, but they won't need to learn Mandarin Chinese—or Internetese. You don't have to take lessons in car mechanics to be a transportation planner, or to know how an automatic transmission functions to be a skilled driver. It helps, however, to understand how brakes work, as anyone who's skidded on an icy road will attest. In the 1980s, many firms spent large amounts of money to train senior managers in computer "literacy," only to find that what they really needed was a basic level of comfort with computers, not in-depth knowledge about them. They needed to be able to evaluate investment decisions about computer technology for competitive positioning, not to explain the difference between, say, X12 and EDIFACT or the meaning of acronyms such as APPN or MPEG2.

Over the past decade business managers have abstracted from the vast terminology of information technology, both computers and telecommunications, a small subset of terms useful for finding their way around a still often bewildering field. Most managers, for instance, have a sense of what an operating system is and that Microsoft's Windows family is now the dominant product. Many terms that just a few years ago were technological jargon are now part of the everyday language of business, such as interface, multimedia, online, database, RAM, CD-ROM, Pentium, floppy disk, and so on. Indeed, many managers have difficulty recalling how intimidating these terms once seemed. (Much of IT's more specialized and recently-evolved jargon and concepts, of course, remain mystifying to most people outside the field.) The terminology used to discuss the Internet will undergo the same shift from technology jargon to management vocabulary, a process that has already begun; few managers today would acknowledge ignorance of concepts such as Web site, home page, virus, and downloading. What purpose, then, does a book such as this serve? If business managers can be expected to become comfortable with the language and concepts of of the Internet over time, why worry?

For several reasons. First, the time frame for building business understanding of the Internet will be much more compressed than was that for doing the same with PCs. The PC is now in its third decade. When the Apple II, Wang's word processing software, and the spreadsheet package, Visicalc—the first PC "killer application"—first began changing the office landscape in the late 1970s, most business executives could comfortably ignore computing's new direction. Even in the late 1980s, relatively few of them used electronic mail, had laptops, or were directly involved in bet-your-company decisions involving information technology. Now, information technology is so central to business operations that it is nearly impossible for any manager to ignore it. Here are just a few examples. In retailing, technology's effects on point-of-sale and quick response are make-or-break factors. In the travel industry, computerized reservation systems and 800 numbers are the core, not the periphery, of operations; when the telecommunications network is down, so, too, is the business. In financial services, "product" innovation basically means IT, as does customer service. In manufacturing, electronic data interchange and electronic payments are the glue of logistics and just-in-time business. Designing a new product means using IT tools such as computer aided design and manufacturing, virtual reality, groupware, and many others. And so on and so on, across more and more industries—even law is now high tech, with multimedia animations routine in court cases.

The Internet will have at least the same degree of impact on business basics as did the previous waves of IT-enabled change, but it will do so in a far shorter time period. In 1990, the Internet was merely a specialized, almost elderly network used only by academics and computer scientists. Even in 1994, as the World Wide Web attracted more and more attention, users, and uses, no business *had* to make a decision about it. Today, all businesses do have to respond to it. The stakes are getting bigger. Several industries show signs that the Internet is changing the competitive rules, although other industries do not. Many ambitious, optimistic, large-scale efforts to exploit Internet opportunities have turned out to be duds, but some very distinctive niche innovations point to more general opportunities and impacts. These industry-shaking developments all unfolded between 1994 and 1997. With PCs, firms could wait and see. With the Internet, companies face a lack of data and experience from which to act along with a lack of time for waiting until the data is available.

In addition to time pressures, business managers coming to terms with the Internet face a high degree of leading edge–bleeding edge risk. IT professionals' somewhat ruefully term bleeding edge the hasty innovator's frequent waste of money, project-management and implementation fiascoes, and great high-tech ideas that turn out to be hype-tech ideas. The field traditionally has been guilty of overhyping, raising overexpectations with overpromises. The Internet may well end by continuing that history, especially given its inherent risks of overload, unreliability, and weak security. So while it is almost certain to continue to grow in use, especially for education and communication, businesses and consumers may ultimately opt not to make it the base for their business.

On the other hand, the Internet may end by continuing another aspect of IT history: continuation of its *business* rather than its technological side. Again and again, imaginative business exploitation of relatively standard technology has changed an entire industry, leaving the laggards so far behind that they do not get back into the competitive mainstream for a decade or more, if ever. In retailing, the competitive surge to leadership of firms like Wal-Mart, Circuit City, and Dillard was built with point-of-sale as the cornerstone for getting the right goods on the right shelf for the right customer at the right time. K-mart missed the boat. In the airline industry, American Airlines sustained fifteen years of industry dominance through its early exploitation of reservation systems, while Delta slid from leadership largely because it neglected them. For the last thirty years, Citibank's IT-based ATM and credit-card systems have contributed to its industry leadership after rescuing it from near-bankruptcy in "traditional" banking areas.

If the Internet meets even a fraction of its potential as the extention of *existing* trends in the role of IT at the core of business, then Internet laggards may be putting their businesses at risk. If, however, it follows the too-frequent pattern of technical innovation that fails to gain consumer acceptance, then the leaders may waste resources and credibility in the same way that home banking pioneers did in the 1970s. In a more recent example, media firms have spent have an estimated $60 billion on interactive TV, with zero profits thus far. The Internet challenge for businesses is not technological, although the technology will continue to be volatile and to pose many challenges to the people responsible for quality of operations. The challenge for business decision-makers will lie in understanding which basics matter to business and why, what business moves seem to work and why, and how to think about the Net in business terms while respecting its technical complexity, risks, and trade-offs. This challenge can only be met by business-savvy decision-makers who possess not Internet literacy, an abstract knowledge about the Internet, but Internet fluency, the ability to move fluently, conversantly, comfortably through the Internet's very new, foreign, and complex space.

Many excellent books are available that help to build Internet literacy. The aim of this book is business Internet fluency. We want to brief managers about the business Internet, not to predict its direction, advocate it, or hype it. We don't take a position that it will or won't become the base for a massive new consumer market somewhere in the range of $500 billion in sales by 2000. We very much doubt the consumer market for Internet electronic commerce will grow anywhere near as fast as its most ardent enthusiasts proclaim. We sense that over the next five years the main area of Internet growth and explosion in utility will be in intranets, the use of Internet technology within companies, and in electronic catalogs for industrial goods. We do, nonetheless, have a number of hunches about the Net's direction in the last years of this millennium.

- The low-cost hardware devices called Internet computers, network appliances, or network computers that are today beginning to challenge the standard Intel-based PC loaded with Microsoft software will be far more successful than many technical professionals believe;

- Cable modems will be a major factor in providing the telecommunications "bandwidth" (speed and capacity) needed to reduce Internet traffic jams and the time needed to download videos and high resolution graphics; and

- The computer programming language Java, designed for Internet- and network-based software systems, will transform the nature of information systems development.

Our predictions, however, are irrelevant to the basic task of building business Internet fluency. Everyone else's predictions are just as irrelevant. No matter which predictions turn out to be correct, managers today must learn to treat the Internet as a business resource and to accept that they will be involved in business decisions concerning it. This book, therefore, does not attempt a complete review or analysis of the Internet; it is a management *guide* to it. It helps managers to find a practical, reliable, and straightforward set of answers *now*, regardless of the Net's future possibilities, to this simple, but crucial question: What, exactly, is the Internet, *from a business perspective?*

Business Internet Vignettes

The single question about the Internet to which most managers want a reliable answer is "How do you make money on it?" No one knows. Yet. Given that it is only in the last three years that firms have targeted the Internet as a business opportunity, it's clearly too early for general patterns and lessons to have emerged. The hype about the Internet, however, has led commentators to make huge claims about its future on the basis of a few examples from the present—or, in some cases, without any evidence at all. A fairly typical dust jacket blurb for a 1994 book, for example, promises readers will learn "how to do what [the authors] did so successfully—make a fortune advertising on the Internet. . . . You'll discover that with some fairly simple ideas, a PC, a modem, and a telephone line, you can 'cybersell' your way to wealth." Three years later, in 1997, no firm (including that of those authors) has yet made a fortune through Internet advertising, and the most touted examples of Internet business success are, in fact, decidedly dodgy on turning "success" into profits. Amazon.com, for example, a brilliant innovation in book retailing with a burgeoning customer base that grew its sales from zero to almost $30 million per year, was in 1997 nowhere close to breaking even in terms of profits.

The hype and hope view of the Internet business opportunity doesn't help managers to reach their own practical decisions about the appropriate scale and focus for their firms' Internet investments. The following nineteen vignettes provide both a survey of the business landscape and a pretty clear picture of the state of good, though not necessarily best, practice today. We hope that these "snapshots" will give managers some ideas for their own firms' strategies, but, perhaps even more importantly, we hope that they convey a sense of what's really going on, rather than what may happen, what a vendor wants managers to think will happen, or what a journalist claims will happen.

As shown in Table 2, the organizations treated here cover a wide range of industries. Most are large, mature firms, although a variety of start-up Internet ventures, public sector organizations, and a few small companies are also included. We chose mostly large, well-known companies, because of the greater availability of reliable information about them and their Internet activities and because readers can more easily perceive the relative importance of such companies' Internet activities to their overall business concerns. One of the ever-present problems in writing about information technology is that small scale successes are very easy to find, but too often that's all they are—isolated, limited, and, in the end, peripheral to the firm's competitive and financial health.

Each vignette provides four kinds of information: a brief review of the company itself; what it did with the Internet, and why it did it; what the impacts of its Internet policies have been and what these impacts imply for the firm's future; and general lessons managers can take from the firm's experience. We do draw attention to any general lessons or reliable strategic messages raised by a firm's experience, but these vignettes are not meant as models or exemplars. They just tell managers what's happening on the business Internet.

Table 2 Business Internet Vignettes

	Public Sector	Transpor- tation and Distribution	Manu- facturing	Retail and Publish- ing	Petro- chemicals	Software Distri- bution	Real Estate	Page
Alain Pinel							X	70
Amazon				X				81
American Airlines		X						66
Cisco			X					60
FEDEX		X						73
General Electric			X					90
Hewlett-Packard			X					85
HotWired				X				93
Kenny's Bookshop				X				100
Knight Ridder				X				112
Lockheed Martin			X					55
McAfee						X		106
Millipore			X					50
Schlumberger					X			102
Silicon Graphics						X		109
Sun Microsystems			X					96
Uncover				X				108
USAID	X							94
Virtual Vineyards				X				77

Millipore <*http://www.millipore.com*>

Millipore is a $600-million, high-technology company that applies purification technology to research and manufacturing problems, such as monitoring bacteria levels in municipal water systems, reducing viruses, harvesting cells, testing for biological and chemical pollution in air and soil, and sterilizing biotechnology-derived drugs. Its products include disc and cartridge filters and housings, filter-based test kits, precision pumps, and other supplementary equipment and supplies. Millipore has a worldwide sales and marketing infrastructure, offering several thousand products and accessories targeted at many different industries and market niches. In each market, it has become the number one or number two player.[1]

Headquartered in Massachusetts, Millipore employs 3,482 people in seven manufacturing plants and more than thirty subsidiary and sales offices around the world. It sells its products to the microelectronic manufacturing, biopharmaceutical manufacturing, and analytical laboratory markets in more than one hundred countries. Millipore reported total sales of $618 million for the 1996 fiscal year.

Millipore used the Internet to create an on-line information and communication channel to the bio-research community that extended its information resources from a very basic, locally accessible internal capability to a fully interactive, global one. Millipore is in a knowledge-based business. Its products and their uses are complex, and the customer buying decision is very individual and requires scientific and technical data. This represents a substantial marketing challenge.

Millipore saw the Internet as a means for transmitting information faster and more efficiently, simplifying data collection, speeding up transactions, and providing more information to researchers through, for instance, color catalogs, newsletters, Internet designed annual reports, customer case studies, marketing brochures, notices of employment opportunities, and hyperlinks to major customers.

In each phase of Millipore's Internet experiment, its goals and expectations were met. The company derived the following major conclusions from its experience.

- *The Internet is practical for reaching key customers worldwide with the information they need.* Millipore now receives electronic-mail requests for service and information from customers around the world. The two-way flow of communication made possible by e-mail has strengthened customer links and their ties to the company's marketing infrastructure.

- *The Internet cuts costs and accelerates the flow of information.* Locating and downloading files is quicker and easier over the Internet. In addition, it has made Millipore's publishing more cost-effective: Millipore has eliminated printed quarterly reports, produces its catalogs faster and less expensively, and saves money on mailings.

- *The Internet accelerates research as a competitive edge.* It has increased research speed and enabled researchers to obtain more data faster: One analyst reports that "research that might have taken several weeks can now be accomplished in several hours."[2]

- *The Internet is a tool for customer service.* The Internet cut the turnaround time for responding to customer requests from six weeks (when processed through the U.S. postal service) to a few minutes or even seconds; responses to customer service issues and complaints have been similarly improved, along with interaction between the technical community and Millipore's customers.[3]

- *Internet marketing growth is a function of external awareness.* The Internet helped Millipore build content on its Web server that attracts customer interest, rather than merely meeting the company's internal information needs. Millipore learned over time that attracting the "right"

Navigator, and houses its Web site on the server at Johns Hopkins University. In just over a year, nearly eight thousand external users access the site.

- *May 1994:* Due to rapidly growing response to its Web site, Millipore installs its own server and creates its own home page. In the first fifty-six weeks of implementation, more than one hundred thousand files are accessed from about 9,500 different computers in around 14,500 different sessions originating from fifty countries.

- *1995:* At least 10,000 files per week are downloaded from the Millipore server, with Millipore providing hyperlinks to more than three hundred databases and key customers' Web sites.

- *1997:* Millipore's biopharmaceutical content is the most frequently visited area on their Web site—with over 26,000 hits since being added to the Web site in January. The biopharmaceutical area contains an online catalog of products, training documents, and forms, as well as hyperlinks to databases, universities, regulatory agencies, related companies, virtual libraries, and other related resources.

Throughout this development period, the Internet became more and more an everyday part of Millipore's marketing and customer relationships. Millipore reported total sales of $618 million for the 1996 fiscal year and had a market value of $1,792.7 million. The firm's sales and profits grew consistently by 10 to 30 percent per quarter; in January 1997, Millipore reported a 16 percent sales increase from the previous fiscal year.

It is obviously difficult to assess the direct contribution of the Internet to Millipore's continued growth and success. Millipore employees rate the Internet connection very highly. Two comments, taken from the Millipore home page, convey the tenor of its internal acceptance. In terms of the customer link, one employee noted the following:

I think the Internet really enables our customers and any interested parties in Millipore, kind of, excuse the expression, get real time access to what's going on in our company. I think it's also going to really help us from the standpoint of marketing in terms of creating market segments of almost one person if we can customize or tailor information that our customers need to their individual requirements.[6]

Another employee makes a similarly positive assessment from the technology perspective:

I would like to add to that from a perspective of dealing on the technology side, with customers as well, the fact that this alliance is a global alliance, and the world turns around every twenty-four hours, the time zone difference makes it very difficult to communicate live. And the advantage of having Internet access is that as we do more global activity such as with Celsis Connect or various information activities with customers, they are going to be able to access this on their terms and it will facilitate communication as we go forward in trying to find new ideas for products, deal with regulatory challenges and so forth.[7]

The Millipore Internet experience is very representative of the Internet experiences of other information-intensive companies, such as vendors of high tech computer and telecommunications equipment and, as here, providers of goods to the scientific and research community. In this area, marketing and information go together. Millipore built its experience in the pre-browser Internet of the late 1980s; it had established contacts with the Internet community when it decided to put its product data online, which led to its use of the Johns Hopkins server. When demand took off it looked for ways to minimize the traffic and reliability problems endemic to university Internet sites, which are heavily used by students, researchers, and others, Millipore did not hesitate to set up its own site in-house. These straightforward strategic decisions highlight general questions it is useful for any manager to ask.

- Which of our customers request substantial amounts of substantive information before they make their purchase decisions?

- How quickly do we respond to customer requests for information and service?

- How important is a stable customer link to our marketing and service functions?

- In what areas of our business is information a key element in ensuring customer satisfaction?

The Internet provides as obvious a vehicle for building and sustaining information-intensive and information-dependent relationships with customers as a 1-800 phone number is for consumer relationships. In an information-intensive relationship enhanced by the Internet, customers can ask and answer their own questions.

Lockheed Martin's Research and Development Division <http://www.lmco.com>

Lockheed Martin's Research and Development Division, headquartered in Orlando, Florida, employs more than 4,000 people and has been in business for almost forty years. The Lockheed Martin Company is now the world's leading aerospace and defense contractor, although the planned merger of McDonnell Douglas with Boeing will bump it down to number two in aerospace. The U.S. government buys almost 70 percent of Lockheed Martin's services and hardware, which include the Trident and Hellfire missiles, the C-5 Galaxy transport plane, and communications gear for defense satellites. The F-16 Falcon fighter jet, generating 8 percent of total revenues, is Lockheed Martin's largest program.

Through its management of the Department of Energy's Y-12 plant at Oak Ridge, Tennessee, and several other such projects, the company is the DOE's single largest services provider. In addition, as part of an effort to expand its customer base, Lockheed Martin has pursued and won several contracts outside U.S. borders. Among these have been contracts to outfit the Apache attack helicopter with night-vision systems and armaments for the United Kingdom and the Netherlands (potentially worth $1 billion) and to build an advanced communications satellite for the China Orient Telecom Satellite Company. Following Lockheed Martin's formation and acquisition of Loral's defense electronics and systems integration businesses, the company continues to consolidate facilities and shrink its workforce.

Lockheed Martin's Research and Development Division (R&DD) works on the technologies required by LMSC (Lockheed Missile and Space Company). R&DD communicates electronically with other organizations within LMSC, with customers, and with non-Lockheed partners. In the early 1990s, to meet changing customer needs and demands for improved efficiency, to reduce cycle times, and to create better value, Lockheed Martin adopted a new business model for the company based on information— about the customer, customer values, competition, alternatives, and costs. The company's previous model, as described by one analyst, had been founded on "research by individual contributors to development of product-focused technology by cross disciplinary teams that often partner with non-Lockheed companies to share technology development."[8]

The need for an intranet to meet the new model objectives quickly became apparent: It was the only practical way to deal with legacy systems, a problem faced by just about every large firm. *Legacy system* is the somewhat inappropriate term used in the information systems field to describe the often elderly core software and hardware systems that handle the bulk of a firm's transactions and provide the bulk of its information resources. The term is inappropriate in that legacy suggests something of value, a bequest in a will and an asset to be treasured. Most legacy systems are really burden systems, developed at a time when every computer manufacturer's equipment used proprietary tools, software and database management systems exclusive to a given type of hardware that could not link to those in use in incompatible technology bases. Systems built on Digital Equipment Corporation's mini-computers, for instance, the favorite of engineering departments in the 1980s, were incompatible with those built on IBM mainframes, the workhorses of finance, sales, and accounting. Incompatible telecommunications systems, personal computers, office automation, software packages, and hardware types compounded the problem, as departments made their own case-by-case technology choices. In addition, much of the information needed by and generated in R&DD was on paper documents stored in filing cabinets.

Lockheed's corporate growth history was typical of many large firms. According to William Buonanni, Program Manager of Lockheed's intranet initiative, "I really did not have a way to send a document to 20 different people. Now suddenly, there is a very easy way to do that. I could see the light bulbs going off as people realized what this could do."[9]

The Internet provided Lockheed Martin with the means to implement an entirely new approach to the access and exchange of information with independent but cooperating companies. R&DD developed five fundamental concepts to manage information:

- *Deliver information to the desktop in a unified form that meshes with how the user thinks.* Information from many disparate databases and sources is delivered to users without their having to know anything about where it comes from or how it is organized. The browser, in effect, hides the systems that generate it. R&DD became a single information provider, even though it drew on information from many sources. This was significantly more cost effective than trying to provide multiple internal systems as well as access to multiple external providers.

- In addition, R&DD's intranet allowed the automatic transfer of data through TCP/IP, the telecommunications protocol. This set of message formats and transmission procedures constitutes the foundation of the Internet's ability to end the incompatibility curse. The constraint on interoperability among hardware, software networks, and data resources has been that the connecting computers must "know" something about each other. TCP/IP removes that restriction and, in doing so, has transformed the very basis of information technology. In many ways, TCP/IP is inferior telecommunications in terms of reliability, security, speed of delivery, and network management when compared with the protocols used in business core transaction processing systems; but it gets the message from here—anywhere on the Net or an intranet—to there—anywhere.

- *Supplement existing systems.* Instead of wrestling with adapting legacy systems to meet new needs for information access, R&DD used the intranet to focus on developing fast, flexible "front ends" to those systems. It was able to reduce the time needed to modify the Internet information delivery systems to between two and four hours, systems development time to between thirty and forty hours, and system deployment times to fifteen minutes. For the legacy systems, substitute weeks or even months for hours for each of these tasks.

- *Reuse information from internal and external sources.* As one analyst notes, Lockheed's R&DD intranet capability achieved "significant savings in labor and implementation systems that enable its scientists to reuse information provided by others rather than having to re-create the information themselves or rely on laboratory personnel to find the information. [The company] refers to this leveraging of existing information systems as 'information reuse' internal and external to the LMSC."[10]

- Lockheed's intranet provided automatic information links among pages through hypertext. This almost magical hypertext feature derives from HTML, the simplest software tool for designing Web pages, which makes it easy to include a pointer to any other Web site or page on a Web site. By clicking on an item highlighted on the screen, the user can move between databases as if they were all in the same file.

- *Utilize information experts.* Lockheed's R&DD designed a tool set and an approach that allowed creation of customized information catalogs in a timely and cost effective manner. These catalogs match the mental models and work processes of different customer groups, using the very same information elements. Rather than relying on already overburdened computer programmers with limited interest in or knowledge of the information in the legacy systems or its uses, R&DD was able to draw on skills of people focused on users' needs, not on technology, and to customize its Web pages to those needs.

- *Provide a standard and common interface.* On R&DD's intranet, the software browser provides the interface (the link between a user and a system) between the PC and the information resources. To the user, the interface *is* the system. The interface hides the complexity of the technology behind it, just as the two- or three-pin cable that plugs into the wall hides the complexity of the electrical system. Instead of learning and adapting to many different screens and menus of commands and procedures, the user relies on the browser, which presents a consistent view of the system and the means available for accessing the information it conceals. The interface defines the system's look and feel.

The intranet did not change the basics of Lockheed's R&DD, but it augmented one of its key organizational resources: It made information that had been merely available, *accessible*. Overall, R&DD's business increased during a very tough time for defense contractors; after the end of the Cold War, the entire industry fell into a structural recession. In 1991, the laboratory won 37 percent of the jobs for which it submitted proposals; that figure increased to 52 percent in 1992, 78 percent in 1993, and 95 percent in 1994. R&DD has increased the value generated by each employee by 45 percent between 1990 and 1994. Lockheed Martin continues to exemplify excellence in utilizing its intranet to integrate business goals, customer satisfaction, quality, and corporate vision. In August 1997, Lockheed Martin was listed by the magazine *CIO* as one of 100 companies that use information technology to achieve and exemplify a high level of excellence. Sales at Lockheed Martin for fiscal year 1996 topped $27 billion.[11]

Legacy or burden systems represent massive roadblocks for information flow across organizations and among organizations and their trading partners. Intranets built on Internet technology remove these roadblocks. They offer a pragmatic solution to the problem of sharing information that will be beneficial to any organization whose vision statement talks about collaboration, learning, teams, intellectual capital, and knowledge workers. Lockheed Martin grabbed an organizational opportunity that only Internet technology could provide.

Cisco Systems <*http://www.cisco.com*>

Cisco is a California-based company specializing in internetworking equipment, a field in which it has been as much an innovator as Microsoft has been in personal computing. It is the number one supplier (owning 70 percent of the market) of routers, switches, and hubs, the devices that allow computers to talk to one another, and markets its products in seventy-five countries. Cisco ranks #2 in overall network equipment sales, after 3com. Cisco's Internetworking Operating System (Cisco IOS) software lets networks running under different telecommunications protocols interoperate, creating a seamless information and communications system. A rise in the scope, scale, and use of online applications and services has led to an increase in demand for the company's products, which also serve as on-ramps to the Internet. Cisco has almost 9,000 employees (note: in 1989 Cisco employed 94 people; in 1996, 4,000), annual revenues of more than $6 billion, more than $900 million in profits, and a market value of more than $40 billion.

Not only does Cisco make money by building Internet infrastructures, it uses the Net to generate income—a lot of income. It has by far been the most successful firm to date at selling products over the Internet; experts estimate that it accounted for around 10 percent of Internet electronic commerce revenues as of mid–1997.

Since 1992, Cisco has been developing electronic customer communications, moving from the Web as a tool to the Web as a service to the Web as a business in itself.[12] Cisco has been selling its products on the Net since August 1996. Web sales of networking equipment have reached $5 million a day, and more than $1 billion a year—one-quarter of its total revenue. As of July 1997, Cisco's on-line revenues surpassed $2 billion a year.[13]

In April 1992, Cisco launched Cisco Connection Online (CCO), which was accessed by Cisco's customers through direct dial-up to a public data communications network. By October 1992, it had had four hundred users since its inception. By April 1993, the company had added automatic registration and a guest system that allowed potential customers to look at the benefits of online service. It also added tools to download software and a fax option. By June 1993, Cisco Connection Online had two thousand registered users, with fifty new accounts and more than six hundred logins every week. In July 1994, Cisco's Web site logged its five thousandth user. By the end of 1994, Cisco was receiving two hundred new registrations per week.

Much of the early Web traffic came from customers asking for information and help in solving problems; most of these inquiries could be quickly answered by Cisco's engineers. To provide customers with an opportunity to share more complex queries, Cisco launched Open Forum in April 1995. The Forum, created to air less straightforward technical support questions in a private news group managed by the customer service staff, has grown steadily. Out of some six hundred queries in a typical week, only twenty-five percent make it to the Open Forum, meaning customers are finding their answers earlier in the search process.

Cisco's Web site was very popular with customers, who continually pushed for more. A company spokesperson described the effect of this agitation. "Once customers could see 'X' on the Net, they wanted 'Y' and 'Z'. Our usage and satisfaction results supported the drive for online automation. . . . We've been able to turn our ears to the customer, without turning our company on its ears."[14] In order to leverage its many channel partners (the companies selling Cisco products as part of their broader offerings in networks, systems integration, and equipment), Cisco created PICA (Partner Initiated Customer Accounts), which allows its partners to create user accounts on Cisco's Web page. PICA resulted in more than a thousand new company accounts and in thousands of individual registered users. By June 1995, Cisco's PICA had registered fifteen thousand users and twenty thousand logins per week.[15]

In the fall of 1995, Cisco introduced two so-called commerce agents: the Pricing Agent, which allows qualified customers to examine pricing in local currencies, and the Status Agent, which enables customers to check the shipment status of their orders. The Status Agent is used twenty thousand times each month, and a company representative extolls its usefulness in terms of "time saved all around. No more bulk faxes between harried customer service and purchasing agents, with an hour delay in international relations."[16] According to Cisco's Chief Information Officer, the Web is used to deliver more than 70 percent of the firm's customer support. "We're using the Web to revolutionize our relationship with customers. We want quantum-leap results: lower costs, higher customer satisfaction, leadership in service. We're achieving the highest impact on the Internet of just about any company around. . . . More than 500,000 times each month, an existing customer with a service contract contacts our company to report technical problems, check an order, and download software. More than two-thirds of those contacts now take place electronically."[17]

Cisco doesn't just use the Web as a marketing tool. Rather, it has made it the means to move customer relationships to a new level: to let customers do their own work—a self service system that reduces the number of telephone calls needed and the consequent delays and administrative involvement, thus saving Cisco time and money. These benefits were all made possible through relatively simple applications of Web technology. The multifaceted effort involves customer service, marketing, sales, technical support, public relations, operations, and human resources. A company spokesperson states "this is a channel by which we reach the outside world."[18]

In March 1996, Cisco set up a European "mirror" site. This site contains the same software and information as did the original site, but reduces the traffic congestion inevitable on such a popular Web site, thus improving user connections worldwide. The further across the Web a user's message has to travel to access data, the more telecommunications delay is added; when many users are accessing the same server, traffic jams often result at periods of peak use. Mirror sites reduce the load on the main server.

March 1996 also saw the launch of Cisco Connection, Cisco's full online marketplace. By the end of the first month of operation, Cisco had registered 28,000 customers, recorded 130,000 visits, downloaded more than 30,000 software images, checked

the order status for 20,000 users, and answered 5,000 price inquiries, 4,000 technical queries, and tens of thousands of other queries related to products, solutions, job availability, and documentation. If Cisco eliminated its online services, it would have to
double its support staff.[19]

The Web site generates higher revenues and lowers costs for
Cisco. Late in 1996, Peter Solvik reported booking almost $17
million per month on the Web.[20] Cisco's goal was to exceed $150
million per month, which equates to 24 to 30 percent of the
company's total sales. This goal has now been met. Cisco's cost
savings can be illustrated by the following example: 50,000 Web
logins per month eliminate a corresponding number of phone
calls to Cisco's technical centers. With each service response
estimated to cost $200, this translates to an $11 million savings
per month, or $130 million per year. During that same month,
Cisco had 50,000 software downloads, at a savings of $500,000 for
FedEx charges alone, and an annual savings of $6 million.

In the future, Cisco envisions *total* automatic service. It is
planning a system, still in the R&D stage, whereby its *products*
report the problems and Cisco fixes them without anyone needing to log in to the Web site: Cisco will be connected to each
customer's network. Software will monitor the network, check for
problems, determine the response needed, and make suggestions
for alleviating the problem—without anyone initiating the transaction.

In March 1997, Cisco added forty-nine country-specific pages
and content in fourteen languages to CCO. Continuing its efforts
to make Internet electronic commerce more global, it added
remote distribution servers with local access points in China,
France, Japan, the Netherlands, Hong Kong, and South Korea.
Of Cisco's fifty-four thousand registered users, 38 percent are
outside the United States and Canada, but only 9 percent are
from Asia. To address this, the company added local language
content in Chinese, Korean, and Japanese to its existing content
in French, Spanish, Dutch, Portuguese, German, Italian, Danish,

Swedish, and Norwegian. Currently, 70 percent of its customer-support activity and 15 percent of its product orders are completed via the Web site.[21]

An interesting aspect of the Cisco Internet story is how ordinary and undramatic it is. The company uses no gimmicks and nothing particularly innovative in either its Web technology or its chosen areas of application. Maybe that's the lesson. Cisco focused its Internet strategy on the basics of customer relationships and evolved its Internet marketplace incrementally. It made the Internet a lever for and extension of its business basics, instead of looking to it for some exciting, jazzy application. Cisco used the Internet to sustain its business efforts rather than timidly launching a small-scale pilot system or making a bold leap forward. On May 21, 1997, Cisco Systems received the Tenagra Award for Internet Marketing Excellence. Cisco continues to use the Web to simplify the product ordering process for their customers and partners, as well as to provide in depth customer service. The Tenagra Awards were initiated in 1994 as a means of recognizing substantive achievement and contributions to the field of Internet marketing.[22]

As the following comments from Cisco executives and technical professionals indicate, the driving priority in all of Cisco's Internet developments has been the customer *relationship,* not "information" or "surfing" or "marketing." Cisco has shown sensitivity to and sophistication about the key elements of electronic relationships and their organizational context that surely contribute importantly to the commercial success of Cisco's site.

- "Nothing will frustrate a customer faster than having a problem on a Web site, only to be foiled by people on the telephone who aren't familiar with that particular page or feature."[23]

- "The Web completely changed how the corporate communications and marketing departments felt about electronic publishing. With their interest running high, more tools, more training and more content were made available to all involved."[24]

- "[I]f you go to a movie, and don't like the ending, you shrug and leave the movie theater talking with friends about how it could have been different. With an imperfect Web page, people e-mail the Web master or author directly, and demand changes to suit their tastes. Once people see something on the Web, they want the author to iterate the creative process. Fix this; tweak that. It'd be perfect except . . ."[25]

- "We're tracking online sales by order volume, not total revenue. The goal is not to generate dollars. It's to reduce cycle times and costs—and to increase customer satisfaction. We know we are doing that on every online order we take. . . . We really believe the business-to-business is the Web's killer app."[26]

Cisco's success partly reflects its customer base, which is technically very sophisticated and for the most part already comfortable with and experienced in using the Internet. The users' culture and style are also very similar to Cisco's: The Cisco Web connection gets engineers talking to engineers, with all participants looking for sound technical information and advice and remaining very task-focused—Cisco's customers don't need any soft sell. Perhaps the general lesson for all firms here is this: *Adapt the Internet to your relationships, not the other way round.* A bank, retailer, or wholesaler might copy every detail of the Cisco Internet strategy and fail completely; the relationship base in those fields is different. That said, the underlying principle of Cisco's Internet use applies to all firms: Think relationship, not system.

American Airlines <*http://www.americanair.com*>

American Airlines set the pace for innovations in the use of information technology as a competitive resource from the late 1970s through the 1980s. Its computerized reservation system,

Sabre, changed the nature of competition as American used it to capture 40 percent of the travel agent business. It invented frequent flyer programs. It became the leader in yield management, the exquisite and information-dependent art of pricing and discounting every single flight so that it has no empty seats at takeoff that could have been discounted and sold but is not so oversold through discounts that the opportunity is lost to sell full-fare tickets. American routinely wins awards for its use of computer-based mathematical modeling techniques for crew scheduling, fuel optimization, and other forecasting and optimization applications. All in all, American Airlines must be ranked one of the top ten companies in the world in terms of its use of information technology as a competitive resource.

Its success dipped in the 1990s. The airline industry was hit with cost pressures and price wars, and Southwest Airlines took a major share of the domestic market by operating point-to-point on selected routes, rather than running a complex hub and spoke system, and by offering a so-far unmatchable combination of low price, low operating costs, and superb service. In addition, American itself faced major labor conflicts with its pilots and crews. The airline business is a very tough industry in which to make money consistently; it has seen many former leaders go bankrupt, including Pan Am, TWA, Eastern, and Continental (twice). American remains a dominant force in the industry, however, and if its merger with British Airways—the other leading airline innovator—occurs, it will continue to be a formidable competitor.

The difference between a profitable and a bankrupt airline is approximately five tickets per flight. The most distinctive feature of the industry is the perishable nature of its products. An empty seat is lost revenue; much of any airline's marketing strategy focuses on how to determine whether an otherwise empty seat must be sold. Equally, though, an airline that sells too many seats at cut-rate prices loses the chance to sell at full fare. American's yield management planners thus monitor every flight for a full year ahead, constantly adjusting forecasts and prices to maximize not the revenue but the yield—the operating profit; this concept is increasingly being applied to other industries with perishable products, such as hotel rooms and car rentals.

It's hardly surprising that American was one of the first airlines to use the Internet to extend yield management, specifically through ticket auctions. American's Web site provides the equivalent of an in-person airline reservation agent who can help with fares, itineraries, package deals, hotel reservations, car rentals, and flight reservations; American also provides interactive travel planning software to its frequent flyer passengers.[27] But many other online travel agencies offer similar services over the Internet; the entry barrier is low, and the industry is already so computerized that firms like CitiTravel (a subsidiary of Citibank), Travel City, and many others have full-service Web sites through which they pass on to consumers some of their cost savings from electronic self-service in the form of discounts. Even though sales of plane tickets are one of the largest segments of the as yet embryonic online electronic commerce market (computers, books, and records are the other major components), only a very small fraction of consumers prefer to book their own flights; for years, American Airlines has offered its EasySabre self-reservation system for use on PCs or via online services such as AOL, but its use has been fairly limited. In an attempt to make on-line booking more attractive to potential customers, American Airlines has recently updated its Web site, Americanair.com, to allow customers to shop for tickets in a variety of ways—by price, by schedule, or through NetSaver fares—that correspond to their specific needs. This strategy, combined with postings of fare sales on their home page, has generated record activity for the airline. During a fare sale in February 1997, bookings via the American Airlines Web page increased fourfold.[28]

If AA offered just another Web site for travel information and services, it would merely be keeping up with the pack. What it has added could—just could—be a simple and apparently small innovation that, given the importance of yield management, may have fairly substantial impacts on profits. The innovation is to reach out directly to Internet users to sell tickets at the last moment through auctions and electronic mail.

In May 1996, American Airlines began offering discounted fares to Internet users. Every Monday and Wednesday, registered users get an e-mail from AA listing about twenty discounted airfares on domestic and international routes, respectively. Called Netsaver Fares, these tickets are 70 to 80 percent lower than the already discounted twenty-one day advance purchase fares. American does this in order to sell seats that otherwise would very soon go empty. Discounts are for weekend travel only and are available until the end of the posted week. Although most of the transaction occurs electronically, the tickets cannot actually be purchased directly from the Web; prospective purchasers must call an 800 number and pay using a credit card.[29] Other airlines have followed American's lead: Southwest, Alaska, Delta, United, USAir, Trans World Airlines, and Northwest Airlines are among those already offering some type of online ticketing. Using the Web for ticketing saves the airlines money, including the commissions they would otherwise pay travel agents and their own reservation desk costs. "The motivation is financial," said Carl Lehman, a technology analyst at the Meta group. "They also hope to keep in touch with customers and their needs."[30]

American Airlines also offers an Internet Silent Auction. After entering the Silent Auction room, potential bidders find the items to be auctioned (specific flights, with brief descriptions), the date and time that bidding will open, the minimum bid and raise, the current high bid, and the date and time that bidding will close. Bids are time-stamped as they are received, and items are awarded to bidders based on the highest bid and earliest time-stamp. Bids of equal value are ranked according to the time-stamp. Winners are notified via e-mail within twenty-four hours.

American Airlines' use of the Internet evolved from its existing systems and operations, with the exception of the auction feature. In an industry already dominated by online services, no vacuum waited to be filled—the air is already alive with the sound of keystrokes, and a new travel service or airline Web site would be just another Web site. Travel agents provide fast and responsive service and are easily accessible through America Online. It is difficult to add something new and different.

The American Airlines auction is both new and different. Sales figures are not available, nor is data on the auctions' impact on American's yield management; the service may turn out to be just a modest contributor to its profits. The venture does, however, provide managers with useful food for thought. The Internet can very quickly shift customer relationships out of a one-way, passive mode and into a two-way, interactive one. American clearly needs urgently to sell the seats it auctions or lists as discounted by electronic mail, or they would not be offering them online. Previously, the only way to get this message to potential customers was through newspaper promotions or incentives to travel agents for pushing the fares and flights. The Web site adds a new dimension to the customer relationship, giving the customer the initiative: a reason to actively search out the site, to read electronic mail from American, and to search for bargains.

The second message for managers is that JAWS—"Just Another Web Site"—won't work. To induce people to go to *your* site, you must provide something special in the relationship. Log onto the Web and browse for cheap airfares, and you'll see a flood of options and bargains. You probably won't even remember the names of the companies offering them. Through its site, American, the leading airline innovator at exploiting computers and telecommunications for competitive advantage, may have found yet another edge.

Alain Pinel Realty <*http://www.apr.com*>

Alain Pinel is a rapidly growing real-estate firm in California that makes use of the Internet central to its strategy. Its 1992 sales were $259 million; those for 1994 were $690 million. With five offices and more than three hundred agents, sales volume in 1997 is expected to be around $2 billion. Between 10 and 20 percent of that business is directly related to Pinel's Internet presence. According to Pinel, "Real estate benefits a lot from the Internet. It works with peoples' natural curiosity. When they drive through a neighborhood and see a sign, they wonder: 'How many bedrooms does that house have? What is the square footage? What is the price?' With Alain Pinel, they can get on the Web and find out."[31] As soon as a house is listed, the information is distributed via e-mail to all of Pinel's agents, and one of them often makes the sale before agents at other firms even know the house was for sale. Each agent pays a technology fee to defray the cost of their computer and beeper.

The company is working to become a one-stop-shopping provider for real estate sales in the Silicon Valley area by offering full service worldwide. It offers a direct ISDN line to an experienced broker with access to more than eleven hundred loan sources and to home and title insurance, as well. (ISDN is a specially-installed phone line that offers roughly double the transmission speed of a standard household line.) In early 1997, Pinel's Web site added hyperlinks to Yahoo, a search engine that provides classified ads for commercial and residential real estate listings across the Unites States, with plans to include Canadian listings in the near future. Executives attribute most of the company's success and its fast growth, even in a period when the California real-estate market was depressed, to the Pinel agents' business cards and the agency's brochures, all of which contain the company's Web-site and e-mail addresses. Pinel uses the Internet to "provide superior marketing information in the pre-sale phase at no more cost than other real estate agencies."[32]

Pinel argues that real estate agents are basically just a link between a wide range of parties: brokers, home buyers, mortgage companies, banks, inspectors, title companies, and builders. He sees the Internet as a proven, easily accessed, low-cost "log on and go" infrastructure that can speed up transactions and reduce costs for all the parties involved. His firm spent $2 million to set up a network for electronic mail that links to the Internet; the internal network adds efficiency and reliability to the less efficient and reliable but wider reaching Internet.

The main limitation of the Internet-based communication strategy to date has not been technology or cost but simply tradition and inertia. As of early 1997, only 20 percent of Pinel's clients were able or willing to accept e-mail messages, even though several of the firm's offices and associated brokers are located in California's Silicon Valley, the highest tech area of high tech. Most buyers still prefer face-to-face meetings, which are of course almost always required for handling signatures at settlement. Most real-estate agents are not yet online, although more and more are getting up on the Internet, driven by fear, fashion, curiosity, or their kids. Building and termite inspectors, people who are very mobile and don't spend much time in an office, are less likely to be able to receive and send electronic mail. A senior executive at Pinel commented in late 1996 that online businesses were in a transition period: "The learning curve of the general population needs to catch up."[33] Pinel's $2 million investment has paid off, though, in terms of streamlining the sales process, eliminating paperwork, and improving responsiveness to customers. Evidence from real-estate industry studies shows that, whereas the average customer looks at fifteen houses before buying, the online customer with access to information and pictures looks at half that figure, a definite productivity gain and time saver for both customer and agent.

Pinel is not a giant firm ($2 billion in home sales amounts to around five thousand units sold). Its Internet system is a simple communication vehicle, with no online transaction capabilities, yet it still cost $2 million. Business managers must always keep this lesson in mind: the cost of getting on the Net may be negligible compared to the costs of staying on the Net and making it an integral part of doing business.

Federal Express <*http://www.fedex.com*>

Federal Express, the Memphis-based shipper of things that absolutely, positively have to get there overnight, delivers to 212 countries in North America, Europe, Asia, and Latin America. FedEx has 43,000 package drop-off locations and offers services in 7,000 retail outlets, including Target stores and Kinko's Copy Centers. It also operates 1,400 storefront FedEx World Service Centers. Not everything FedEx ships gets to its destination overnight. The company offers a variety of services for shipments of varying urgency. Most items sent through FedEx reach their addressees within forty-eight hours, but the company also offers same-day delivery service in the United States.

Federal Express has put its core competency onto the Internet. FedEx went online in November 1994, spending less than $100,000 to launch an intranet site; it already had such a comprehensive and powerful existing infrastructure and skill base that the intranet was an evolution, not a revolution in its systems. Interestingly, the intranet idea came not from the top executives, but rather from individuals and groups much further down in the organization who took the initiative to implement a Web server and the original sites.[34] These employees had observed that while Federal Express had superb systems for tracking packages from pick-up to delivery, its internal information resources were scattered and fragmented. The Internet gave staff a single point of access to a wide range of data. According to Robert Hamilton, manager of Electronic Commerce Marketing, "We don't know how much we saved, but we are convinced on anecdotal evidence that we crossed over the break-even point in the third month."[35]

FedEx had for some years provided larger customers with its PC-based system, allowing them to handle some of their own transactions, such as filling out the forms for sending packages, informing FedEx electronically that a package was ready for pick up, and tracking the progress and delivery of their packages. This saved the customer time and effort and saved Federal Express money. This win-win situation is commonplace with self-service technology applications that make life more convenient for customers and reduce the provider's staff and administrative costs. ATMs are another obvious example. The Internet allowed FedEx to extend this strategy at an absurdly low cost, because the online systems were already in place and FedEx had rolled out the needed PC software years before; accessing the Internet instead of the company's own internal telecommunications network was basically a matter of changing the dial-up phone number. The Web page itself was straightforward to design.

The Internet version of FedEx's existing online customer service and package-tracking systems is just a base for the company's planned long-term thrust to make the Internet not just a complement to business as usual but a core component of operations and service. FedEx's Web site now functions in various ways: as a resource for customers who are ready to do business with FedEx as an online presence; as a showcase for talking about, showing, and making available FedEx electronic commerce tools for people exploring their own EC applications; and as a communications vehicle to explore new services, new enhancements, and changes in services for customers and prospects.

The company realized immense cost benefits through savings from decreased agent interactions with customers and reduction in calls to its 800 number, and gains from new volume that followed the new, better service that the Internet provides. One company executive stated "I can't tell you how many calls and messages I've seen from existing customers saying 'We've decided to move all of our shipping over to FedEx,' especially those customers who ship on a global basis. Finally, there's no easy way to measure the intangible benefits of instant customer gratification that the Web site provides."[36]

FedEx ships 2.5 million packages each night. Not surprisingly, it has an Internet capability for accepting payments. Shippers set up a FedEx account, which validates the user without having to obtain credit information for each shipment. In July 1996, FedEx released interNetShip, the first automated shipping transaction on the Internet. As of July 1997, FedEx had 650,000 total electronic users. For FedEx, its executives maintain, "the Internet represents a conviction for us, not just a hobby. We are doing research among our customers, asking people to comment directly. We're looking for low hanging fruit and to deliver it in the order our customers want."[37]

In June 1997, FedEx added a new feature to its Web site called "Rate Finder." Through this service, customers can obtain a quote for how much a package with specific shipping parameters will cost. By indicating the zip code of the originating city, the zip code of the destination city, the value of the package, the type of delivery wanted, the shipping date, and the full address, the FedEx Rate Finder will determine the cost for shipping this particular package.

The following results and benefits were directly generated by FedEx's use of the Internet:

- A significant portion (although still a minority) of customers use the Web site to conduct business rather than the 800 number. If the current growth rate continues, the Web site will save FedEx millions of dollars annually.

- Customers track about 20,000 packages per day using the Web site.

- Customer service currently takes 300,000 calls nationwide per day; as many as 60 percent of the people who track packages through the Web site would call customer service if the Web site were not available.

- Customer service representatives use the time made available by the Web site to focus on the higher-leverage interactions with customers.

Admittedly, these are relatively small scale operational benefits. FedEx, however, sees the Internet as a business springboard, as the following comments from executives show:

- "Our ultimate goal? To have 100 percent of our transactions come through some online media. . . . [T]he Web obviously is the very powerful tool to make that happen. . . . [F]or one thing, it's got a worldwide reach, so anything we do, any minor changes we make, a new feature or function, is almost instantly available worldwide. For another, it allows us to have a presence on desktops, in parts of corporations that we never had access to before."[38]

- "The Internet is an incredibly intense focus at Federal Express. We've got departments with titles like Internet Technology and Internet Engineering, and we've got a standing meeting of senior executives every week where we discuss the Internet and electronic commerce as a common opportunity."[39]

- "One thing about the Internet that has fascinated us is that we put the home page up and we put the tracking information on the home page and we never advertised it. In fact, to this day, we really have not advertised that capability. And, before we could even turn around, we were exceeding a million hits per month on the home page and exceeding fifteen thousand tracks and traces a day. Without saying anything, just by putting up a dynamite home page, we were getting a lot of transactions that would have come through 800 numbers and now would have come through our customer service means. They're now coming through the Internet, and we never said boo about it."[40]

Federal Express has always had "an incredibly intense focus" on turning strategy into action. That made it a leader in the use of technology for its tracking systems, an innovator in the basics of package and courier services, and an award-winner in its total quality management programs. Any firm's Internet strategy needs intensity and focus. It's so easy to just put up a Web site and gain the obvious benefits of lower communication costs. But if FedEx's site were no more than a cost substitution for its 800-number phone bills, none of the plans and ideas implicit in the above quotes would be likely to emerge. FedEx is *committed* to the Internet as the base for its thinking about the customer relationship. That's very different from using the Internet to supplement the relationship. Obviously, many firms don't depend on information and communication as the foundation of the customer relationship in the same way that Federal Express does; for such companies, making a similar level of commitment to the Internet would be inappropriate and unnecessary. But many companies talk about the importance of the Internet without ever making a corresponding level of management commitment to it. These companies are likely to find themselves stuck between the proverbial two stools: in the game too deep to avoid spending a lot of resources but not in deep enough to make a real impact.

We offer a conjecture here (and it is no more than that) that firms whose culture is one of commitment, rather than consensus, and whose management style balances very aggressive top-down strategic directives with space for individual initiative, will naturally pick up on the Internet opportunity and turn that opportunity into commitment. We suspect that other companies, lacking this dynamic culture, will make the investment but not the organizational commitment. They may be better off not spending the money.

Virtual Vineyards <*http://www.virtualvin.com*>

Virtual Vineyards is one of the two companies most often cited as successes in Internet electronic commerce. (The other is Amazon, the online Internet book retailer.) Virtual Vineyards sells wine and gourmet foods exclusively on-line. Using the Web as a means of providing in-depth information to potential customers in a comfortable and unintimidating setting was a key to their quick on-line success. Virtual Vineyards' staff consists of an operations manager, a support person, two engineers, a designer, and a founder. On January 25, 1995, Virtual Vineyards went on-line with wine from thirteen wineries. Just over two years later, they carried wine from seventy-five different wineries.

Virtual Vineyards spends 20 to 30 percent of its revenues on advertising, including purchasing Web banners (ads that appear on a Web page as small pictures within the screen display) at sites such as Yahoo! and Infoseek, which attract millions of Internet users daily. (These are two of the leading Internet search engines, the software that locates Web pages containing information specified by users.) Virtual Vineyards also advertises on America Online and CompuServe, promotes its products through Internet service providers, does joint marketing with other companies, and maintains a hot link on its site to Wells Fargo Bank and CyberCash for handling electronic payments. Many sites have linked to Virtual Vineyards because of its success; they want to point their own community of users towards it: Company president Robert Olson estimates the number at "from 30–40 to hundreds. They don't tell you anymore when they link to you."[41] Virtual Vineyards makes it extremely easy for customers to make purchases, accepting payment in any form, both online and offline; Olson has stated "we never received cash . . . but we would take it."[42]

Virtual Vineyards was one of the first companies to accept CyberCash as a method of payment. CyberCash, one of the pioneers in electronic money, aims to expand the scope and scale of electronic commerce on the Internet and to be a major player in electronic payment transactions. CyberCash uses an electronic wallet (a software element on the user's hard disk that stores digital cash to be used for transactions with participating Internet merchants) to facilitate rapid, secure, and simple Net purchases. In contrast, credit card transactions are comparatively expensive to process, requiring online authorization. Digital cash is the electronic equivalent of coins and notes—a new legal tender, anonymous and simple to transfer from the electronic wallet to the electronic till. According to Olson, CyberCash "seemed to offer mostly information-oriented, small sized transactions, and our customers don't want to spend ten minutes to transfer $120 from their account over to First Virtual [another Internet bank] before they could transfer it to us."[43]

In February 1997, Virtual Vineyards signed on as a publisher with Intermind Corp. (www.intermind.com) in an effort to boost personal service. With the Intermind communicator software, users can find content pertaining to their special interests; for example, connoisseurs of Merlots who want regular updates on what's available can receive notices of the latest information via their browsers.[44]

Virtual Vineyards is praised almost daily in the press. Here are some representative comments:

- "Like one of the vintage vinos it proudly hawks, Virtual Vineyards just seems to be getting better as it matures."[45]

- "Virtual Vineyards is what every Web merchant should strive to be: an improvement, in significant ways, over its real life counterparts."[46]

- "The secret to Virtual Vineyards' success is that it doesn't simply sell wine. It entices people into an informative, interactive world where they can do everything from tour the site to pose questions to the Cork Dork."[47]

- "One of the first retailers on the Internet . . . [Virtual Vineyards] has become one of the most popular because it goes beyond the pure sales pitch."[48]

One of the myths of Internet commerce is that, because it is so cheap to offer information and goods on a Web home site, it is easy to build a business on the Internet. It isn't. The founder of Virtual Vineyards, Robert Olson, had a very clear business model for choosing the target for his start-up company and a very realistic understanding of costs.

The first thing is that information had to be crucial to the sale. I believe that most people on the Web today are information professionals. They're trained to be highly analytic; they like to make considered choices. The second thing is that it had to be a business that could hold its margins. . . . Also, whatever you're selling has to have a distribution problem, so you're not competing with Safeway. Finally, it had to be something that I could find an expert about. As it happened, I was talking to my brother-in-law, Peter (now the sommelier at VV), and he told me my description fit the high-end wine business perfectly. The small wholesalers and retailers are getting squeezed out. These wines aren't carried by the large retailers—a whole vintage might be five thousand cases. What's that, one hundred cases per state? It's not worth their time or their shelf space. . . .

Most people think of the Internet as a low-cost option. In fact, it's a high-cost option. By the time we're cash-positive, we'll go through $1.5 to 2 million. People going into this area today need to figure out how to leverage the characteristics of the medium to get (1) volume *and* (2) premium prices. It's possible to do the Internet inexpensively, but it usually looks it. To get a quality product, you have to spend the money. In the future that may change, since there will probably be a lot of off-the-shelf solutions, which will cut down the labor costs. But your personality always shows through.[49]

Olson describes the combination of volume and premium price as resting on a choice between just two practical models. One is rock bottom prices, but "you—the customer—had better know exactly what you want."[50] (What he seems to mean is not a premium price but a premium margin built on low prices and ultra-low costs of operation.) The "discretionary" model reflected by Virtual Vineyards is one in which the seller, as adviser and expert, is partly responsible for the choice made by the customer. One of the keys to Virtual Vineyard's success is the availability of on-line, interactive expertise. Olson's brother-in-law, Peter, provides recommendations on the Web site, and customers also leave comments about the wines they've bought. Virtual Vineyards seems to have been one of the earliest firms to recognize that a key to Internet electronic commerce is to allow appropriate interaction, not to create passive electronic billboards or hyperactive multimedia.

Virtual Vineyards is one of the most successful and most widely-publicized Internet electronic commerce companies. As such, it is one of the few Internet ventures about which reliable estimates can be made on the costs and revenues other start-up firms would need to succeed. Virtual Vineyards spends about $80,000 per month on its Internet operation. Its goal is to maintain a 30 percent margin, so it must generate around $250,000 per month, or $3 million per year, to break even. Olson stresses the need for high-speed telecommunications lines: "It's important to be snappy if you want repeat traffic, much more than being beautiful."[51] The service uses the T1 communications link that has for decades been a standard for larger companies' data communications networks. T1 lines move data at speeds fifty to one hundred times faster than those of standard phone lines. For Virtual Vineyards, the link provides low costs per user, as many PC messages share the high-speed connection.

Amazon Books <*http://www.amazon.com*>

Amazon Books, in business since July 1995, sells books solely on the Web. Along with Virtual Vineyards, it is by far the most widely-cited example of a start-up firm that became successful by targeting the Internet as the base for its offerings. Amazon has certainly transformed the book retailing industry. It reported $15 million in sales for 1996, compared to $511,000 in 1995, and in the first quarter of 1997 it sold $16 million—more than the total sales for 1996. In fact, throughout 1997, Amazon's revenue growth rate was topping 25 percent per month, with Internet sales for the second quarter of 1997 reaching $27.9 million.[52] And yet, even though the company successfully launched an initial public stock offering with an opening price of $18 a share in May 1997, Amazon hadn't, as of late 1997, made a profit. Its share price soared on the day of the issue, only to drop rapidly. In August 1997, Amazon's stock was up once again—at nearly $27 a share. This volatility reflects both Amazon's potential and its uncertain future. At approximately the same time it made its IPO, it had for the first time to prepare for new competition, from such giants as Barnes and Noble and even from the book wholesaler that supplies about half Amazon's books. As of June 1997, however, Amazon reportedly had a base of customer accounts that totaled 610 thousand, and was continuing to rise. This figure represents an increase of 79 percent, up from 340 thousand accounts at the end of March 1997. Fifty-percent of all orders taken in the second quarter of 1997 were from repeat customers.[53] Regardless of whether Amazon can leverage its unique position in the Internet marketplace—including its very strong brand, one of the first on the Internet—its achievements have been remarkable. Its innovations go well beyond just offering a catalog of books online. They include the following:

- An inventory of 2.5 million book titles, most of which can be purchased online and delivered in as few as one to two days, though specialized titles from small publishers may take three to six weeks for delivery. About this record Amazon.com says "the point is the million books that consumers have access to, regardless of what's on hand in the warehouse. And while [our] inventory may not be enormous on any given day, the bookstore rotates its stock more than seventy times a year."[54]

- Comprehensive search and browsing tools for locating books on specific topics or by specific authors. The software includes a value-added feature: It asks customers if they want to receive automatic electronic mail messages from Amazon when any new book is published on the topic they have searched.

- Opportunities for customers to write book reviews and to access other customers' reviews, as well as editors' reviews.

- In addition to standard e-mail services, Amazon.com offers a very specialized and unique type of e-mail called "Eyes." Eyes is a free service that enables customers to track new releases by author, title, or subject. If a customer inquires about a book that is either not yet published or out of stock, Eyes will send a personal e-mail message to the customer when the book is released or restocked. These inquiries can also be made about authors, and the service will respond when the author in question publishes a new book.

- On-line author interviews.

But by far the most far-reaching innovation affects publishers rather than customers. Book publishing is a high cost, low margin business because of the need, first, to ship so much inventory to stores and, second, the difficulty of matching supply to demand, the determination of how many copies of a new book a publisher should print in the first run. Print too many, and a $29.95 product will be on the remainder table for $2.98. Print too few, and a sale is lost, often for good. In addition, books that are shipped to stores but which go unsold are returned to the publisher, with the publisher refunding the price.

Amazon orders from publishers on the basis of demand; it maintains no inventory except for copies of the very hottest books at the very top of the best-seller list. Publishers thus don't have to ship books that may get returned; an Amazon order is a real sale. In addition, by listing books that are to be published in the next few months in its on-line catalog and taking prepublication orders, Amazon gives publishers automatic e-mail feedback that provides an entirely new basis for forecasting sales.

Because so many books are in print, it can be difficult to locate particular titles. Few bookstores stock more than a few thousand of the many thousands available. The World Wide Web offers a natural infrastructure for browsing a topic area, singling out a title or author, and placing an order. Two and a half million book titles dwarfs the CD market's mere 200,000 titles. According to Amazon.com's CEO Jeff Bezos, "The only thing on Earth that there are more of in one category are insect species, and I don't think there's a big market for that."[55]

So much—perhaps even too much—has been written about Amazon that we have little to add. It will be 1998 before Amazon will be able to answer the questions every business manager asks:

- Will Amazon be able to make a profit? And if so, how? Will it gain an advantage through pricing, through sheer volume, by building a loyal customer base with an increasing proportion of Amazon to bookstore purchases, or by attracting customers who don't haunt bookstores but buy books from Amazon because of its convenience and low prices? The underlying general question is how does a firm identify the factors that will drive Web profits, not just revenues?

- Will Amazon's Net beachhead and its brand be enough to ward off Barnes and Noble and other well-funded giants? The Internet has no barriers to new online electronic commerce entrants, and, equally, no barriers to imitation. One analyst describes the situation this way: "[T]he Web's radical efficiencies present Amazon with a start up's dilemma: if the service offered is so easy that a couple of hundred computer jocks can pull it off, it should be equally easy for a billion-dollar behemoth to shoulder you off the road—so better stay ahead every mile of the race."[56]

- Can the very distinctive style of interactive customer relationships that Amazon is building be sufficient basis for creating and maintaining a competitive edge? If so, how can other firms design similarly effective relationships for the Business Internet? If not, what other base exists for attracting and retaining customers other than great prices, great inventory, and ease of use?

The last set of questions could hold the key for businesses seeking profits from the Internet.

Hewlett-Packard *<http://www.hp.com>*

Hewlett-Packard, one of the first Silicon Valley high-tech start-ups, has also been one of the most successful companies in the computer field for well over three decades, only occasionally straying off its path of continuing innovation, profitability, and reputation. Through its diverse products and alliances and its skilled choices of niche markets, HP has maintained a strong position in the mainstream computer industry. HP's more than 25,000 products include computers, networking products, electronic test and measurement instruments, and systems for chemical analysis, electronic components, and hand-held calculators.

Founded in 1939, HP employs 112,000 people across 73 divisions worldwide, and has 600 sales and support offices and distributorships in more than 120 countries.

HP operates one of the largest intranets in the world, with 140,000 host computers transmitting more than 10 terabytes of information per month—that is, 10 trillion characters or the total hard disk storage capacity of about five thousand personal computers. HP maintains more than 400 sites worldwide, a 1,200-seat worldwide customer support organization, 110,000 PCs, 23,000 Unix desktops, 6,000 servers, 70,000 Netscape Navigator browsers, 2,500 Web servers, and 170 proxy/caching servers (special-purpose servers designed to optimize the speed of Internet message flows). In addition, HP receives approximately 1.5 million e-mail messages per day. That is a very large network indeed, a mini-Internet in itself.

Hewlett-Packard uses this network capability for global electronic communication, software distribution, document management, staff training, and collaborative teamwork. According to HP's own internal case study, the intranet creates greater organizational flexibility and has generated an explosion of information sharing among employees that has ultimately increased employee productivity. It contributes to faster time-to-market, improved customer relations, more competitive and profitable products and services, reduced cost structures, and improved communication. Company CEO Lewis E. Platt has stated that "HP's corporate culture has always encouraged open communication among employees. But with the advent of our intranet, information sharing has taken off like never before."[57]

In the early 1980s, HP recognized the need to link its global operations and to speed up its time-to-market. Time had become the new currency of business, with FedEx and fax machines beginning to change communication, and just-in-time manufacturing methods becoming a key competitive strategy. A company executive defined HP's goals this way: "We wanted to be able to place an order from anywhere in the world and send that order automatically to the factory that would deliver the product. To do so, we needed a common interface."[58] The intranet was part of this evolution; Netscape's Internet browser, Navigator, provided an easy to learn and use interface, a single standard format, and a set of procedures for users accessing a wide range of information and transactions.

HP's information systems department (IS) directed implementation of its intranet. That decision proved essential, but it was also a little unusual. It was essential because, while a business unit can build and maintain a single Web site using people with Internet-specific skills and training—meaning that they are sure to be fairly young—the task of coordinating an enterprise infrastructure of 140,000 host computers providing information to 110,000 personal computers demands the expertise of computer professionals who understand the details of large-scale, high-performance, high-volume, high-security systems. HP is unusual in that very few companies to date have worked top down rather than bottom up in their Internet and intranet ventures.

HP's priority has been innovation, experimentation, flexibility, and speed of development in its efforts to find ways to exploit the business opportunities opened up by the Internet. None of these have traditionally been hallmarks of most information systems groups, whose strengths—often underrated or dismissed as IS bureaucracy—are discipline and structure in the management of very large-scale systems. Business innovators focus on building Internet applications quickly; IS plans ahead to maintaining and operating applications once they have been built. IS can be seen as (and, in some cases, it really is) a roadblock to experimentation. In the case of HP, IS was the enabler, not the blocker; HP combined business innovation with technology discipline.

During forty-eight hours in January 1997, HP rolled out new intranet applications to one hundred thousand users—just one routine example of the IS team's maximization of the firm's global intranet. The intranet is now the vehicle for HP's IS department software distribution, with automatic electronic installation over the network instead of physical installation at the desktop. The intranet is thus a major source of productivity for IS itself. Implementing the relatively inexpensive TCP/IP Internet telecommunications protocol saved countless operating dollars, and the subsequent cost of operation has been one-fifth that of the old and very efficient corporate network that had been built on other protocols. IS was able to cut its 150 worldwide data centers to eight. According to recent figures, configuring PCs electronically via the intranet has saved $2,000 per PC each year,[59] and that figure may be low if the cost of time lost as business departments wrestled with manuals and piles of floppy disks is added in. HP's IS department uses the intranet for technical support; problems can be diagnosed and often solved online by engineers worldwide at central sites. A technician will only go to a site after all intranet options have been exhausted. HP also uses the intranet to distribute software upgrades and common tools, to manage documents, to transmit and store employees' personal records, and to enhance staff training through intranet-delivered courses. One thousand HP business users take advantage of on-line learning opportunities every month.[60]

Hewlett-Packard soon discovered that it could use the intranet to undertake one of the major challenges facing almost every large firm: ending desktop anarchy. A useful analogy is electricity. All of us take electricity for granted. We simply plug the cable into the wall socket without thinking about voltages, pin sizes and shapes, or how the electrical signal is transmitted, modulated, and synchronized. We don't have to worry about differences among appliances by Sony or Panasonic or Sharp. We simply plug in and turn on. We want the same capability from our PCs—switch on and log on—and we are beginning to expect to be able to do just that.

Alas, information technology infrastructures differ substantially from the electricity paradigm. Information systems planners struggle every day with PC software upgrades, network operating systems, virus protection, local area networks, servers, routers, hubs, protocols, and network management. Each of these issues affects the desktop. When every type of desktop system can be as different from one another as a VCR is from a cellular phone, the problem of coordination is compounded. HP has more than eighty thousand personal computers running either Microsoft Windows 3.1, Windows 95, or Windows NT, plus more than twenty thousand workstations using the UNIX operating system. These all require tweaking and special network software and hardware to enable them to participate in the common network infrastructure. The task of supporting a multiplicity of operating systems, PC applications, database management systems, and local area networks is as complex as that of managing an electrical utility, except that the utility is stable and has evolved over a century while the IT utility is unstable, incomplete, and ever-evolving.

TCP/IP offers a solution to this problem. It is the only telecommunications protocol that can operate with and "interoperate" among devices using any operating system. It can thus deliver information created on, say, a Sun Microsystems workstation operating under UNIX to a PC running under Windows. The Web browser provides a standardized and hence easy to service and support interface that, again, makes information and communication between disparate systems practical.

HP used the Internet technology as the base to define its Common Operating Environment (COE) and to establish desktop standards without requiring business units to adopt a single operating system and set of core software packages for word processing, spreadsheets, and electronic mail. UNIX lovers didn't have to switch to Windows.

The HP intranet serves many distinct applications and projects:

- *Data Broadcasting:* Employees are kept up-to-date through daily downloads of company and industry news directly to their PCs.

- *Human Resource Management:* Distribution of personnel policies and guidelines.

- *Product Design and Information:* Coordination and communication of design iterations and change orders, and a home page that provides sales and marketing information.

- *Software Sharing:* Internet access to a central server that reduces the number of copies needed of common PC applications, such as word processing and presentation packages.

- *Electronic Sales Partner:* Delivery of sales and product information to the field, allowing sales reps to spend more time with their clients. (In addition to significant savings in mail and printing costs, an internal HP survey revealed that four thousand sales reps calculate that ESP saves them five hours of wasted time every week.)

HP's intranet strategy is almost certain to become standard for large organizations. TCP/IP has its limitations and could not have been used in the mid-1980s as the foundation for an internal network. The improvement in telecommunications transmission speeds, lower costs, and the ever-increasing power and cost-effectiveness of computer hardware, however, have made it a very practical tool for harmonizing the mass of incompatible hardware, software, and networks that IS organizations have to support. But, as the HP example shows, exploiting the intranet opportunity rests on having a strong, skilled, and credible IS unit to lead design and implementation.

General Electric <*http://www.ge.com*>

General Electric operates in more than one hundred countries around the world, with 250 manufacturing plants in twenty-six different nations, and it employs 222,000 people worldwide, including 150,000 in the United States. It is the world's largest diversified manufacturer and a leader in many of the major markets of this century: among them jet aircraft engines, electric power generation, television broadcasting, home appliances, and industrial materials such as plastics. The Connecticut-based conglomerate is among the world's ten largest industrial firms and, with a market value of $120 billion, the highest-valued company in the United States. GE Capital Services, which provides consumer and specialized financing and property and casualty reinsurance, is the company's largest revenue source.

GE's long-standing goal is to have each of its segments lead its industry. The National Broadcasting Company (NBC) is enjoying its most profitable period ever, with strong ratings leading to higher advertising revenues. GE and one of its joint ventures won more than half the world's orders for commercial aircraft engines in 1995. Its lighting business had developed a global presence, and its plastics unit has achieved record growth by supplying the computer and consumer electronics industries.

GE set up its Web site in response to customer requests for speedy, accurate information and business transactions performed on their terms, and GE's goal was ultimately to handle all dealings with suppliers and customers through the Web. In October 1994, GE's Web site went public with about fifteen hundred pages of technical information.[61]

GE's short- and long-term strategic Web objectives are, respectively, to encourage customers to do business at the Web site and to make their buying decisions there, and, over time, to raise the level of customer decision making, whether at the consumer or the business-to-business level. After scrutinizing many company Web sites, Eugene Marlow, author of *Web Visions: An Inside Look at Successful Business Strategy on the Net,* comments on GE's Web site: "GE is one of the standard setters in the relatively new intranet communications medium. For the consumer, business and employee alike, this site accommodates many needs and offers information that previously would have often been unattainable or at the very least, difficult to obtain."[62]

GE's latest endeavor is to create a consulting practice for customers and GE Capital units that provides electronic commerce services. This includes the roll-out of a Web-based ordering and tracking service (at its $1.6 billion electrical products distribution unit) and the addition of seven business units to GE's Web-based automated procurement system. John McKinley, chief technology and information officer at GE Capital in Stamford, Connecticut, defines the program this way: "Electronic commerce traditionally was niche focused, like credit-card purchases over the Internet. . . . But we have a much broader definition of electronic commerce. It's a ubiquitous network business model for prospecting customers, order management, and order fulfillment."[63]

In the summer of 1996, GE launched its web-based Trading Process Network to allow approximately fourteen hundred suppliers to compete for contracts with the firm. The Trading Process Network, now referred to as TPN Register, has since evolved to include an Internet-based trading network that allows buyers and sellers to engage in business-to-business electronic commerce. By June 1997, GE expected to have done $1 billion worth of business through its Web site.[64] The Trading Process Network, which automates purchasing by GE's Lighting Unit in Cleveland, started as a pilot project and has succeeded in cutting the unit's average purchasing cycle in half, from fourteen to seven days. Because of the Web's openness, the project gained an immediate payoff of a 10 to 15 percent cut in prices; many smaller companies and ones that had had no prior relationship with GE accessed the site and made bids on proposals, increasing price competition among suppliers.

In the future, GE's Web site will become more transactional. Richard Costello, corporate marketing communications manager, summarizes GE's position:

> Many of the businesses we are dealing with are quickly shifting themselves to their own intranets for internal communications. Once you do that, you also get access to the external Net and so you are getting very high levels of penetration. . . . [A] year ago this month, there was less than 10 percent penetration of access. I checked last week and we had about 80–85 percent penetration. . . . I think intranets are going to be very, very rapidly disseminated, so that suddenly a medium that was penetrating at 10 percent, 15 percent now has 80 percent, 90 percent access to your customer groups, at which point it becomes a very, very viable alternative distribution mechanism to paper, telephone calls, catalogs, telemarketing, and other things that we're using other than traditional distribution systems.[65]

GE's intranet, like that of HP, serves as a signal to all large organizations: Enterprise intranets are rapidly becoming essential tools. Between 1994 and 1996, the Internet attracted all the interest and excited attention: 1996 was the year of the Internet. But we predict that 1997 will be known as the year of the intranet.

Combining the Internet with an intranet will be the agenda for the near future for every large firm.

In GE's case, the Net has significantly changed the company's procurement process. GE posts requests for proposals on its site, thus attracting new bidders, who respond electronically; both partners' transaction costs are reduced, which shows up in more aggressive pricing. At an extreme, this may lead to commoditization: Suppliers will be so squeezed and will face so many new competitors pushing to capture business with large firms like GE that only pricing will matter. In this regard, the Internet may reduce gross margins over the long term. Since using the Net can only reduce transaction costs, the overall impact may be not only lower prices but substantial profit, as well.

HotWired <*http://www.hotwired.com*>

The *HotWired* Web site, launched in October 1994, is unquestionably a state-of-the-art E-zine (electronic magazine). It combines the design and editorial style of its printed sister magazine *Wired* with multimedia, hyperlinked, interactive resources of the Web. *HotWired* attained its reputation as a premier advertising site on the Web by using the now common Web banner ad format that allows interested parties to click on a small picture—the banner— to access an advertiser's Web site.[66] *HotWired*'s homepage recently reported that the company had acquired 235,000 subscribers in just one year.

In 1995, *HotWired*'s revenues were about $25 million; in 1996, they increased to approximately $30 million. Andrew Anker, president of *HotWired,* the company's World Wide Web "cyberstation," says *HotWired* gets four hundred thousand to six hundred thousand hits per day and that the staff working on *HotWired* is larger than that working on *Wired* magazine itself, with *HotWired* hiring two new employees each week.[67]

HotWired may or may not succeed; many E-zines have come and gone, and despite all the claims and predictions about advertising on Web as the wave of a glorious future and about the death of print, online magazine publishing has had few successes. The Web changes all the rules—about advertising, writing, publishing, and even reading. *HotWired* is worth tracking, however, because it is produced by one of the field's leading print publications and targets the mainstream Internet community using the best of available Internet software and multimedia tools. It thus represents a potential new mainstream for publishing.

One key factor in *HotWired*'s success thus far has been its audience, which, true to one of the E-zine's primary tag lines, constitutes "mainstream culture for the twenty-first century." Nearly one-third of *HotWired*'s readers (28 percent) report visiting the site to view product information or advertising; 80 percent visit for entertainment; and 50 percent visit to read the magazine. Seventy-two percent of *HotWired*'s readers are college graduates or have post-graduate degrees. The average member is a thirty-two year old male earning $50,000 per year who has been a Web user for less than six months.[68]

AT&T was *HotWired*'s first advertiser, signing on in April 1994. In its first year of online publishing, more than forty advertisers made use of *HotWired*'s Web site, from Fortune 500 corporations such as IBM and General Motors to emerging technology leaders such as Xircom and Personal Library Software. Ads make up 95 percent of the E-zine's revenue, with about 90 percent of the buys coming through agencies.[69]

For the three-month period ending August 31, 1996, the *HotWired* Network had an average of more than 24,000 visitors and approximately 9.7 million page views per weekday. It had more than 430,000 registered members and a staff of more than 125 reporters, editors, designers, and sales personnel. Revenue estimates for 1997 are in the $30 to $40 million dollar range.

USAID <*http://www.info.usaid.gov*>

USAID, established in 1961 by president John F. Kennedy, is an overseas provider of economic aid and humanitarian assistance with the goal of advancing U.S. economic and political interests. The Internet was almost literally a lifeline for the struggling organization. According to Joe Fredericks of USAID's Legislative and Public Affairs Department, "one of the central motivations for the agency's development of, first a Gopher site, and then, a Web site was survival: survival of the agency in the Washington, D.C., context of government contraction and budget deficit reduction."[70] (Gopher is an Internet software tool for accessing and sharing data files, developed at and run by the University of Minnesota, the sports teams at which use the nickname Gophers.) USAID began using the Internet in the spring of 1994. It built a straightforward Web site, and in doing so extended the effective reach of the organization immensely.

When an attendee at a trade conference commented that he wanted to do business with USAID but didn't know anyone or have any contacts there, another attendee in the back of the room responded: "I manufacture medical supplies. I happened onto their home page and I looked at the business opportunities and, looking through there, I managed to find three I could bid on. Electronically, I got the solicitation document, bid on all three, won all three; I provided the supplies, submitted a bill, got paid . . . and I still don't know anyone at USAID."[71]

USAID's effectiveness rests on communication of information and on contacts. Those are expensive items when they depend on offices, people, and publications, and in today's cost-cutting environment the organization's budget can only go down. The Web provides USAID with international offices that don't require staffs and transforms the publication flow. Many companies find that the Web's main value is to provide them with an international presence, establishing two-way links with customers that they could not otherwise afford. For USAID, this has been a matter of survival. For others, it will be more a matter of opportunity and incremental growth: Their Web sites won't change the basics of their business but constitute sensible additions, rather like adding a 1-800 number for customer service. These companies can expect cost savings or other benefits in such areas as printing and customer communication, additional sales leads, and closer relationships with some customers due to improved response times and information flow. These benefits will result even though the Web sites are not linked to internal transaction processing systems, which adds cost and complexity to both application development and operations.

At some point, probably before the end of 1999, what is now an opportunity will become a necessity, as at USAID. Customers will expect to see an electronic mail address on their suppliers' business cards and in their marketing material. In this eventuality, having a Web site may not add revenues and profits, but not having one may well cut them, just as not having an ad in the Yellow Pages is not a smart choice for a take-out pizza delivery service.

The USAID example shows that even an organization with limited resources and information technology capabilities can move the communication and information components of its customer relationships onto the Web at low cost. Relationships, not technology, are the issue. In light of USAID's experience, business managers should consider the following questions relative to their own firms' situations.

- If we make it possible for existing customers to access information and services via the Web, will this capability make a marginal or a major difference for them and for us *now?*

- Will a Web presence make a marginal or a major difference in our efforts to attract new customers?

- Looking ahead three years, what will be the answers to the above questions?

Sun Microsystems <*http://www.sun.com*>

Sun Microsystems, based in Mountain View, California, ranks number 244 on the Fortune 500 list. Its business strategy has always been based on its aphorism "The Network Is the Computer." In the 1980s, Sun was an early Internet user. Today, as a company with more than $8 billion—this figure from fiscal year 1997 reflects a 21 percent increase from 1996—in annual revenues, it continues to expand its Internet applications and to discover new network challenges.

Sun will succeed or fail because of the Internet. Its high-performance workstations use the UNIX operating system, the core software on which the Internet was built. Before the creation of the Mosaic Web browser, the base for the browsers at Netscape, America Online, and others, the Internet meant UNIX. Sun's cofounder and chairman, Scott McNealy, has been a passionate advocate of "networkcentric" computing; in an earlier era, marked by slow and expensive telecommunications, the PC as Microsoft's private software preserve, and a pre-Web Internet, McNealy was largely seen as mildly eccentric. Now he's leading a sustained assault on Fortress Microsoft by enabling an entirely new approach to computing through networking. Instead of a heavy-duty PC handling and storing all software, a stripped-down network appliance gets software as needed from the Internet. That software is built in small, self-contained "applets," something like a software Lego block, written using the Sun-sponsored Java programming language. Java is transforming Web software development by letting users add animation and real-time video to their Web pages. But Sun built its reputation on hardware— workstations, servers, and microprocessors—and its UNIX-based servers run about half the networks that make up the Internet, while its microprocessors power its own and others' workstations and servers. Commercial accounts make up one-third of Sun's revenues.[72]

As a leading provider of innovations for the Web, Sun is also an innovator in using it. The Web is becoming, in effect, its organizational structure in action, and it permeates all of Sun's operations and customer relationships. The cost of the Web per U.S. branch is in the $50,000 to $60,000 range. Jerry Neece, enterprise training program manager at Sun University, comments on the meaning of this figure to Sun:

> To put that into perspective . . . this is the justification we used to fund it. If for example there are three thousand sales people in the field and the average cost of a trip for a week to take training from Europe is about $2,200 and from Asia about $3,000 and the number of trips those three thousand people take is reduced by one each year, take the three thousand and multiply it by $2,500, and that's how much Sun saves. Just in reducing the air travel cost and hotel expenses, it more than pays for the network. In terms of intranet applications, the one that will pay for itself fastest is probably training, simply because it has such a large cost elimination associated with it, that is, travel.[73]

Sun's extensive use of the Internet and the World Wide Web allows it to address many issues simultaneously, while at the same time lowering the costs of distributing information, facilitating collaboration, and keeping international customers in close communication. Global reach is an essential component of its overall Internet strategy.

One seemingly trivial Internet application that saves Sun a lot of time, money, and frustration, for example, is Sun's system for filing online expense reports. Before implementation of the system, forms were filled out and sent to an approval desk, after which employees would wonder what happened to them. Reports often got lost, leaving employees to scurry around, wasting time and getting irritated trying to find or recreate them. Just as often, the reports would be returned to the employee for more information. Now, when filling out online reports, employees find that the system won't forward reports with incorrectly filled or empty fields. The report, once accepted, is e-mailed to all approvers, and the employee knows exactly who has and has not approved it. The entire process happens online, with a savings to Sun of at least 50 percent over the cost of doing it the old way, before the Internet.[74]

The following are some of the benefits Sun has gained from its strong presence on the Internet.[75]

- Staff at the university where Sun housed its first Web site projected, by the end of the server's first year, ten thousand hits per day as an optimistic goal. After several months, the volume of traffic was so great that Sun upgraded the hardware at the Chapel Hill, North Carolina, Sun SITE. By 1993, the server was getting one hundred thousand requests for information daily, and traffic was so heavy that Sun provided the Sun SITE with a separate high-speed T1 (leased line) connection to improve access and response time. Daily hits at the Chapel Hill Web server quickly reached three hundred thousand.

- By June 1995, Sun had fifteen Sun SITE servers in place, handling well over one million hits per day, bringing Sun's brand name and corporate presence to desktops everywhere. Visitors associate Sun SITE with current, accurate, useful, and interesting information that is well organized and easy to access.

- The Imperial College, London, server is the second-busiest Sun SITE, with more than two hundred thousand hits per day, and its collection of public domain software makes it the most heavily used ftp (file transfer protocol) site in Europe.

- Katherine Webster, manager of Sun's Internet marketing program, estimates that in 1994 SunService saved more than $4 million in traditional customer support costs because so many of its customers went directly to a Sun SITE to obtain software upgrades and patches or to find product solutions.

- Sun's corporate home page receives one hundred seventy-five thousand plus hits every day.

Innovators in the computer industry don't necessarily benefit from their leadership. Wang, the pioneer in easy-to-use word processing, and Digital Equipment, the inventor of minicomputers and for twenty years IBM's only successful competitor, are now examples of technology leaders and business losers. That could happen to Sun. It's vulnerable on many fronts, and its invention of Java may well create a vast software industry from which Sun, primarily a hardware firm, will not make money. That said, Sun remains a very well run company with superb products, imaginative leadership, and shrewd market sense. Perhaps the main message managers can glean from Sun's use of the Internet is this: Well-run companies use every edge they can get, and the Net adds an edge, even if only for expense reporting and training; by compounding small savings and streamlining processes, only a few years yields a leaner, faster machine.

Kenny's Bookshop and Art Galleries Ltd., Galway, Ireland <*http://www.iol.ie/resource/kennys/*>

Kenny's Bookshop, in operation for fifty-six years and specializing in new and secondhand books on Irish topics, reports annual sales of approximately $1.5 million, of which 60 percent comes from export sales to libraries and individuals through its direct mail book club. Kenny's employs twenty-two people, has just one retail store, and operates an extensive mail order business. It quickly spotted the opportunity offered by the World Wide Web for a simple extension to its core business. Kenny's goal was to provide customers with information electronically and to enable them to make their purchases online.[76] Table 3 summarizes the benefits that Kenny's reports having gained from its Internet presence. To maintain a tradition of personal assistance to each customer, everyone sending an e-mail request to be added to Kenny's mailing list receives a personal e-mail response, followed by a telephone call.

Kenny's has seen many other benefits from its Internet presence, including the following:

Table 3   Kenny's Bookshop: Benefits from an Internet Presence

Business Process	Pre-Internet	Post-Internet
Marketing	Creation of company brochure (expensive)	Large and regularly updated interactive brochures via WWW
Weekly Mailing List of New Books on Irish Topics	Labor intensive preparation of paper copies for postage	Sent via e-mail to 40 percent of existing list recipients; 200 percent increase in list
"Irish Book Parcel"	Limited access to potential new customers	Greatly expanded access to potential new customers
Customer Inquiries Turnaround	Days, due to use of post by customer	Minutes, due to use of e-mail
Secondhand Book Catalog	Paper-based catalog quickly out of date and reaches existing customers only	Electronic online catalog updated weekly; existing and new customers due to WWW pages
Customer Relations	Telephone calls limited due to time zone differences	Reduction of time zone problems by using e-mail
Publicity/Corporate Image	"Old and Staid"	"Modern and Progressive"
Monitoring Existing Customer Stocks	Telephone and library	Telnet into the libraries' online database

Source: Adapted from the Proceedings from the Ninth International Confrence on EDI - IOS, p.297.

- During its first year, Kenny's Web site received inquiries resulting in two hundred new customers for its Irish Book Parcel; these new customers represent $50,000 in per annum sales on an on-going basis.

- Due to the increased speed of response made possible by the Internet, time lag in replying to customers has been eliminated.

- The currency and availability of the secondhand book catalog has been considerably enhanced.

- Kenny's has realized some of the benefits to small companies in areas of limited local market size of the ability to sell products globally.

- The Internet reduced Kenny's advertising costs while extending the reach of its advertising campaign.

- The Internet provided a non-proprietary, low-cost medium for organizations from anywhere in the world, regardless of size, to trade with Kenny's via computer networks.[77]

Maryse Collins, Kenny's marketing manager, believes that "on the Internet all organizations are equal in the sense that the e-mail address or World Wide Web pages of large and small companies are indistinguishable."[78]

The Web is a gift to small firms in industries in which (1) customers know what they want and don't need to inspect goods before placing orders; (2) existing retail systems are limited in inventory and ease of access (try locating, say, a biography of the Irish patriot Wolfe Tone anywhere in the city nearest you); (3) goods can be shipped by mail, Federal Express, or UPS; (4) the gross margin on a single sale is high enough to cover the costs of the Internet service (books typically have a 20 to 40 percent margin); and (5) two hundred extra customers would make a significant contribution to profits.

Schlumberger (*http://www.slb.com*>

Schlumberger is a New York-based $7.5 billion multinational company. It manufactures testing and measurement equipment and provides high-tech services to oil companies. When customers need key information about existing oil wells or technical support in exploring potential oil and gas deposits anywhere in the world, Schlumberger finds the answers. It helps oil exploration companies rejuvenate aging production fields in the North Sea or the

Gulf of Mexico. This Franco-American oil services firm, with its close links to the world's premiere semiconductor maker, Intel, has also developed sophisticated electronic systems that allow oil companies to extend the life of wells that less technologically equipped oil companies might otherwise give up on.[79]

The company's equipment, which allows precise monitoring of oil reservoirs and fluid movement, can recover about 50 percent of the oil currently being overlooked in existing fields, according to the company's CEO, Euan Baird. About 75 percent of the company's revenues and income are derived from activities outside the United States. Schlumberger employs more than fifty thousand people of seventy-five nationalities operating in more than ninety countries (with some located in extremely remote, desert locations).[80]

Schlumberger uses Internet technology to bring its organization and employees together. Its intranet network uses the TCP/IP protocol and serves twenty-two thousand users in more than five hundred locations. It has more than one hundred internal Web servers and thirty Gopher servers. (Gopher is the file transfer equivalent of the Web, a software service for finding and downloading computer files.)[81]

The Schlumberger intranet (SINet) was designed to connect everyone, everywhere. The firm created satellite links to remote sites, making global communication possible and providing the basis for many otherwise impractical IT projects, which in turn save money and create new revenue.[82] Bill Macgregor, a scientist at Schlumberger Labs, observes that the company's interest in the Internet is not solely a matter of geographic convenience: It is also a natural outgrowth of the firm's pursuit of the best technological solutions for international research and communication. On the road, the network keeps Schlumberger's employees connected to ongoing discussions and decisions. This combination of long-distance travel and electronic teamwork puts a premium on information-sharing at all levels in the company. The Internet bridges differences in locations to promote a culture of communication and collaboration. The Schlumberger strategy for global competitiveness includes using the Internet to speed development projects, to serve customer information needs effectively, and to foster a sense of community and collaboration among the company's far-flung locations.[83]

In addition to creating global connectivity, SINet has benefited Schlumberger in other ways. Teams of employees can now download design tools on the computer, which has significantly reduced the time from oil-field research to well-site launch from four years to eighteen months and made possible real-time updates of technical documentation and hazardous waste manuals. Information sharing fosters global collaborations that help solve customer problems quickly, reduces duplication, and enhances employee productivity.[84] Given the multi-billion dollar cost of developing oil fields, the forty-eight to eighteen month reduction in launch time is in itself a massive economic and competitive gain.

In early 1984, before corporate networking was "in," Schlumberger set up a new communications network. The company connected, through a series of proprietary (vendor and product specific) networks, research labs in Paris, Tokyo, Houston, Ridgefield, Connecticut, and Cambridge, England. In 1991, Schlumberger instituted its Internet-based strategy for its international network. According to Victor E. Grijalva, executive vice president of oil-field services, "the biggest obstacle was technical. . . . Nothing like SINet had existed before."[85] David P. Sims, technical manager for information technology at Schlumberger's Sugarland, Texas, office, further comments on the utility of the system: "Because we'd had a private corporate network since 1985, the evolution to Internet-style, open architecture networking was seen as a way to improve performance and achieve a high level of interoperability—Schlumberger has at least one of every kind of computer ever invented—while at the same time reducing costs."[86]

Between 1989 and 1996, Schlumberger invested $72 million

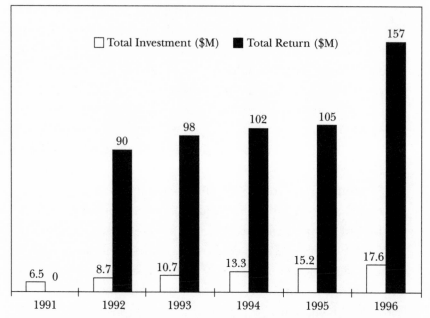

Figure 7 Schlumberger Internet Investments and Returns, 1991–1996.

Source: E.B. Baatz. "Net Results." *CIO Magazine,* 1 February 1997, 80. Reprinted through the courtesy of CIO. © 1997 CIO Communications.

in its network. On average, the demand for network service increases 4 to 10 percent every month. Since 1991, the company has tracked communications costs, including expenses for airline travel for face-to-face meetings, telephone and network charges, and overnight mail and courier services. Its findings for 1993 showed that total communications costs had decreased by 2 percent, a $2 million saving. Since 1993, product data management and resource planning software deployed worldwide in the oil field product services centers have saved the company $55 million in IT costs.[87]

The network helps fewer people accomplish more tasks. Prior to SINet, the company had one sales representative for every forty customers. Today the ratio is one to three hundred. Sales per employee per year amount to $149,000, outperforming Schlumberger's nearest competitor by 50 percent. Between 1991 and 1995, head count fell 6.3 percent, while revenues grew 26.5 percent. From 1992 to 1996, Schlumberger calculates that revenues were enhanced by $552 million due to SINet. (See Figure 7.) In addition, the company was able to reduce the number of seismic data processing centers around the world from fifteen to two. Exceedingly important to serving its clients, Schlumberger's network allows the company to keep up with fast-moving emergency situations.[88]

Schlumberger's total $72 million investment on its network generated a direct gross return of a phenomenal $552 million: a net ROI of 668 percent. In 1996, two spin-off companies, Omnes (the Schlumberger/Cable & Wireless telecommunications joint venture) and GlobalSoft (a new software development company), also generated significant additional revenue income ($70 million) for the company.

McAfee Associates <*http://www.mcafee.com*>

McAfee Associates, a California-based software development company and leading supplier of enterprise-wide network and security management software, was started in 1989. Since the company's inception, its homepage reports, McAfee Associates has registered thirty-three consecutive quarters of revenue growth, and the number of employees has grown from four to four hundred and one. According to Bill McKiernan (former president and CEO at McAfee), electronic software distribution is the essential ingredient in the firm's success. He strongly believes that given the impressive advantages, doing business electronically will soon be the norm in his industry. In just six years, McAfee's net revenue went from $1.5 million (in 1990) to $13.7 million (in 1992) to $181.1 million in 1996.[89] Just packaging and mailing a floppy disk and manual costs at least twenty-five dollars. Sending it electronically costs less than twenty-five cents.

The firm's business plan was to develop basic software needed by the majority of businesses and then to post the software on various bulletin boards and networks, encouraging organizations and individuals to download the software for free on a trial basis. During this free test period, McAfee offered high quality technical support services to every customer. It then collected licenses and fees from the businesses and individuals who decided to keep the software.

Comments from company executives emphasize the enhanced flexibility as well as the cost savings of the McAfee system. Bill McKiernan, former president and CEO, stresses the initial advantage to both company and customer.

> It makes no sense to take a product like software, that starts out in electronic format, download it onto a disk, wrap it up in cardboard and plastic, weigh it down to two or three pounds of paper documentation, then ship it out to the customer. . . . Think of all the overhead, waste, and delay in that process, compared to letting customers download software and documentation onto their own computers. Delivery is instantaneous; the software can be up and running as soon as it is needed . . . and because software is distributed electronically, enhancements and upgrades can be passed on to the customers at much more frequent intervals. . . . We can reach customers in Europe or Asia as easily as companies in the United States. It provides us with an electronic channel to reach literally millions of users in minutes at incredible cost savings.[90]

The follow-up advantages are equally significant, as this comment, also from McKiernan, attests.

> When someone posts a message on the Internet asking about a specific technical issue related to our software, we can respond to it at once; the answer will remain on the Internet and be available for other users to read. If anyone has follow-up questions, they can also get them answered on-line. This is a big advantage over answering the same question five hundred times on the telephone; it represents another way to realize significant savings in support costs while actually improving our support to customers.[91]

By 1999, sending software upgrades through the mail by floppy disk will obviously be a quaint eccentricity. Almost all software will be downloaded from an Internet or intranet site.

Uncover Inc. <*www.uncweb.carl.org*>

Uncover, launched in 1988 by CARL Systems Inc., is a database featuring the tables of contents from thousands of journals. According to Rebecca Lenzini, president of CARL,

> People thought we were crazy at the time, putting all this information into a database that existed only on a network, with no printed equivalent or even a CD-ROM. From the beginning, Uncover was a product intended for customers with network connections. Some people simply could not believe that it was a real market. They predicted Uncover would never become self-supporting. By the fall of 1988 it became clear that the Internet was going to be the primary vehicle for reaching a large number of organizations and individuals. So we began focusing on how to get Uncover up on the Internet and how to market access to it.[92]

By spring 1993, Uncover was generating enough business to spin off as an independent enterprise.[93]

Uncover has experienced a growth rate parallel to that of the Internet itself. In 1990, the database was accessed nearly five hundred times each day. By spring 1993, the rate of use had increased to more than nine thousand hits daily. A major growth spurt occurred when Uncover added a document delivery service linked to the articles in the database. Direct payment for journal articles made it possible to expand their customer base from primarily educational institutions and libraries to a broad base of researchers, consultants, and professional and business people. An internal system was set up to handle the anticipated large volume of individual traffic and credit card orders. Since the inception of direct payment, Uncover has delivered about fifty thousand documents, with a 300 percent increase in the last eighteen months. This pace shows no sign of slowing. The delivery business has generated so much revenue that Uncover can now offer its original product, the table of contents database, at no cost.[94] By mid-1997, Uncover's services included more than 17,000 English-language periodicals in its database, and over 7 million articles available through on-line delivery—with 5,000 citations being added daily. Nearly every publication is delivered on-line at the same time it is delivered to the newsstand. In addition, most articles can now be sent directly to a customer's fax machine within 24 hours of order placement; more often, delivery time is under one hour.[95] The company was hopeful that by late 1997, it would be able to deliver an individual article, with the permission of its original publisher, directly to their customer's desktop.[96]

Some information is best provided in paper form, and paper will have the advantage for many decades. Some information is too expensive, too varied, or too specialized for potential users either to be aware that it exists or to be willing to pay $50 to $500 to subscribe to the journals in which it is published. (A 1980 survey found that the average readership of an article in the leading academic journals was just six people—probably the author, his or her proud parents, and the professor's tenure committee.) Through Internet services such as Uncover, the six readers are already becoming six hundred or six thousand. The Internet is also making it easy for anyone to find even the most obscure journals.

Silicon Graphics Inc *<http://www.sgi.com>*

Silicon Graphics (SGI) brings fake things to life. Founded in 1981, the California-based company is the world's number one maker of computers used by engineers, scientists, and Hollywood special-effects artists. Silicon Graphics pioneered many developments in visual and 3-D computing. It offers high-performance

workstations, multiprocessing servers, advanced computing platforms, and application software. Silicon Graphics is probably best
known for its graphics subsystems, which enable computers to
process 3-D imagery and real-time animation without slowing the
performance of more general computing tasks. Its computers
were used to make computer-generated images seem like the real
thing in the movies *Forrest Gump, Jurassic Park,* and *Men in Black.*

Silicon Graphics's intranet, Silicon Junction, is accessible by
all 10,400 SGI employees in 195 locations. It has more than 2,000
servers and provides access to more than 150,000 Internet addresses (that is, URLs, or Unique Resource Locators) and to more
than 200,000 Web sites.[97]

SGI began developing the intranet in early 1994 as a small-
scale grass roots project. Now, *every* project at Silicon Graphics has
its own Web site on the intranet, and every desktop computer is
set up to be its own Web server. Employees are free to create as
many sites as they wish.

Before the intranet, Silicon Graphics used a typical purchase
requisition process. A paper form listing the requested items was
manually filled out and sent to appropriate management for
approval. After signatures were obtained, the requisition was forwarded to the purchasing department, where a purchasing coordinator entered data into a software application. The output was
then routed to a purchasing manager for review and authorization. Problems were frequent, ranging from incorrect part numbers to employee inquiries about the status of overdue orders.
Consequently, as the number of employees increased, the number
of purchasing personnel needed increased correspondingly.

SGI mandated the creation of an intranet infrastructure, open
to the entire company, to be supported by its central Information
Systems organization. Important to the intranet strategy was the
participation of employees and departments, who were encouraged to create what they needed when they needed it, without
waiting for approval from either corporate headquarters or IS.

The Purchasing Department created an application called Electronic Requisition. Offering a graphical interface, it is used as the front end to the requisition process and automates and streamlines standard item purchases. This post-intranet requisition process is much quicker and more efficient than the old one. Using it, an employee logs onto the system, selects an item from the electronic catalog, complete with description, and adds the requested items to a "virtual" shopping cart. When the order is complete, the requisition is routed for approval, based on the department number and signature authority input by the employee at the beginning of the process. The approval process consists of codified signature authority rules so that, when the order is sent via e-mail to the appropriate authority, with the aid of a Web jumper, the manager can click on the order and approve, modify, or reject it. The requisition is then sent to the purchasing department, and a purchase order for the items chosen is sent either electronically or by fax (without human intervention) to the supplier. The order is then drop-shipped directly to the employee's desk. Managers must still place orders for non-standard items; but SGI's goal is to put as many items as possible in the pre-approved catalog.

SGI's intranet has saved the company money; an estimated $250,000 per year savings in computer training costs as well as $3 million per year in reduced travel for sales force training. In addition, SGI's intranet has allowed the company to streamline business processes and reduce the time, errors, and steps necessary for employees to do their jobs. Less easy to quantify has been the observed impact the intranet has had on meetings. Because information is so easily obtained and so readily available, employees are better prepared, and meetings are less frequent, shorter, and more productive. There are fewer follow-up phone calls made and fewer documents need to be circulated. SGI reported $3,552.6 million in revenues for fiscal year 1997.

NBD. No Big Deal. The Internet is nothing new or special.

Yet that may be the salient message here for managers. NBD. Purchase requisitions, HR job listings, coordination of software upgrades . . . NBD. Just do it.

Knight-Ridder <*http://www.knight-ridder.com*>

Knight-Ridder, a Miami-based company, prints thirty-eight papers (accounting for about 80 percent of its revenues), including the *Detroit Free Press,* the *Miami Herald,* and the *Philadelphia Inquirer.* The second largest U.S. newspaper chain (after Gannett), the firm also has a significant presence online: its Knight-Ridder Information subsidiary offers information retrieval services such as DataStar and Dialog, which provide abstracts and full texts of more than four thousand business, news, and science publications. The company also seeks to publish World Wide Web versions of most of its newspapers.

KR-SourceOne is the electronic document delivery arm of Knight-Ridder Information (KRI), a Knight-Ridder company. It is a full service document provider and possibly the largest user of Internet services for commercial document delivery, with two hundred thousand customers in almost one hundred fifty companies. It offers more than six hundred online databases and delivers documents quickly and efficiently through a variety of order interfaces including Web sites and DIALOG (sm), the Knight-Ridder Information online information service.

Knight-Ridder and IBM received the first Internet and Electronic Commerce Award for Internet infrastructure, presented by the Gartner Group and *Information Week* magazine. The award was given in recognition for the "dramatic results achieved by the state-of-the-art document image order management system." Using a combination of Lotus Notes and Domino's interactive Web application server, IBM developed Knight-Ridder Information's KR SourceOne document delivery service.

Document requests are processed online through the Lotus Notes software system, which tracks orders, customer information, and order status updates automatically via Internet e-mail. Document sources are expedited rapidly through an identification process that accesses an electronic catalog of 1.5 million document sources. Using this catalog, orders are instantly routed to sources around the world, linking the system to state-of-the-art image depositories as well as archived hard copy collections.[98]

By leveraging intranet technology to automate and enhance key processes, KR SourceOne generated impressive gains in efficiency and customer satisfaction. An independent survey found the following:

- Ninety-seven percent of SourceOne customers report being either "very" or "extremely" satisfied with the service.

- Ninety-three percent of customers are "very" or "extremely" satisfied with the ease of using the service.

- Ninety-four percent of customers would recommend Teltech's document delivery service to colleagues.

- Ninety-seven percent of customers expect to contact SourceOne again for their document delivery needs.

Customers are able to search the document catalog, check real-time order status, place orders, review their profiles, and download KR SourceOne's "DocView" image view software, at no charge. The combination of image workflow, improved order management, and custom Web interface capability has thoroughly integrated the work environment. This cultural change has boosted productivity, reduced costs, and improved responsiveness to customers and customer satisfaction. Specific improvements include the following:

- A 25 percent reduction in costs of goods sold.
- A 20 percent increase in productivity.
- Decreased order turnaround times.
- Increased percentage of requests filled to 97 percent, considered the highest of any full service document supplier.[99]

Summary

These are just twenty or so of the companies that have found ways of exploiting the Internet as a business opportunity. These vignettes clearly show how each company has not had to rely on technology innovation. As is always the case in the computer and telecommunication fields, they have had to deal with the often complex and expensive issues of implementation and operation. However, their experience shows, using the old cliché, that the business Internet is "ready for prime"—as were the managers in these companies.

Glossary of Terms

Agents Agents are smart software programs that find or filter information or make transactions. Sometimes referred to as intelligent agents, software agents, smart agents or just agents, they act on the user's behalf as the equivalent of a travel agent, secretary, or caterer, carrying out tasks without waiting for explicit requests; they don't tie up the user's time, making him or her wait around as they complete their tasks. Agents are among the most important emerging innovations for Internet services because they offer many value-added features without adding extra complexity for or demanding extra effort from the user.

Eyes provides an example of a simple agent at work. This automated Personal Notification Service is offered by Amazon.com, an online Internet bookstore with a catalog of over two million titles from thousands of publishers, all of which can be purchased from anywhere in the world. When users search the Amazon Web site for a particular author or subject, Eyes asks if users would like to be informed of any new book matching the established criteria. If users respond "yes," Eyes will track for them every newly released book by the specified author or in the specified area of interest, automatically sending e-mail messages about it. The agent does the work—the user need not even think about it. This service is free, entails no purchase obligation, and can keep the user fully up to date about areas of interest without even bothering to visit Amazon to find the information. In the future, agents will make many Web sites increasingly "invisible," as they work in the background, contacting users only when the agent has something for them to look at, rather than their having to contact the agent or site.

"Andersen Consulting developed Bargain Finder, a software agent that searches the Web for the lowest prices on consumer products. Although the results of this experiment had not been reported publicly, managers interviewed during the summer of 1996 expressed concern about the destructive potential of Bargain Finder and other agent-based capabilities. Some reported that, as a countermeasure, their firms were attempting to utilize a variant of agent-based software to block unwanted agents from visiting their Web sites."[1]

Agents represent an inevitable, not a potential Internet growth area. Common-sense applications of fairly recent software development tools, they can add value to just about any Internet-based application. Below are several emerging uses for agents.

- *Locating information or products via Internet search engines or directories.* As in the Amazon example, at the user's instigation agents providing this service roam the Web, searching for relevant Web pages (search engines) and Web sites (directories), analyzing the content, and reporting back the information without any further effort on the part of the user.

- *Receiving personalized information based on a predetermined profile.* Used mostly to provide personalized news services, this type of agent is central to the rapidly increasing number of "push" services, which push information automatically to users, who do not then have to pull it from the Web themselves. These agents monitor the Net and feed the information to their subscribers. Many Internet news sites, for example, ZD-Net's Personal View, PointCast Network, and NewsPage, act as agents, keeping their subscribers informed up-to-the-minute about the issues they have specified. A stock analyst, for instance, may request to be alerted about new bond issues or IBM product announcements.

- *Searching for comparative information based on user needs.* BargainFinder, an experimental agent from Andersen Consulting, allows shoppers to check the availability and to compare the prices of music disks listed by nine

Internet CD retailers. Agents Inc. positions its Firefly as a personal software agent that intelligently navigates the Firefly community space, discovering information relating to tastes, opinions, preferences, and idiosyncrasies that is then used to recommend new music and movie choices to the initiator. Andersen Consulting has recently introduced another experimental agent, called LifestyleFinder, that develops demographic profiles of users from very small amounts of nonpersonal information: Obviously, the plan is to sell the profiles.

- *Building interactive, personalized "smart catalogs."* The smart catalog concept is illustrated by experimental work being undertaken at Stanford University, Hewlett-Packard, and CommerceNet. The experimenters' goal is to demonstrate the efficiency and flexibility afforded by Web-accessible catalogs that allow potential customers to locate products after providing only a broad description of their requirements. By linking information about a product and its attributes throughout the entire distribution chain, buyers can view "virtual" catalogs in real time, as new products become available. A user might specify, for example, that he or she wants the agent to build and maintain an up-to-date catalog of all laptop computers that cost under $2,000, use the Intel MMX chip, have a screen size of X, and weigh no more than Y. From the hundreds of laptop providers advertising on the Web, agents of this type will construct for the user a personal catalog—eliminating the need to carry out a search and access the individual Web sites.

The possibilities for employing agents are almost unlimited. Already intelligent agents monitor the status of telecommunications networks and alert the network management center of potential problems. Agents can bid on users' behalf for, say, discount air fares offered over the Internet. An agent can place an order for a digital camera, waiting until the price drops to a specified level, whether that happens soon, next year, or never: The agent will dutifully look after the user's interests.

Agents represent one of the most interesting and potentially creative trends for Internet commerce and the personalization of services. They will generate many concerns over privacy. They threaten to overload further the already congested Internet as they become more widespread. Retailers may resent and protest what could be viewed as electronic snoopers and comparison shoppers. Consumers, finally, will need to understand that they have set a piece of unsupervised software loose on the Net. An agent a user authorized in 1998 to monitor camera prices falling below $125 may inform him or her in late 1999 that it had found one and placed the order—a year after the user had bought one for $100.

See also **Push Technology.**

AltaVista Search Engine   AltaVista is one of the best-known and most widely used Internet search engines. Search engines build and maintain massive indexes to information available on the Internet; they are the main tool used for surfing the Web. Search engine indexes vary widely in level of detail. AltaVista, probably the largest search engine, contains more than fifteen billion words from more than thirty-one million pages found on 476,000 servers and four million articles from fourteen thousand Usenet news groups and online discussion sites. One of the fastest and most popular search engines on the Internet, it responds to more than twenty-nine million queries per day.

Search engines have invisible programs that continuously and automatically scan the Web for new pages to index and add to their information inventories, a process performed by powerful software programs called spiders. AltaVista's spider (called Scooter) crawls the Web at a rate of three million pages per day and passes the information it gleans to an indexer software that can "crunch" one gigabyte (a billion characters) of text per hour.

Scooter built AltaVista's forty gigabyte index. This book contains around a million bytes; a gigabyte thus represents around one thousand books. AltaVista's library indexes the equivalent of more than thirty million books.

AltaVista can present users with too much information. If a user searches, say, for all references to Michael Jordan, AltaVista will produce a list of every single Web site that contains anywhere in it the words *Michael* or *Jordan*. To circumvent this problem, AltaVista, like all of the other major search engines, provides users with the means for limiting searches. With AltaVista, for instance, typing in "Michael Jordan" + "Chicago Bulls" yields a list of only those sites that contain both "Michael Jordan" and "Chicago Bulls."

The Internet contains masses of information, and search engines are very effective means for accessing it. Increasingly, the problem for providers and users will be to structure both the information and the information search.

AltaVista personifies the Internet. Firstly, it's free and replaces services that previously combined people and software at a cost to subscribers of hundreds of thousands of dollars a year. Secondly, its developers need to make money from their product, yet they don't quite know how. Thirdly, it generates massive information overload; and finally, once you use it a few times, it becomes an indispensable and even addictive tool.

Applet   An applet is a baby software application, a very small piece of self-contained code that can be linked automatically to other software applets. Think of them as Lego blocks that can be assembled to form large structures; applications can be thought of as buildings, or, in some cases, as cities. As each new version of such standard word processing and spreadsheet packages as Microsoft Word and Excel increases in size, it chews up more hard disk space and requires more computing power than did the one before it. Microsoft Word City sits on your disk, but you never enter most of its buildings and rooms. The applet approach attempts to circumvent this problem.

The consensual estimate among experts is that the typical PC application user employs no more than 20 percent of its features. We wrote this book, for instance, without using any of the following commands: *Insert* Caption, Form Field, Sound; *Tools* Mail Merge, Envelopes and Mailing, Macro; or *File* Add Routing Slip. Someone else, writing a promotional brochure, for example,

For over thirty years, the computer science industry has been on a self-imposed diet to try to rid itself of its obesity of software. The goal has been to turn "systems," "packages" and "applications" into "objects," "agents" and now, "applets." Instead of storing massive blocks of code on a hard disk, the Internet will deliver the applet needed, on demand, to a user's PC. It may be a decade before applets become the norm and applications a quaint historical artifact, but the evidence overwhelmingly points to a massive shift in the nature and economics of software. The Internet will soon be a software supermarket where you tote your PC shopping basket around and pick up applets.

might use all of these but not the *Insert* Index or *Tools* Word Count features that we use frequently. As software packages add more and more features on a one size fits all basis, they obviously become larger and more complex. The original Microsoft DOS operating system came on a single floppy disk; Windows 97 requires dozens of floppies.

The growing complexity and size of software applications such as Microsoft's Office and Lotus Smart Suite were made possible through the growing power, speed, memory capacity, and disk storage of personal computers. Until the early 1990s, the computing mainstream followed the path of ever-increasing raw hardware speed making possible ever more complex software applications. Often termed the Wintel model, it entails Intel providing the power and Microsoft using it: As several cynics have commented, "Andy Grove (Chairman of Intel) giveth and Bill Gates taketh away."

Applets are part of a major general shift in software development that presents a massive challenge to the Wintel model. For more than twenty years, computer scientists have been working on ways to design software as objects, small, self-contained units of program code. OOPS—object-oriented programming systems—and object data bases represent this new mainstream in systems development. Applets, a subset of object technology, are changing the basics of Internet systems development and may ultimately change the basics of all PC use of the Internet.

Objects encapsulate all the information and procedures needed to carry out their tasks, so changes to them do not affect other software elements in an application and vice versa. They also possess *inheritance,* crosslinks to other objects that in effect provide any given object with built-in extra knowledge. An object "car," for instance, defined as part of a "class" of objects called "vehicles," inherits information and procedures such as fuel consumption, without the programmer needing to include code defining them. Objects are "invoked" when other objects pass messages to them that provide information needed in the calculations, such as, in this example, miles per gallon.

Applets rent software objects from the Internet as they are needed—they provide software on demand. Applets on the Internet (or on a corporate intranet) can be accessed from any PC with the software needed to manage them; the applet mini-programs become highly mobile and really "live" on the network. Invoked when needed by an application, they get immediately downloaded, run their task, and go back into hiding where they came from, until the next time they get called upon. When it's time to update an applet, the developer exercises complete control of that process, needing neither to modify other applets nor to burden users with work—no "updates" or Version 13.21 need be copied onto your hard disk.

As noted, applets are invoked as needed. If a user doing word processing wants to insert a caption, for instance, the network appliance—a stripped down PC without a massive operating system like Windows 95—recognizing that it needs the caption applet, sends a message through the Net to access it. It does the same to insert a form field or for any other of the myriad commands that constitute the typical word processing program. The designer of the caption applet may update and improve it, as the designer of the form field applet may update and improve that function. Neither need know anything about the word processing software or the other applet. But the next time an application invokes a caption or form field applet, the latest version will be automatically downloaded. New features can thus be added on a continuous basis to thousands of separate applets and delivered almost instantaneously on demand to millions of users without burdening any one of them with identifying and procuring the latest version of a massive single application, such as Microsoft Word.

This sounds great for lightening-up the load on local PCs on which massive operating systems and software applications may take up half the hard disk storage. A "lighter" and lower cost PC (called an Internet appliance, Internet computer, network computer, or, more recently in IT jargon, a thin client, the PC being a fat client) would download the applets from the network, as needed. There is a hitch, though: Hard disks access routines from Word very quickly; the Internet is very slow. In addition, Java, the programming language that has become the main vehicle for building applets for the Internet, creates substantial processing overhead.

Proponents of the Wintel model argue that the Internet is simply not adequate for meeting the traffic demands made by the applet model and that the network appliance is and will remain too slow to handle users' demands. Analysts with this view see no reason to abandon the very successful existing Wintel mainstream, since the power and speed of chips increase at around 40 percent per year, and disk storage and memory increase at comparable rates. Since companies have billions of dollars invested in Windows and Windows-based applications, it makes no sense to adopt an unproven new model for computing fundamentals.

Telecommunications speeds have not, indeed, kept up with microchip speeds and the Internet will not have the bandwidth demanded by the Internet applet strategy for many years to come. But the proponents of the Java-Internet-applet network appliance model argue that the bandwidth is coming and that the Java strategy is more productive, secure, and cost-effective than the Microsoft Windows one, which constitutes a basically 1970s computing model.

The IT profession currently splits evenly about whether Java and applets will beat out the Wintel establishment, become a major niche and complement to it, or lead to a dead end. Commentators take very strong positions on the topic. (We should admit our own bias: We're Java believers.)

Java is by far the most important innovation in computing since the World Wide Web. More than 250,000 Java developers are working to build libraries of applets. Given that Java has only been more than an experimental new language since 1996, applets have yet to become widely available and used. Java was explicitly designed for developing Internet systems, so the evolution of one will greatly affect the other. If the Internet becomes faster, applets will become a more attractive option. If applets become widely available, the Internet will be used to access them.

A distinguishing characteristic of applets is that they can be incorporated into a standard World Wide Web page, just as an image can be. A Java-enabled Web browser used to view a page containing an applet will instantaneously decode it and transfer it to the user's system to be executed by the browser.

"Applet" is now part of the IT trade core vocabulary. The Internet has provided the applets concept an instantaneous conduit and delivery vehicle to millions of potential users. The Java language has greatly facilitated ease and rapidity of applet software development. Gamelan's Earth Web site, for example, has assembled more than six thousand applets. Gamelan visitors can find applets for categories such as arts and entertainment, sports, math, physics, Indonesia, news, special effects, and so on. Software developers can purchase and download these applets instantaneously and incorporate them in their own software application.

The Java-network appliance versus Windows battle will dominate the IT profession for at least the next two years. It is of immense importance for businesses, and at some point business executives will become involved in the discussion. It will be at least as big an issue as the old mainframe computer versus PC debates of the late 1980s.

Authentication   Authentication is the automatic verification of the identity of a person or device. It is a key element in the security of Internet transactions and a vital requirement for the growth of electronic commerce on the Net. In electronic commerce, one of the greatest challenges in processing transactions such as product purchases is the validation of the transacting parties: that they are who say they are, that they accept responsibility for the transaction, and that the messages sent between them have not been altered in any way. Electronic commerce depends on trust, which can be difficult to build when the two parties are either computers or anonymous individuals. Trust becomes even more difficult to ensure when a fraternity exists, however small, of technology-smart individuals specializing in "hacking" and "cracking" telecommunications networks and computer systems.

When a credit card is used to make a purchase on the Internet, the transaction is virtually certain to be encrypted, that is, coded so that no one can intercept and misuse it. But how does the merchant know who is *really* making the purchase? The card and password might have been stolen. The Internet service provider needs more information from the user to verify this, something equivalent to a personal signature or a photo ID. In addition, the provider must be sure that the message came from the ostensible sender and is not the equivalent of a faxed photocopy. Authentication doesn't apply just to people. Any component in an electronic commerce system must be able to conclude that an incoming message came from the claimed point of origin, has not been tampered with, and, all in all, that the transaction is valid and can be accepted. The user must prove his, her, or its identity, and the provider must be able to check that proof.

Some Web sites require authentication of a user's identity before the user can enter them, usually accomplished with a password and/or user identification code established before the user attempts to enter the site. Such systems may be acceptable for gaining access to valuable information, but they are not sufficient to secure money transfers during financial transactions.

In the real world, we use drivers' licenses, photo IDs, passports, birth certificates, and other forms of identification to prove our identity. These various forms of paper can adequately authenticate a transaction because the granting authorities are widely trusted to ensure identity before issuing the given ID. While criminals continually find new ways to forge such documents, the providers work equally hard to add new features that can't be falsified or tampered with, such as the holograms now standard on credit cards. Many documents are also accepted only if they have been notarized; in these cases, a trusted third party has examined the document and verified the signature and identity of the party signing it.

Authentication mechanisms for the Internet serve exactly the same purpose as these everyday paper- and card-based ones, including the use of electronic notarization, called digital signatures, and encryption—the core of Internet security. As you might expect, this immensely complex issue requires ingenious hardware, software, and mathematical techniques to authenticate both people and computers. In identifying people, the issue is to know that the purported sender of a message is, in fact, the sender and that that person is the originator of the information. In identifying computers, especially as increasing numbers of automated transactions take place between unattended computers and without human intervention, service providers must trust the computers to authenticate each other, ensuring that they are conducting the right transactions between the right parties.

While managers need not understand the details of authentication and related security mechanisms, they must understand how important such systems are and determine the exact degree of security in their own firm's links to and from the Net. Stated bluntly, most organizations are wide open to intrusion from skilled hackers or disgruntled employees and former employees (the most frequent source of sabotage, tampering, and misuse). Perfect Internet security is no more possible than perfect credit card or cellular phone security. The issue, rather, is how good is good enough and how much it will cost. Every firm needs to formulate an explicit security policy and to commit the funds necessary to make the policy effective. If security is seen as just an extra cost to be minimized, managers need to assess the resulting risks. Credit card firms, for example, accept a risk of around

2 percent. All companies transacting business on the Internet need to decide what level of risk they will underwrite.

For networks used only within companies, authentication is a secondary issue, because access is only from the inside. But the entire reason for being on the Internet is to provide access to anyone, from anywhere. Intranets fall between the two extremes of the relatively easy to control internal network and the wide open Internet. The greater the number of anonymous people who can access an online transaction system, the greater the importance of authentication.

See also **Certification Authority; Digital Signatures;** and **Encryption.**

Bookmark   A bookmark is the equivalent of the memory-dial phone services that allow users to hit a single button on the keypad to dial a seven- to eleven-digit number. Web addresses can be very long, impossible to remember, and difficult to type without making a mistake. This address, for example, accesses a government agency:

http://www.acl.lanl.gov/~rdaniel/classesJDK/PickTest2.html

Visitors to a site, however, can bookmark it, making it easy to return to. The browser that is being used, Netscape, Microsoft Internet Explorer, or any other, simply adds the site address to a list it maintains for each user. To return to that site, users simply click on its address on the list, without typing anything in.

Many people regard bookmarks as the most useful tool for routine Web surfing.

Browser   A browser is the software tool that users of personal computers employ to manage their interactions with the Internet. The term is increasingly obsolescent in that browsers such as Netscape's Navigator and Microsoft's Explorer, the two main contenders for market dominance, are adding increasing numbers of features with the result that these browsers are becoming Internet operating systems, analogous to PC operating systems like Microsoft's triumphant Windows, IBM's fading OS/2, and Apple's hanger-on, Macintosh System 7. The browser is to the Internet what Windows has been to the PC. The only differences are that, first, it runs "under" Windows on the standard PC and, second, that Netscape stole the market, pushing Microsoft into a catch-up position.

The most basic way to think of a browser is as a graphical user interface—a software system that displays options on the PC screen for users to point to and click the mouse on. This contrasts with a command-driven system, which requires users to type in specific commands. The original Internet was command-driven; the vestiges of this can be seen in World Wide Web Home Page addresses, like "http://www.bigco.com." Prior to the development of browsers, the only operating system that accessed the Internet was UNIX, the workhorse of academic and scientific computing over the last three decades. (UNIX is still widely used on Internet servers, the computers that manage Internet sites and traffic flow, though its share of the total market is declining.) The three main PC operating systems, DOS, Windows, and the Mac, did not provide direct access to the Internet: Only browsers filled the gap between UNIX-based, command-driven systems and PC operating systems. They now provide the interface between the PC and the Internet.

Browsers are simple for almost everyone to use—far more so than Windows itself—and they facilitate the viewing of information scattered across the millions of computers connected to the Internet, without users having to know much about the Internet itself. One of the main benefits to companies of this simplicity is that they do not need to provide training on how to use browsers, and they can assume that anyone who accesses their Web site has a browser and thus doesn't need guidance or support. This is a major step forward in the use of computers in the mass market, and one that will surely over time open up more and more business opportunities. For decades, computers have been difficult to

BYTE Site browser distribution shows Microsoft's Internet Explorer to be gaining ground in market share; it jumped from 12 percent in January 1996 to 35 percent in January 1997. Over the same period, Netscape's relative share dropped from 75 percent to just under 60 percent. No other browser (Mosaic, Lynx, WebExplorer, or the Lotus Notes browser) exceeds ten percent. Most are hovering in the 5 percent zone and no single browser had increased its overall market share since January 1996.[2]

"Wired recently announced on the cover of its magazine that the Web browser is dead. People started saying that two years ago. It keeps coming up over and over again. What's happening is, the browser is expanding into something that is much, much bigger. It's becoming a browser on steroids. And again, it's because of the transformation of computers from stand-alone devices to network terminals. The browser is becoming a complete desktop interface to all these resources on the network—basically everything you need to get work done in a business or to live on the network as a home user. The operating system is becoming irrelevant."[3]

use, however much software vendors boast about their "user-friendly" products. Browsers are user-natural. Very few people who use, say, Netscape, Explorer, or America Online's browser, will have any idea what hypertext means or HTTP. The browser invisibly translates to and from the arcane commands of the Net.

The early browsers did no more than handle the basics of Web surfing: locating and linking to a Web site. They were built around the Hypertext Markup Language (HTML), the foundation of the World Wide Web, which defines the format of a Web page as it appears on the screen, organizes the information that can be accessed, and links a given site with other Web sites and pages. Basically, HTML is a tool for writing a script: "Show this logo at the top of the page. . . . Add a link from this icon to the product catalog. . . . Transfer the user to this Web page and display its screen. . ." and so on. Over time, the simple two-dimensional and static Web displays of text and graphics have been augmented by three-dimensional displays, video, music, telephony, radio, virtual reality, and links to non-Internet software, networks, and data resources.

As a result, the boundary between PCs, the Internet, and networked computing in general have blurred, and browsers have added more and more features, to the extent that they have become operating systems in and of themselves. This development will shape the battle that will drive the entire information technology field for the foreseeable future: Microsoft and Netscape will each strive to make its own browser the de facto operating system in both the consumer market (basically browser-driven) and the business market (driven by the need to integrate all the many components and resources of information technology). Of course, in the rapidly shifting IT business, the foreseeable future may be less than a year; the odds are high, however, that the battle to create the dominant next-generation browser will last for at least the next five years.

What then is the future of the browser? Two trends are likely to dominate near-term developments.

- The continual addition of productivity and "plug-in" enhancements that add to viewing capabilities. (Plug-ins are software routines that can be automatically added to an application with no additional programming needed.) In the case of Microsoft's Explorer, for example, its ActiveX library of add-on components provides rich multi-media and animation features to the basic browser. Netscape has opted for a different approach, publishing the specifications for writing plug-ins to its browser thus allowing developers to do their own work. Some of the enhancements to browser function provided by plug-ins include 3D, animation, audio/visual enhancements, image viewers, and presentation and other business utilities such as calendaring, document management, and pointcasting software. (Pointcasting, in contrast to broadcasting, delivers customized information to a PC.)

- A migration of browsers (or light-browsers) to non-PC devices, such as automated teller machines, televisions, palmtop devices, and other information appliances.

The direction of browser evolution is illustrated by Netscape Communicator, introduced in 1997. Primarily a browser, it also includes an e-mail application and a groupware tool. (Groupware is the industry term for software designed to coordinate and support the work of teams whose members may be in different locations and time zones.) Communicator also includes multi-media capabilities, financial transaction features that allow it to function as a virtual point-of-sale device, and "information-pull" capabilities that make it in effect a television receiving information as if tuned to a news channel. Future versions will support personalized "Web casting," customized information displays from intranets or the Internet that filter and organize information as it arrives on the desktop. In addition, "roaming" access features will allow duplication of a given desktop environment from any ma-

"Remember last year's Browser Wars, where Netscape Navigator and Microsoft Internet Explorer faced off against each other, each desperately debuting new features to top the other's? In the end, we all won, because both products became better, and Web browsing went from the underground to the mainstream. Now we're entering a new phase. Instead of arguing about browsers, both companies want nothing less than to control your desktop— and what you see when you turn on your

computer. Both want to control the browsing function, your electronic mail, the format of the 'push' content you get delivered, and the basic way you view your system. . . . Both companies now say the Browser Wars are over. They're right. Instead we are entering the Desktop Wars, where the competition now is about how your desktop will look and act."[4]

chine in any location throughout the world. Netscape has a vision of the future browser as a "dashboard" of windows, as opposed to a single window to one Web site. The network will filter and track information on the user's behalf.

In early 1996, Netscape held a dominant position in the browser market and was building a very strong base in the corporate market for the large scale software systems that manage the flow of Internet traffic and applications into and out of firms. By early 1997, Microsoft had struck back, and while Netscape still held around 60 percent of the market, Microsoft was exploiting its Windows base to offer its Explorer browser as a free add-on. In addition, its Windows NT product was capturing more and more of the market for the all-important corporate telecommunications infrastructure market. Throughout 1997, both companies launched a continuous flow of enhancements to their flagship systems, including tools for developing Internet- and intranet-based applications, building Web pages with multimedia, linking to and from each other's browsers, simplifying the development of standard Web pages, and so on.

In many ways, any firm's choice of browser represents its choice of a development strategy for its Internet and intranet applications, in that it determines what additional tools it can use in all its Internet activities. The browser constitutes merely the window into the wider Internet–intranet–corporate network infrastructure. While to some extent a firm can use both Explorer and Navigator as the base for its enterprise platform, switching from one to the other, that will become increasingly difficult as more and more systems adhere to specific browsers. Many solid reasons support the choice of any particular browser, but, increasingly, firms will be constrained to make a choice.

Certification Authority (CA) The term *certification authority* refers to applications of the creation and transmission of encrypted—coded—messages across a network that require an unbiased third party to mediate the exchange between two entities of the "keys" for decoding data and ensuring the integrity of the message. Establishing the trustworthiness of such authorities is an emerging issue for buyers and sellers of services and goods via the Internet. Such authentication is the electronic equivalent of purchasing goods by check after producing verification of your identity acceptable to the merchant. Your driver's license and employee identification card may each contain your photo and signature, but the store is likely to accept only the license, because it recognizes the authority and trustworthiness of the issuer. Internet electronic commerce requires such mechanisms, monitored by equally trusted sources.

Documents can be certified as valid by a notary, acting as the certification authority, who verifies and attests to the identity of the signer. Other familiar trusted certification authorities include the government, financial institutions, or airline companies, each of which is entrusted with issuing certain documents that are then commonly and widely accepted as authentic. Governments issue passports and driver's licenses, for example; financial institutions issue credit cards and checks; notaries authenticate death, birth, and marriage certificates; and airline companies issue airline tickets. In the physical world, a predetermined chain of interoperability and acceptance links the various certificates validated by various authorities. Businesses and consumers alike understand and trust this system of authorities to conduct standard transactions. To conduct similarly worry-free business in electronic markets, an electronic chain of trust is needed. Translating the familiar physical process into an electronic equivalent is not as straightforward as it might seem, however. Most obviously, no established and universally trusted certification authorities or transferable documents exist: No one has an Internet passport or Internet driver's license.

A new breed of electronic certification authority is beginning to emerge, particularly over the Internet. A CA in this context is a trusted entity that determines the identity of a person, computer, or other message source and then confirms that identity to

"We need legislation that will essentially indemnify key recovery agents from liability if they obey the rules and provide penalties for key recovery agents that don't, because we have to establish credibility for the agents. . . . Otherwise no one's going to go into the agent business if you can be sued every time something goes wrong. They're going to want protection."[5]

others. The CA then can provide a "certificate" for this verification, in the form of an electronic key or value that can be presented electronically by a trading partner to the CA for verification and confirmation at any time. This system makes practical the anonymous conduct of electronic commerce, or at least of transactions where the parties have no prior relationship. This service is analogous to the ready acceptance and payment authorization of credit cards in thousands of stores and restaurants worldwide. The merchant doesn't know the holder but can verify his or her identity and right to use the card. Electronic certification authorities provide the equivalent guarantee, although not all of the necessary procedures have been established.

The CA also handles the issuing and management of the digital certificate. The certificate represents electronic identification credentials equivalent to passports and drivers' licenses. Digital certificates, which are electronic documents, allow approved businesses and individuals to conduct secure electronic transactions by verifying the authenticity of each party in a transaction. They usually include the holder's name, the name of the certification authority (CA), a public key for cryptographic use, and a time limit for use of the certificate, usually six months to a year. The public key decodes a message identifying the holder to a potential supplier of services or goods. Once signed by the CA, the digital certificate binds the holder, whether an individual or an organization, to that public key.

In mediating the exchange of keys and digital certificates, certification authorities act as unbiased parties. They also are responsible for the certificates' proper use. CAs could revoke a particular certificate if it lapses, if the holders change their status without informing the CA, or if the user violates usage policies.

Several corporations are setting up systems to own and operate private certification authorities, either for internal use by employees, to ensure secure, private and authenticated company transactions, or for external use, to enable companies to conduct business as usual with their trading partners. CAs help to ensure

trust in business relationships. Digital certificates enable businesses to know with whom they are doing business, what organizations they represent, and whether they are empowered to commit their businesses to the transaction; they establish the business
credentials of the party with which they are interacting.

The CA allows instantaneous business relationships to form
in conditions of trust. Typical applications benefitting from a CA
will be payments transactions, secure forms exchange, network
access, information access, secure e-mail, and Internet EDI. The
following companies are already using the certification authority
process.

- GTE's long-distance carrier customers, including AT&T,
  Sprint, MCI and LDDS WorldCom, until last year had
  access to their account information only via a proprietary
  dial-up application. At the end of 1996, GTE's Telephone
  Operations replaced the dial-up application with an
  application based on public keys that uses a combination
  of GTE's CyberTrust digital certificates and its virtual CA
  services to provide secure access and data security for
  information residing on the Telephone Operations'
  corporate intranet. The customer provides final
  verification of clients, and the GTE service issues digital
  certificates on behalf of the virtual CA customer. In this
  case, the customer is GTE Telephone Operations, an
  operating company with headquarters in Tampa, Florida.[6]

- Hewlett-Packard provides all of its employees with a
  unique digital ID to allow them to conduct several
  paper-based corporate processes online. They can use it
  to obtain disbursement vouchers for petty cash, for
  reimbursement of travel expenses without waiting for an
  expense check, and even for direct payroll
  disbursements. For employees working at home or on the
  road, the digital ID authorizes remote access to the
  corporate intranet. HP plans to make its human

resources department responsible for issuing and revoking the digital ID, so that HR will, in effect, function as the corporate CA.[7]

- CyberSource License Clearing House Services facilitates electronic software distribution by issuing passwords, unique product ID numbers, or digitally signed and encrypted End User License Agreements (EULAs). The passwords, IDs, and EULAs provide security and accountability and can unlock and open the digitally encrypted container holding the software awaiting electronic distribution. License Clearing House Services deals with companies that wish to guarantee customers secure transmission over the Internet of electronically distributed software.[8]

- VeriSign, Inc., provides digital authentication services and products for electronic commerce and other forms of secure communications. The business is set up to benefit from the need for trusted certification authorities, and it issues and manages different classes of certificates for various vendors and markets.[8A]

See also **Encryption;** and **Public Key Infrastructure.**

CGI See **Common Gateway Interface.**

CommerceNet CommerceNet is a not-for-profit industry organization set up to accelerate the transformation of the Internet into a viable open marketplace by focusing on areas where no single company alone can take effective action. Its members worldwide include over five hundred leading banks, electronics firms, telecommunications companies, providers of online services, Internet Service Providers (ISPs), online software and services companies, as well as major organizations using the Internet.

CommerceNet's efforts focus on market and business development, technology research, industry pilots, education, and advocacy in legal and regulatory issues. Since its founding in 1994, in California's Silicon Valley, CommerceNet has expanded its network of global partnerships nationally to all parts of the United States and internationally to Canada, Japan, Australia, Malaysia, Korea, France, Italy, Sweden, and Germany. CommerceNet continues to expand and by 1998 expects to have global partners in Spain, Russia, India, Chile, and many other countries. CommerceNet is one of the most respected industry associations for Internet commerce.

CommerceNet creates value by bringing together vendors and end-users who possess key pieces of the Internet electronic commerce puzzle and helping them to fit together. It provides a number of services—vision, technology, project management, public relations, and legal or policy advocacy among them—delivered in partnership with its members and simultaneously opening up business opportunities for them. Because of its high-powered membership, CommerceNet is expected to be a major player in the Internet's evolution.

Evidence of CommerceNet's likely impact is shown by the announcement in October 1996 that the World Wide Web Consortium (W3C) and CommerceNet had established final specifications for the Joint Electronic Payments Initiative (JEPI). (W3C is an association of leading Internet scientists the mission of which is to help develop, through influence and expertise rather than formal authority, the next generation of Internet technology and standards.) JEPI constitutes a universal payments platform that will allow merchants and consumers to carry out transactions over the Internet using many different forms of payment. W3C and CommerceNet spearheaded the effort to agree on JEPI specifications to be implemented by providers of hardware, software, telecommunications, and electronic commerce services such as IBM, Microsoft, British Telecommunications, and CyberCash. JEPI's underlying principle is that the relevant Internet component systems—those of the merchant, the bank, and the customer—negotiate acceptable types of payment, including credit cards,

In November 1996, CommerceNet and the Electronic Frontier Foundation (EFF) joined together to form TRUSTe, which aims at establishing consumer confidence and trust in electronic transactions. It will certify companies that meet specific security requirements; they will be allowed to post the TRUSTe logo—"trustmark"—on their Internet Web sites. Today, distrust is high among consumers—they fear their privacy will not be respected and protected and that the Net is not secure. The Executive Director of the EFF claims that if you ask a roomful of people if they immediately leave a Web site that asks them to register their names, half the hands go up and that many of those who do register put in bogus data.[9]

bank account debits, or, more exotically, digital "cash"; these can then be piloted around the world with automatic resolution of technical issues associated with the communication of information and payments among the parties.

JEPI is a significant move forward in the process of making the Internet a base for consumer rather than corporate electronic commerce. The prestige of CommerceNet's membership makes it a strong force in this effort. Whether that force will translate into implementation is difficult to predict. Electronic commerce is moving so rapidly that changes in the technology and individual players' wishes to establish their own products as the marketplace standard often get in the way of cooperation.

Commerce Server A commerce server is a Web server (a computer that provides information or transaction services) or a collection of servers specializing in managing and supporting a company's electronic buying and selling processes. For firms undertaking large-scale Internet commerce, commerce servers provide the various technical components necessary to support business-to-business ordering and payments, consumer transactions, credit card authorizations, online electronic catalogs, customer information database management, and many other processes. The electronic commerce server may link to many existing, continually operated, maintained, and updated transaction systems and databases, such as order processing, inventory, customer records, and many others. It may require new components, as well, such as Web sites with ever more interactive features, multimedia, and dynamic links.

A simple way to think about a commerce server is to view it as a gateway to a firm's current systems, that is, as the single contact point through which trading partners (suppliers and business customers, other industry members, banks, insurers, distributors, and the like) and customers access those systems. The Internet thus extends the reach of the firm's systems beyond its organizational boundaries to build new relationships.

Allowing customers and prospects to tap into a firm's electronic universe requires creating an "electronic back-office" environment for handling orders, transactions, payments, and so on. This requires a commerce server. Commerce servers are defined by their function; they do not comprise a specific hardware/software combination, although they do make use of server technology. Servers handle the flow of communication and information. An Internet server, for instance, manages the traffic to and from the Web sites that store software and data on it, and a file server manages access to and updating of computer databases.

A commerce server includes most if not all of the services needed to ensure that customers' or trading partners' messages are handled efficiently as part of the wider business process and not merely as a single, specific transaction. A customer message may send a purchase order, but the process triggered includes credit management, audit trails, inventory checking, order scheduling, payments, and many other processes. The commerce server coordinates the relevant processes.

Desirable features in a commerce server include security and compatibility with various types of payment transactions and instruments. The server must be able to accept messages, data, transaction inputs, and results from other servers, within a context of standard message formats and procedures. Finally, technical and business process integration are key to making an electronic commerce environment a part of the firm's extended enterprise. Building an electronic commerce environment requires establishing the following elements.

"The whole world is realizing that the Internet is becoming critical, and we looked at it as really the first new medium to emerge since the forties. When you take a look at the penetration rate of both television and the telephone over the course of the first 30 years and extrapolate the Internet over its initial existence over the same 30 years, it actually can grow to reach a larger base."[10]

- *Digitally formatted content and services:* A digital inventory includes information about products or services and can be automatically downloaded by customers. Most content today goes beyond presenting text alone to use a more engaging multimedia format.
- *Merchant services:* Firms moving into electronic commerce become electronic merchants, with electronic (or digital)

storefronts, requiring electronic versions of shopping carts, cash registers, and product display and layout choices.

- *Transaction management:* Transaction management involves processing digital orders and receipts, with the consequent need for authentication, order management, and record keeping.

- *Payment mechanisms:* Credit card and other types of payment require that firms have the capability to interface with the relevant financial institutions and internal accounting systems.

- *Order fulfillment:* Firms must establish a connection between the order process and the appropriate delivery system, depending on the type of product being sold, managing the transportation logistics system for delivering hard goods or the electronic downloading of "soft" goods, such as information or software.

- *Customer service and support:* Electronic customers want instantaneous and efficient customer support online, including detailed statements of their own transaction history and efficient responses to their queries.

- *Data reporting and analysis:* Necessary data reports and analysis include internal controls and data reporting on customer and Web site activity. Measurements vary from recording the "hits" on a site to building and analyzing customer profiles. The electronic marketplace requires new decision making, requiring new kinds of data to support it.

Several vendors offer their own versions of commerce servers. Some are bundled with features such as those mentioned above, while others have a modular design that allows users to add features as needed. The task of a commerce server is complex, requiring commerce services that are themselves complex. A firm must make a very big organizational and technical jump to move from operating a Web site to operating a Web business.

Common Gateway Interface (CGI)   CGI (Common Gateway Interface) is a protocol, (an electronic procedure) for linking a standard World Wide Web page (the display that appears when you access a Web site) to a wider variety of information displays, transactions, forms, and data. CGI is a technical term that very few managers will ever hear or use in planning their organization's Internet and intranet activities, but it is one that will permeate technical professionals' planning, and it may thus be useful for managers to understand it and, perhaps more importantly, the issue it addresses: how to link Web pages written in the standard HTML language (HyperText Markup Language) to other software programs and data.

HTML allows relatively fast and simple design of Web pages. Unfortunately, it doesn't take long to reach the limits of its capabilities, so that differentiating one Web page from the millions of others becomes more and more difficult. In response, a wide range of tools has been developed for adding virtual reality, three-dimensional computing, applets, objects, and the like, to the basic Web page, tools such as VRML, HotJava, ActiveX, and Dynamic HTML. HTML on its own is useful for placing static information on the Web. To keep content up to date, however, links to corporate databases and other information sources are essential. A common (shared) interface allows the mapping of information to the data source. Mapping occurs, for example, when you enter your employee number on an onscreen form, in order to get information on your company retirement fund contributions. The HTML program can't access the information directly, so it sends a request to the firm's human resource database management system that it be pulled up and sent to you.

CGI provides the common interface in the form of a programming protocol. When users complete an HTML form, the browser bundles all the requests up and sends them to the Web server, which passes them on to a CGI script for processing. A CGI script constitutes the program that can read this data. CGI has become a standard for running programs on a server from a Web page. By incorporating CGI scripts into your Web pages, you enable anyone with an Internet browser to execute programs on your computer systems, even though their own systems cannot directly link to yours; that is, a consumer using a standard browser, such as Netscape Navigator, Microsoft Explorer, or America Online's software, can carry out transactions on a computer that uses, say, Oracle's database management software, IBM transaction processing applications, and C++, the programming language widely used to build interactive systems.

CGI scripts are an essential part of building Web pages. They represent the "middleware" between basic HTML programming and more advanced "mission-critical" software development and can be written in a variety of special-purpose programming languages.

CGI illustrates how a simple HTML Web site, built for a few thousand dollars to display information and link to other pages, can become a six- or seven-figure investment when extended to handle transactions. Internet and intranet applications are designed to be simple to use and to make it easy to move around the Web while at the same time accessing a wide range of often complex information, resources, and transactions. Hiding the complexity is neither simple nor easy. CGI contributes to keeping the user's side simple by handling the links to the complex stuff.

Communication and Collaboration   One of the major applications of the Internet and intranets is the improvement of communication and collaboration among people and organizations. Electronic mail is the primary communication application. E-mail has revolutionized business communication. Internet e-mail allows companies to communicate with one another without having to worry about the compatibility of their e-mail software. Even smaller companies can communicate across distance without having to set up expensive networks to connect their various offices.

Collaboration involves using the Internet to work more effectively while minimizing time, distance, and organizational barriers. Teams of engineers, developers, or marketers, for example, can collaborate on specific projects despite being thousands of miles apart. The Internet glues them together.

As part of intranet development efforts, companies should invest in enhancing collaborative applications for their various business entities and departments. Collaboration can also occur between organizations and their trading partners, crossing intranet boundaries. Some examples of collaboration and communication include discussion forums, video and audio conferencing, global calendaring, and project and team management. Lotus Development Corporation pioneered the concept of collaborative software with its Lotus Notes suite of products, later adapted for the Internet and intranets.

Collaboration is an essential element in firms' efforts to build learning organizations, substitute teams for hierarchy, replace "stovepipe" business processes structured by department with cross-functional workflows, and create partnering relationships with key suppliers and customers. Notes, a very complex software system, goes well beyond the communication facility it provides through electronic mail: It aims at creating new styles of interaction and relationships, a feat that is complex technically but far more complex organizationally.

The Internet doesn't reduce either source of complexity, but it obviously opens up the interaction space, providing an invitation to work together. That's why so many companies that have implemented intranets or that use the Internet for business-to-business electronic commerce report that one major result is a strengthening of both communication and collaborative links. More generally, the Internet, online services such as America Online, and bulletin board services have built strong electronic

"We're using the Web technology to access information so that we can have a valuable conversation with the customer. Before the Internet we would say 'Yes, we would be happy to sell you three lines,' write up an order, and then come back four days later and say, 'I only have one.' That's a big problem. Nobody wants it to be that way. It's not that we are idiots; it's just that the systems have not allowed easy access to information that exists but is buried way in, practically in the code. Now that information is on the salespeople's desks or however they are accessing it . . . the biggest part of what we're doing is not the demonstration of technology at all, it's the demonstration of community."[11]

communities that could not exist without the reach and ease of electronic mail and discussion groups.

The Internet extends the full spectrum of interaction: communication, cooperation, collaboration and community—the four *C*s. In the long term, that may well be its most important social impact. In the short term, this provides businesses with a major opportunity to expand the scope of their existing business relationships and to add new ones—and see what happens.

Component Software   Component software can be described as the equivalent of using LEGO blocks when building model houses, instead of customized construction materials. In the software industry, "component" refers to putting pre-assembled pieces together, while customization involves a major development project. Constraints of tools and technology (and to some extent, of experience and skill) have for decades meant that software was built in very big chunks that could not be simply and directly linked to chunks written in a different programming language or run on a different type of computer.

To understand component software and its impact on Internet computing, one must consider its origins in object-oriented programming. Object-oriented programming addresses one of the longest standing concerns in IT: how to improve the quality and productivity of software development, which has always lagged behind improvements in hardware. Ideally, software should be designed in building-blocks, one component at a time, with each block representing a distinct software object. Entire systems would be assembled by putting components together, with components being reusable and shared among many software systems, thus substantially reducing the time required to build new applications. Most standard business transaction processing applications, for instance, repeat basic routines, such as checking the validity of an account number, calculating an interest payment, and changing an address; it makes sense to build libraries of reusable components, rather than crafting them anew each time a system is developed. Such libraries have been a goal of developers for over three decades, but it's only relatively recently that the tools for building truly reusable objects have become both available and practical for wide-scale use.

The costs of supporting or debugging component software are much lower as well. It is far easier to isolate errors in a short block of program code than to try to track the origin of an error in logic in a complex application, in which the results of such errors may show up only thousands of lines later on; in addition, the design principles of object and component methods ensure that all the logic and data needed in a given object is self-contained and isolated from those of other objects.

Component software introduces modularity to software development, a long sought after and much welcomed evolution in modern software engineering. Component software contrasts with what was referred to in the old days as "spaghetti code," never-ending series of intertwined lines of codes subject to numerous errors and in which changing one piece automatically and inadvertently affected other pieces.

Object technology is widely seen as the next-generation approach for application development, providing the mechanism for more efficient programming and more rapid responses to business needs and opportunities. An object is a self-contained package comprising both code and data about code attributes. Distributed objects are spread across a network to better utilize system resources, a capability not possible previously. Objects also allow an "open" environment in which the pieces of an implementation can be developed and tested, at different times, by different development teams or independent software vendors, and later assembled for final execution.

The Web is a perfect platform for encouraging component software to flourish, to the extent that just about every development in software methods is both targeted to the Web and relies on components. The benefits of this approach are direct savings resulting from speed of development (due to reuse); speed of integration (due to the assembly of components, most of which will have been fully proven in use and hence will be reliable and error-free); and lower overall costs of deployment (because a part of the costs has already been shared by others). The component software approach ensures a higher level of quality because components can be tested separately, making troubleshooting much more efficient.

Companies must learn to exploit the massive opportunity provided by software components and such related tools as the Java programming language (the first fully modern, Internet-focused, component/object development language for interactive and multimedia services), Microsoft's ActiveX, and many others. They must, first, attract and retain a new generation of software developers and, second, maintain existing software systems, built using very different tools on very different hardware and in very different telecommunications environments, while linking them with systems developed using an entire new philosophy and design strategy. The field of software development has always been short of first-rate talent, but the proliferation of new tools, technologies, and targets for their application, plus the massive demand for entirely new Internet-centered interactive and multimedia systems, makes the shortage even more acute.

See also **Applets.**

Content Providers   Content providers own information and related resources that they make available to Internet users via Internet service providers. Content is, in effect, the Net's inventory, and service providers are the means of accessing it. The broad term *content* is industry shorthand for information ranging from simple text to complex multimedia publications, entertainment, and data stores that include animation, video, and audio capabilities. Content can be also "live," that is, readily available as it is updated, in a manner similar to what broadcasters mean by live programming. In electronic commerce, content refers to the actual products or services being offered, bought, and sold. Owners of publications, libraries of photographs, databases, and so on, recognize that information turned into digital content can be delivered over the Internet with great ease and minimal reproduction cost.

Content liquidity refers to the ease with which content, via the Internet, can now be obtained, processed, searched, encrypted, classified, converted, disseminated, and reused; the term suggests the value of information as a form of liquid asset that can be readily turned into currency. Software applications, for example, are routinely downloaded over the Internet. Electronic newsletters and e-zines (electronic magazines) can be created from new material or existing print inventories. Soon, more and more CDs and videos will be downloaded over the Internet, as well, raising the possibilities for and increasing the volume of this type of electronic commerce.

Today, the Internet offers a wide array of free content, which is one of its most appealing value propositions. (Some of the free content providers rely on other revenue sources, such as Web advertising.) Increasingly, however, much content is being made available only to paid subscribers or users. In these cases, subscribers typically pay from a few dollars to $100 a month for the service. Most content providers that charge for their services offer free access to a section of their Web site, displaying a sample of the available content, as a way of attracting new subscribers. Content providers that charge for their services include the following:

- The Wall Street Journal Interactive Edition, which includes more than fifty thousand pages, changed daily, and augmented with multimedia delivery capabilities.

- NewsPage (from Individual Inc.), which provides thousands of daily press releases from the major wires, indexed using hundreds of categories.

- Quote.com, which provides real-time stock market prices and financial information and reports on thousands of companies.
- ESPN Sportzone, which includes in-depth sports statistics and events coverage and which can offer information personalized to the user's interests.

Online content in both intranet and Internet environments is exploding, as content developers and providers rush to build up their digital inventories by creating new or converting old content. With the proliferation of content, and with Web sites fighting for as many eyes and as many moments of attention as they can, content has to be compelling. Interactive content thus gains an edge, with its capability to allow users to interact with and modify content to suit their personal needs, rather than passively receiving a one-way flow of information.

Designing content for a Web site involves considerations of quality versus quantity, navigational requirements, and education versus entertainment. Pricing constitutes today's most critical and complex issue. Web users have grown accustomed to information being free and are now largely unwilling to pay for it. In addition, mechanisms for charging a few cents or fractions of a cent for each online microtransaction must be instituted and widely adopted before purchase of small units of information, such as articles from electronic newspapers, will be practical.

The chairman of America Online summarized his company's view of online services by stating that "content is no longer king." Ted Leonsis, chief executive of AOL Studios, is convinced that, in the end, the companies that succeed on the Web and in other online services will be those with strong content brands that distribute content on a large scale. He stated his position in a recent interview.

Interviewer: Won't there be a lot of competition? For example, there are competing Web sites for almost all your content.

Leonsis: I call them grave sites. We're about to enter an incredible Web winter, and the new model that will emerge is that the big distributors like AOL will use their distribution footprint and power to launch new interactive brands, just like Time Warner launched HBO. There will be twenty to forty winners in this business. Take newspapers—there are nine thousand in the country, and the top twenty-five account for 85 percent of the circulation. And those top twenty-five newspapers are owned by seven companies. So, I laugh when I hear newspaper companies saying there are going to be millions of Web sites that are going to be successful. . . .

Interviewer: Then what's your advice to businesses setting up Web sites?

Leonsis: They have to realize it's no longer new media, it's media. It took radio almost forty years to penetrate almost fifty million homes. It took television more than twenty years, and it will take the Web seven years to penetrate fifty million homes. We're in year three of that phenomenon. Then, the dabbling has to stop. It has to become part and parcel of the way you are delivering services. If you are not spending at least 20–25 percent of your marketing and advertising dollars on this, you're missing out.[12]

Given Leonsis' outstanding track record and the fact that the most successful content providers on the Web are distributors like ESPN (ESPN.Sportzone) and Playboy, his views are well worth considering.

Cookie A cookie is a little nugget of information sent to a browser from a Web server with which a user is interacting. Once it arrives, the cookie stays on the user's hard disk until it expires. (That could take minutes or months.) Cookies allow the interacting Web application to record and access personal preferences or specific actions or information, unique to each user, that can be used when the user interacts with the same application a second

Wells Fargo Bank uses cookies during online transactions to make certain that the individual accessing specific accounts and the account holder are the same person.[13]

A cookie placed in a client computer can store an enormous amount of information. For example, at the Netscape General Store, the server needs to account for multiple shoppers making selections simultaneously. This is accomplished by updating the cookie each time a new selection is made. The cookie, therefore, is literally the shopping cart itself. The client's own computer, not the server, stores the information as a cookie, and when the final tally is requested by the shopper, the server retrieves the cookie and sends back a Web page displaying all of the items selected.[14]

time, thus simultaneously personalizing the site and providing the site owners with information.

A cookie may contain information about buying preferences, for example, so that, if the user returns to the same site even months later, the site will "remember." Or the cookie may store the user identification codes and password for a given Web site so that the information doesn't have to be entered again and again. Cookies can also be used to display only a customized part of a Web site. The first time a user visits the site, he or she is asked to specify his or her interests, generating a cookie that then resides on the user's disk; the next time the user visits the Web site, the cookie is sent to the server, which then recognizes the previously specified preferences and sends only the relevant displays or information. Bank of America's Web site, for example, automatically displays a screen specifying "what's happened since you were last here." Finally, cookies, which constitute unique identifiers of the people accessing a Web site, can be used for more accurate Web site tracking. Web tracking software on the firm's server reads the cookies and interprets the data to distinguish forty individuals accessing the site from one hitting the reload button forty times.

The positive aspect of cookies is two-fold: first, they customize a site to fit the user's profile, thus increasing convenience and value and removing extraneous displays, steps, and information; and second, they provide data of value for the site owner, in terms of feedback and market research. But, on the negative side, cookies can easily be used to invade privacy. Many Web users do not even know that they exist. Legally, firms could sell cookies to other companies, just as credit card companies and publishers sell mailing lists. TRUSTe, a service created by the well respected Electronic Frontier Foundation, the goal of which is to help build consumer confidence about the security and privacy of Internet commerce, offers levels of certification for Web sites, allowing owners to display the TRUSTe logo, effectively stating that they either will not collect and store personal information or, if they do so, will not sell it or pass it on to other parties. Users that do not wish to have their personal information shared with other Web sites can activate a special program on Web sites displaying the TRUSTe logo. This program disables all cookies, thus ensuring the ultimate protection of a user's privacy.

Cost of Web Sites Web site costs vary as widely as do the costs of bicycles, cars, planes, and space shuttles. When they first became *de rigeur,* the costs of a company Web site might have included a single Web server, its connection to the Internet, basic Web server software to publish Web pages, and the salary or fee for a Web master to develop and maintain the site. Today, a Web site for even a small company may consist of an intricate set of servers and services not physically in the same location; may involve several more people, from both the technical and the business sides of the firm; and may interface with other existing internal and external software systems and databases. The lines that once defined Web sites are thus blurring and melding very rapidly with the rest of the organization, resulting in the costs of rolling out a Web site being mixed with other costs, making them more difficult to track on their own. In addition, a large organization's Web site might consist of thirty different physical sites, mirrored across the Internet universe to reduce the traffic congestion that occurs when too many users try to access a single server. (Mirroring a Web site consists of duplicating some or all functional parts of that site in various geographical locations, a tactic common for sites with heavy traffic or that run complex transaction-based applications. Mirroring speeds up message flows by enabling users to access servers near their own, since the greater the distance an Internet message has to travel, the more network "stop signs" it encounters, thus slowing delivery.)

Web site costs vary tremendously depending on whether it is intended to provide information, interactions, or transactions. Information may be expensive to turn into digital content, but it is cheap to deliver. Transaction online processing is generally

A constant theme in the trade press concerning Web sites is that the real costs come after *they are developed: "Getting into this business and putting up a Web site is a lot like having a baby—not only do you have to put this thing through college, but it's probably going to come back and live with you for awhile. You're in for the long haul. I think you need to be committed to it, because like anything else, the more you put into it, the more you get out."*[15]

The cost of Sun Microsystem's intranet per U.S. branch is in the $50,000 to $60,000 range. "To put that into perspective . . . this is the justification we used to fund it. If, for example, there are three thousand

salespeople in the field and the average cost of a trip for a week to take training from Europe is about $2,200 and from Asia about $3,000, and the number of trips those three thousand people take is reduced by one each year, take the three thousand and multiply it by $2,500, and that's how much Sun saves. Just in reducing the air travel cost and hotel expenses, it more than pays for the network. In terms of intranet applications, the one that will pay for itself fastest is probably training, simply because it has such a large cost elimination associated with it—that is, travel."[16]

expensive. Generally, costs can be spread into the following five categories.

- *Technology platform:* Costs in this category include those for hardware, Web software and tools, "peripherals" such as printers and modems, telecommunications links and supporting hardware and software, security devices, and Internet connection costs.

- *Content:* Content costs include those for acquiring, creating, and designing digital content (information, publications, videos, music, photographs, etc.); updating and enhancements; electronic catalogs; Internet applications development; and software customization.

- *Integration:* Costs of integration include ensuring that Internet components interlink to corporate databases, that transaction processing systems' data-mining interfaces function appropriately, and that Internet applications interconnect smoothly with each other and with other existing information systems.

- *Human resources:* The costs of technical support can easily dwarf the direct technical costs: Special expertise is required in such areas as security, education, updating, responding to customer electronic mail, and many other areas of support and service.

- *Promotion and marketing:* Affecting both online and offline procedures, promotion and marketing costs of a Web site will include advertising, public relations, links to other sites, and direct mail and other print media.

Adding up all of the above costs could easily result in a multi-million dollar project with on-going support and enhancement costs.

Country Codes The Internet country code, a two letter convention introduced by the International Standards Organization, accompanies the address of a Web site, called a uniform resource locator (commonly abbreviated to URL and pronounced like "earl"). A few examples of official Internet country codes for those countries whose names begin with the letter "a" would be: af for Afghanistan; al for Albania; dz for Algeria; and as for American Samoa.

Preceding a country code in an Internet address are other somewhat standard abbreviations that describe the type of organization the Web site represents. For example, commercial institutions are identified through the use of ".com" or ".co"; educational institutions by ".edu"; and government institutions by ".gov." The following are examples of several different types of Web addresses:

www.ibm.com (main IBM Corporation Web site)

www.barclays.co.uk (a commercial institution in the United Kingdom)

www.utexas.edu (a university in the United States)

www.whitehouse.gov (a government Web site)

An Internet country code is also part of an individual's e-mail address. For example, somebody@somewhere.com.af is the address of an individual living in Afghanistan. The address of a commercial company (IBM.com) is indicated by ".com," while in the United Kingdom the corresponding code is ".co."

Cryptography   Cryptography is the mathematical discipline of coding and decoding messages. Its origins lie two thousand years ago, with the so-called Caesar code, used by Julius Caesar to conceal his writings about the Roman war in Gaul. His code, involving a shift in letters—so that, for example, *B* became *J, C* became *K, D* became *L,* and so on—was easy to break.* Protecting electronic messages today is much more difficult because it is necessary to devise codes that cannot be broken by intruders

* Those are not the exact transformations used by Caesar, they are illustrative of the way in which he transformed the alphabet into code.

using banks of computers to churn through all the possibilities on a trial-and-error basis. Cryptographers essentially multiply and combine massive prime numbers to generate keys for encoding messages. (A prime number is indivisible by any other number; 2, 7, 11, and 13, for example.) The prime numbers used in modern cryptography are hundreds of digits in length and can represent numbers with no corresponding value in nature, being more than the estimated total number of atoms in the universe. A would-be code-breaker would have to try out all the possible combinations of smaller numbers to find the primes that are the basis for converting, say, the message "send money fast" into an apparently random stream of bits rendered in a form such as *101001010010101010100 . . . 100000101010.*

So far, the cryptographers keep a little ahead of the code-breakers, but the race is neck-and-neck. Every time some article announces that trying out all the possible combinations of numbers necessary to break a key would take today's most powerful computer twenty million years to carry out, some mathematician counters that "theoretically" it could be broken in a few weeks, while a security specialist points out that the computers of 2008 or 2018 will be so powerful that the twenty-million-year estimate will drop to two years.

Responding to the importance of cryptography in electronic communications, the U.S. federal government's National Security Agency (NSA) has amassed what is believed to be the largest single assembly of computer hardware in the world and employs the largest number of mathematicians. These are industry estimates, of course, because the NSA, being very secretive, doesn't publish such figures; even its existence wasn't made public for many years after its foundation in the 1940s. NSA's role is to monitor and decode foreign communications that may indicate a threat to U.S. national security. Cryptography for electronic networks pushes the frontiers of computer science and mathematics.

Cryptography is a highly specialized subject that underlies a very general issue: ensuring security on the Internet. Business managers must take responsibility for their firms' security policy, allocating funds to ensure an appropriate level of "good enough" security and training at least a few staff members in the commercial state-of-best-practice in cryptosystems.

See also **Encryption.**

CyberCash   CyberCash, a company founded in 1994, provides secure financial transactions services over the Internet, including credit card transactions, electronic checks, and microtransactions (those for a few cents or even a fraction of a cent, such as might buy a snippet of online information). It is a main contender for leadership in the emerging but still embryonic market for electronic payment mechanisms on the Internet.

The essentials of a CyberCash consumer transaction are shown in Figure 8. The figure shows a consumer viewing information about goods available from an online merchant. If the consumer elects to make a purchase, a six-step process follows.

1. The customer decides on the product to be purchased and the place to which it will be shipped. The merchant server returns to the consumer a transaction summary, listing the item, item number, price, transaction ID, and so on.

2. The customer clicks on the "pay" button, launching the CyberCash software and opening the CyberCash wallet window. The customer chooses a credit card from his wallet and clicks "OK" to forward the order and encrypted payment information to the merchant.

3. The merchant receives the message, strips off the order information and forwards the payment information, digitally signed and encrypted with its own private key (electronic code key), to the CyberCash server. The merchant does not see the consumer's credit card information, and the transaction is private.

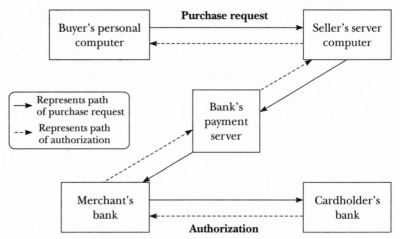

Figure 8   CyberCash Secure Internet Credit Card Payment
Source: Adapted from CyberCash, Inc., 1996

4. The CyberCash server receives the packet and takes the transaction behind its firewall (the hardware/software system that screens its incoming messages and protects it against intruders), thus pulling it off the Internet and into its own secure processing environment. The CyberCash server then unwraps (decodes) the data within a hardware-based crypto box (the same ones used by banks to handle PINs shipped between ATM networks), reformats the transaction, and forwards it to the merchant's bank over dedicated telecommunications lines.

5. The merchant's bank then forwards the authorization request to the issuing bank via the telecommunications facilities of the credit card association, such as Visa, or directly to a nonbank card issuer, such as American Express or Discover. The approval or denial code is then sent back to CyberCash.

6. CyberCash returns the approval or denial code to the merchant who passes it on to the consumer.

From step one to step six typically takes approximately fifteen to twenty seconds. All encryption is at the message level and is therefore independent of the Internet software browser technology used; it makes no difference if the customer got onto the World Wide Web through Netscape Navigator, America Online, or Microsoft Internet Explorer. CyberCash manages the processing within its own boundaries.

CyberCash is designed to combine ease of access, simplicity of use, speed of service and absolute security. It employs the strongest tools of cryptography and processes the key elements of transactions offline, so none of the many hackers roaming the Web can sabotage it. The CyberCash process may or may not become a market standard, but it looks like the blueprint for secure electronic commerce on the Internet.

CyberCash has some problems, of course. By late 1996, it claimed that about 500,000 CyberCash wallets had been downloaded from Web sites. A wallet is a software container that includes several electronic payment choices such as an encrypted credit card or electronic cash. But this number does not represent the actual number of active users for two main reasons. First, users may download the electronic wallet for its novelty element but end up not using it. Second, a limited number of merchants and financial institutions accept CyberCash: By mid-1997, only about one hundred merchants and fifty financial institutions did so. Although the CyberCash wallet includes most major credit cards, its reach is far from being universal because it links to a limited number of merchants and it doesn't interoperate with other Internet payment instruments. Using a CyberCash wallet, for example, consumers can purchase goods and services only from CyberCash merchants, who can, in turn, process these transactions only through CyberCash financial institutions. The institution of interoperability standards, an effort now being spearheaded by the Joint Electronic Payments Initiative (JEPI), will resolve the interoperability issue.

Some merchants accepting CyberCash include ArtQuest, an image-listing service for people collecting and selling art; the JD PowerGuide to Automobiles, published on CD-ROM by J.D. Powell; The Louisiana French Market Online, delivering Cajun foods to all fifty states; Virtual Vineyards, marketing wines around the world; World of Casino Gaming, a casino gaming information company specializing in providing products and services to casino players; CigarSnob, a club offering premium cigars from the Dominican Republic, Canary Islands, and Mexico; and Doctor Is In, a service providing access to a group of doctors ready to answer questions or address concerns. Although varied and successful in themselves, the current relative handful of CyberCash-compatible merchants does not yet constitute the critical mass necessary to establish CyberCash as the new, mainstream standard.

See also **Mondex.**

Cyber Currency The term *cyber currency* is one of the many vogue words being used to describe electronic forms of currency, forms that will, in the near future, be as widely used as other non-physical currencies, such as credit cards and electronic funds transfers. No one can predict when cyber currency will achieve that level of acceptance, and its use today is limited mostly to pilots and trials.

Cyber Mall See **Electronic Mall.**

Cyber Notary Few cyber notaries exist today, though there is an increasing need for them. As the equivalent of the notaries who certify in person the validity of documents and signatures, cyber notaries will serve to authenticate transactions over the Internet, as certification authorities do today. The following excerpt from one U.S. legislative proposal summarizes this new role and how it will affect electronic transactions over the Internet.

The proposed specialist will possess a high level of qualification in information security technology, allowing him to electronically certify and authenticate all elements of an electronic commercial transaction which are crucial to its enforceability under U.S. and foreign law. Using digital signatures, the CyberNotary will be able to certify the identity of an originator of a commercial message (thus establishing non-repudiation of the message by the originator), while also providing a very high level of assurance regarding the content terms of that message, along with the time and date of "notarization," and protocolization for archival purposes. These functions are crucial to the success of electronic commerce in open networks, where identity, capacity, and authority to act cannot be established by traditional means. As a security officer in electronic commerce who combines a technical and legal expertise, the CyberNotary will be competent to engage in transactional interventions on a fairly broad scale. The basic certification and authentication functions of the CyberNotary can be applied to virtually any transaction that requires the intervention of a trusted third party. Thus, CyberNotarial practice in a public key infrastructure will encompass activities ranging from user credentialing for registration of public keys upon which certificates can be issued, to certification of identity, capacity, and authority of users for individual transactional purposes, and authentication of the legality and form requirements of these transactions.

See also **Certification Authority;** and **Public Key Infrastructure.**

Cyberspace *Cyberspace* is a vague but evocative term for the almost living realm occupied by those netizens—network citizens—for whom the Net can seem more real than the real world. The term, coined by the science-fiction writer William Gibson, was popularized by his 1986 novel *Neuromancer. Neuromancer* posited a technology accessible to everyone, even punks and street gangs. In Gibson's visionary dystopia, huge multinational corporations with more power and wealth than any government do battle with one another, and knowledge is the capital of commerce and data its currency. Many of Gibson's characters are thieves and fences searching the "matrix" for software and information to steal and sell. Gibson first introduced the term "cyberspace" in his story "Burning Chrome," in which he describes devices called "cyberdecks." These allow their users to override their sensory organs, replacing them with a full-sensory interface to a world computer network; in so doing, they enter cyberspace. Gibson's cyberspace is thus a metaphorical "place" to which one travels by accessing the worldwide Net. Today, the word *cyberspace* is increasingly used to refer to the digital world produced by computer networks, especially the Internet.

Although Gibson's vision of cyberspace is somewhat surrealistic, many in the computing community believe the term accurately captures the Net ethos. *Cyberspace* has taken on an extended meaning, as well, being used to refer to computer-driven virtual reality environments not necessarily connected to the Internet. The word *cyber* has become a frequently used prefix to signal objects and events that have migrated into cyberspace. New coinages appear continually in the press without clarification, as if they had been in use for years. Among them are cyber bucks, cyber currency, cyber guru, cyber journalist, cyber law, cyber mall, cyber notary, cyber wallet, cyber world, and many others newly and as yet to be born.

Cyber Wallet   *Cyber wallet* is one of the many terms floating around the Internet industry to describe electronic currency. Instead of a physical wallet containing dollar bills, coins, and credit cards, owners of electronic wallets offer merchants currency in the form of software on the Internet, a hard disk, or a special card storing electronic tokens. The contents of a cyber wallet will increasingly be accepted on the Internet as "real" money and will be exchangeable for cash (or will be deposited as cash) at participating banks.

See also **Digital Wallet.**

Data Encryption Standard (DES) The Data Encryption Standard, one of the oldest techniques for encrypting data, constitutes the core of the mathematics of electronic security that has evolved over the past twenty years. Data encryption converts numbers and text, such as a name, account number, and purchase amount, into a stream of apparently meaningless digital bits. Cryptographers search for techniques that quickly and reliably code data to protect it from saboteurs and thieves while making it simple and fast for authorized parties to decode it. DES is the grandparent of the growing number of tools aimed at securing the communication of information across networks. DES, while secure enough to be in widespread use, is not totally so; very powerful computers could crack the code by brute force and trial and error. Given that today's supercomputer is tomorrow's desktop, the necessary mathematical procedures (called algorithms) must become ever more complex to keep the good guys ahead of potential or real bad guys.

Behind the scenes, the DES algorithm protects transactions on virtually every ATM in North America and most around the world by encrypting the Personal Identification Number or PIN that is the electronic signature for consumer transactions. The DES algorithm has also found its way into commercial applications, such as electronic data interchange (EDI), where electronic payment transactions must be secured cryptographically.

Developed jointly by IBM and the U.S. Department of Defense in the 1970s for use in both military and commercial applications, and at that time embodying the most advanced theory and practice in cryptography, the algorithm works in combination with the message data and a set of electronic keys. The key is equivalent to the instructions that might have been given to a nineteenth-century spy who didn't have access to computers and needed a simple way to code messages: "105, 3, 6." The spy and his or her contacts would know that these numbers referred to a specific book, say, for example, *The Works of William Shakespeare,* published by Scruton Press in 1876. The numbers instruct the spy to turn to page 105, line 3, letter 6, an *M*, the thirteenth letter of the alphabet; the thirteen indicates that the letters of the alphabet must be shifted thirteen places, with *A* becoming *M*, *B* becoming *N*, and so on, to decipher a given message. Obviously, such a simple code—called a Caesar code since it was used by Julius Caesar in his private writings—would be absurdly easy to break. Modern cryptography relies on massively complex ways of generating massively big key numbers. DES is in the mid-range of massiveness.

DES is known as a symmetrical or private key-based cryptographic scheme, because both sides or partners in a transaction must use the same electronic key values as well as the DES algorithm in order to encrypt and decrypt messages. (In our simplified example above, both spy and contact use the same reference book and key number, 105, 3, 6.) In contrast, a public or asymmetrical key process allows each party to use a different key, thereby protecting the sender's private key while making public ones available for decoding use only; public systems require that a third party, a key certification authority or agent, look after the keys.

See also **Cryptography; Encryption.**

Demographics The demographics of Internet users—age, income, interests, and, most of all, buying habits—are a matter of immense, and at times frantic, interest to businesses exploring the opportunities for Internet electronic commerce, for firms specializing in Internet surveys and forecasts, and for journalists. When the Internet was a specialized niche in the academic and technical community, its users were, of course, mostly researchers, students, and technical professionals, who were highly unrepresentative of anything but the Internet. Such people remain the Internet's core population, and they continue today to influence strongly the types and volumes of purchases made over the Internet and other patterns of its use.

As more and more millions of people from more and more

"Perhaps over time, the Internet will become a giant collection of affinity groups. As it grows bigger and bigger, it will feel less like a community. It has already lost some of that feeling for me since the old days. To me, the Net is measured anarchy."[17]

countries and more and more walks of life become Internet users, the question arises how and to what extent Internet demographics are changing. A multitude of research and consulting firms continuously carry out surveys and make predictions on these points. Most of them capture a few headlines but offer little real insight into what is going on. That is partly because the rapid pace of Internet growth along with the absence of any central repository of information about users make it close to impossible to gather reliable figures.

Accurate reports can be obtained on the number of computers connected to the Internet, the number of companies registered with unique domain names, or the number of dollars spent on advertising or transactions; but one of the hardest questions of all to answer is "How many people are on the Internet?" Every Internet demographic study must estimate that figure, resulting in extreme variations in the numbers reported. Estimates as of mid-1997 vary by as much as thirty to forty million.

Advertisers, Internet service providers, journalists, and electronic commerce services all have a vested interest in the shifting demographics of Internet users. Although many companies diligently track Internet users and publish surveys and estimates about who uses the Internet and how, due to the rapid growth of the number of users and their expanded use of the Internet it is often very hard to interpret or validate these figures. Table 4 compares survey results from mid-1995 with survey results from mid-1997.

The most important question facing those in the area of electronic commerce on the Internet is: How representative of the general public are Internet users? Until recently, the typical profile of the average Web user was a male in a technical or professional job, or a student in a technical field. This average user typically accessed a relatively small number of Web sites on a regular and systematic basis. This profile helps explain the early successes and failures of Internet commerce. For instance, online computer hardware and software sales thrived, while many online

Netiquette is a set of information guidelines for a code of online conduct through which the Internet community governs itself. Netiquette has evolved over time to add the human and social touch to online communication. It reflects the general characteristics and preferences of the core Internet community who are for open communication, against commercial exploitation of the Net, and view information and research as personal and precious. The netiquette list of what not to do includes: (1) never e-mail advertisements or sales literature to anyone unless they have requested it or they give you permission to do so;

Table 4　Comparison of Internet Statistics from 1995 to 1997

Internet Users	1995	1997
Average age	32 years	35.2 years
Number of female users	9.5 million	18.9 million
Average number of sites visited per use	8 sites	20 sites

Source: CyberAtlas.com

(2) never post advertisements and solicitations to Usenet news groups, chat groups, or forums; (3) never make false representations of your products or services; (4) avoid imposture of any kind; and (5) do not violate intellectual property laws.[18]

retail stores failed. Estimates show that women make 70 percent of all types of shopping purchases, and since women only constituted 30 percent of all Internet users, it is hardly surprising that early retail sales did not flourish. Similarly, given how many male college students were hitting the Net, the proliferation of pornography is also not surprising.

The statistics in Table 4 illustrate the trends on the Net that are likely to continue: an increase in female users, an increase in the average age of users, and a more varied, casual use. This casual use can be interpreted from the increase in the number of sites users hit each time they use the Web.

Today there is a great need for more sophisticated ways to measure usage. The number of average hits per use, for example, does not provide companies the knowledge of whether the last visitor to their site was an elementary school student casually browsing, or a potential customer interested in services or products. To measure more accurately who visits their sites and why, companies on the Internet often request, and sometimes require, users to fill out registration forms before providing information about services. Many sites also leave "cookies" on users' hard disks—nuggets of information that allow a site to record a user's personal preferences. This use of cookies has elevated even further the issue of Internet privacy.

See also **Cookies.**

DES　See **Data Encryption Standard.**

DigiCash   Founded in 1990, DigiCash pioneered the development of secure, private electronic payment mechanisms for network systems. DigiCash is based on patented technology in public key cryptography (the coding and decoding of messages to protect them from interception and tampering) developed by the company's founder and chairman, Dr. David Chaum. As of mid-1997, DigiCash was well placed to become one of the main players in a field that has not yet moved much beyond pilots, proposals, and experiments but that will, as inevitably as ATMs and credit cards emerged in the 1970s, blossom into a full-scale Internet electronic payments system. Among the companies licensing DigiCash's technology are MasterCard and the European Commission's CAFÉ Project. (The latter is a cross-border electronic wallet, or storage device, containing the electronic equivalent of paper currency that can be used in any of the participating countries without the need to exchange, say, francs into marks.)

DigiCash's Internet payment mechanism uses the Ecash concept. Ecash provides users with electronic currency that they can use anonymously, as with paper currency; unlike credit cards, Ecash must be placed in the user's electronic wallet. Ecash works similarly to a stored value card, such as a phone card. When a phone card worth $10 on the provider's computer is used, the record of the balance remaining is updated. (On smart cards, the new balance is stored in the memory chip.) Ecash value is stored on the hard drive of a PC, and extra value can be downloaded from a bank at the user's request and paid for with a credit card or a direct debit. The Ecash funds are then available for the purchase of goods and services from electronic merchants. The Ecash software transfers money from the buyer's to the seller's Ecash account.

Ecash's distinctive feature is that it ensures privacy. The bank providing the service moves money from an actual bank account to the Ecash Mint on a PC, where it becomes available as digital currency. Ecash software moves electronic coins from the Mint, the equivalent of withdrawing money from an ATM. The coin, tagged with a unique identification code, is tucked into electronic envelopes that encrypt information about the sender. Merchants can cash in the coins but cannot learn any more about the person from whom they come.

Mark Twain Bank, a small bank operating in Illinois, Missouri, and Kansas, was the first to implement Ecash, in October 1995, and serves, essentially, as the U.S. clearinghouse for Ecash. It is unusual among banks in that it has for years offered consumers accounts in twenty-five currencies. For Mark Twain, Ecash is just one more. Prior to launching Ecash, it had signed up ten merchants who would accept it. By late 1996, the number had grown to two hundred, and customers numbered close to one thousand. The most difficult issue for Mark Twain was pricing, "the cause of much angst," according to bank officials. Fees for consumers range from a set-up cost of ten to one hundred dollars, with monthly charges of two to five dollars. Transaction fees are more significant, with consumers paying 2 to 5 percent of the value of the transaction and merchants 2 to 4 percent of the value of the transaction. Merchants and consumers each have four service packages from which to choose.

As with DigiCash and the other dozen or so schemes for electronic currencies, Ecash is difficult to evaluate, since no one knows which system will attract the critical mass of consumers and merchants necessary for market dominance. Common sense says that some form of stored value wallet card system will join ATMs and credit cards as an integral part of everyday commerce, but it is not at all clear how quickly this will happen. Smart cards, the offline card equivalent of a DigiCash wallet, have been in use for well over a decade, with growing but still limited and fragmented applications and acceptance that lags far behind advocates' predictions. Smart cards have experienced no sudden, explosive growth, just a long and fairly slow evolution. DigiCash looks like being part of an evolutionary revolution in payments.

Digital Certificates   Digital certificates, also known as authorization certificates, offer electronic validation of the identity of the sender of a message and hence of the authenticity of that message. As Internet usage spreads among more and more people and organizations scattered across the world, businesses will be interacting more often with companies and individuals they have never done business with in the physical world; such new relationships will be increasingly intermittent and ad hoc, with no formal contracts and little time for credit checks or even telephone calls to verify the senders' identities or authority to enact business deals. Business relationships in the digital world thus must be established by new means, specifically through electronic documents containing the principals' assigned personal attributes (level of authorization to access services and information, a unique identifier, and so on); digital documents will attest to the authority to act of a piece of computer software as well as of a person. This document is referred to as a digital certificate or an authorization certificate.

A digital certificate constitutes an electronic ID and is as reliable as a driver's license or passport. Issued by certification organizations that verify a given public key (the code to an organization's encrypted messages) as belonging to a specific owner, digital certificates are sent along with an encrypted message to establish the identity and legitimacy of the sender. The certificate typically contains the owner's name, company, address, public key, and certificate serial number and validity dates as well as the certifying company's ID and digital signature.

Digital certificates, by fully identifying any party sending or receiving information, constitute foolproof means for securing an electronic transaction. The sender uses a private key, available only to it, to generate digital signatures for its electronic documents; the receiver uses the public key sent with the digital certificate to decode the message. Without access to the private key, however, the receiver cannot use the sender's public key to fake messages and commit fraud or other crimes against the sender.

Digital certificates can operate within an intranet or across the Internet. In the former case, a company establishes and maintains the certification process. In the latter, a third-party organization, such as VeriSign, certifies the credentials offered by a company and represents them as valid to other companies with which the first seeks to do business. Certificates represent stronger security than can passwords. In addition to limiting access to a particular message, they verify identity, message, and content integrity; ensure privacy; authorize access to information; authenticate transactions; and support nonrepudiation. Digital certificates eliminate the need for cumbersome login and password dialog boxes in connections to secure resources, because each party can be confident of the other's identity.

See also **Certification Authority; Digital Signatures;** and **Public Key Infrastructure.**

Digital Markets   Businesses increasingly compete in two separate markets: physical markets where resources and value can be seen and touched and virtual (digital) markets that are mediated by the world of information. Business activity undertaken in physical markets takes place in the market*place,* while electronically-mediated transactions take place in the market*space.* These digital markets are also referred to as electronic markets, iMarkets, or Internet markets. Digital markets are made up of a constellation of virtual organizations, electronic trading communities, electronic intermediaries, global directories, digital value-adding services, and millions of users, consumers, and organizations. They interact electronically and increasingly efficiently, prospecting for leads, discovering opportunities, sharing sites and advertising, closing deals, conducting transactions, and so on, without ever having a face to face encounter.

The process of buying and selling lies at the heart of digital markets. The sales aspect includes promotion, distribution, display, pricing, order taking, payment authorization, order scheduling, retrieval from inventory, shipping, payment receipt, product support, and market research. Buying includes inquiring or searching for, comparing, and selecting products, negotiating terms, placing an order, receiving and paying for a product, requesting support, and perhaps giving feedback to the manufacturer about the product. All of the above steps described are *routinely* done in the physical marketplace, but require development of many new mechanisms before they can take place smoothly in the digital marketspace. Of the selling operations listed, for example, none is easily transferred to Internet commerce. A recent review in *Internet Shoppers* of the service provided by companies selling computers online (the largest single market segment of consumer Internet commerce) makes this point: "What we found surprising is that the biggest players in the world of paper catalogs weren't always the biggest players in the online world. We also found that experience shows. Companies that have either been online for a long time or are essentially online have better sites than newcomers."[20] As more and more selling steps are performed or supported electronically, the nature of the relationship between buyers and sellers shifts. Especially affected is how value is created for and perceived by the customer along each step of the way.[21]

Successful digital markets will be shaped by a culture of interaction and interdependence; they cannot succeed by substituting electronic ordering for the physical space of a store. New forms of secure electronic payment, for example, will be integral to consumer acceptance of trading in the digital marketspace, with Internet Service Providers and software vendors playing key roles in electronic banking. Similarly, Internet Service Providers, software firms, and retailers will increasingly offer storefronts and malls on their own Internet servers both to build a consumer presence and to provide shared resources for small firms. Digital markets may evolve in a number of ways. They may create new business revenues or they may take revenues away from the

When you buy a $100 sweater at a high fashion boutique, about 85 percent of the price is absorbed by the distribution channels, leaving just $15 to the manufacturer. Direct customer to manufacturer interaction via the Internet diminishes the need for most intermediaries and hence eliminates most distribution costs, resulting in great potential savings for both the consumer and the manufacturer.[19] Companies such as Dell and Land's End have combined telephone ordering and printed catalogs to capture a sizable fraction of the personal computer and clothing markets, offering both high quality and aggressive pricing. Internet selling operates similarly, combining electronic self-service with electronic catalogs.

equivalent physical marketplace. Another possible area for their continued growth may be as new intermediaries in traditional markets. The Internet seems, for example, to be rapidly loosening the nearly century-long hold of car dealers: People are using the Net to access intermediaries who locate the best deal for them electronically or to access car manufacturers' comprehensive electronic catalogs.

Digital markets are emerging as the next competitive battleground for electronic commerce.[22] In book retailing, the success of Amazon.com has already affected the basics of the industry, with leading traditional booksellers looking aggressively to overtake Amazon. Digital markets in discount securities trading and computer hardware and software sales are taking shape fast. In other areas, such as banking, digital markets are as yet undeveloped and fragmented. Obviously, tracking electronic markets is now a key element in competitive scanning. A firm can't afford to miss the digital market. Even if it decides not to be a leader in its evolution, it has to be there when demand takes off.

See also **Internet Commerce.**

Digital Signatures   A digital signature is a code attached to an electronically transmitted message that uniquely identifies the sender. As with a written signature, a digital signature guarantees that an individual sending a message is really who he or she claims to be. To be effective, digital signatures must be secure against forgery, and a number of different encryption techniques have evolved for this purpose.

The term *digital signature* does not signify an electronic, graphical equivalent of a handwritten signature. It is an encrypted description of the contents of an electronic document. American Express, for example, uses digital signatures to verify the identity of its cardmembers, enabling them to purchase products and services while at the same time protecting their identities and credit card information. Just as merchants check to see if a person's signature on the back of a credit card matches the one on the credit card slip, merchants can electronically compare the digital signature transmitted during an online purchase with the credit card holder's original digital signature.

Digital signatures serve three purposes: (1) to authenticate the identity of the sender or signer of an electronic transmission to ensure against forgery; (2) to protect the integrity of data, ensuring that a message has not been changed, either accidentally or maliciously; and (3) to provide lasting proof of who participated in a transaction (a capability called nonrepudiation) so that someone cannot deny having signed or received the data. It is very likely that a digital signature will soon become as legally binding and universally accepted as a written one.

See also **Certification Authority; Digital Certificates;** and **Public Key Infrastructure.**

Digital Tokens Digital tokens are information-based currency values that are stored on a user's smart card or PC hard disk. A token paid for and received allows the user certain rights to access products or services in the physical marketplace.

Companies should continuously ask themselves: "How can we make more information-intensive products?" Since bits usually travel better and faster than atoms across the Internet as a delivery medium, it becomes essential to replace certain existing products with their information-based equivalent. The following are examples of some possible uses of token-based products. These services can be delivered over the Internet and could rely on smart card technology as a storage vehicle for service fees.

- *Smart Telephone Cards:* A tool for use with public telephones that replaces coins.
- *Electronic Money/Prepaid Accounts:* A step towards replacing coins and bank notes in financial transactions.
- *Ticketless Travel:* A repository for tickets and vouchers.
- *Electronic Access:* An efficient way to control access to data and facilities.

- *Storage of Security Tokens:* A convenient location for the storage of security keys and access controls.

- *Medical Records:* A repository of medical history and insurance information.

- *Individual and Multiple Merchant Incentives:* Cardholder storage of "points" as a result of frequent purchaser programs offered by individual and multiple merchants.

- *Electronic Wallets:* A repository of multiple financial, credit, debit, and merchant accounts.

- *Television Top Terminals:* A method of unlocking and controlling in-home access to expanded television services.

- *Smart Device Control:* A tool to control the personality, operational profile, and access to smart devices of the future.

A factor that will fuel the development of information-based products is the development of advanced smart cards that contain personal demographics and dynamic information linked to a remote database. This type of smart card will enable multiple applications, such as those recently demonstrated by the ImagineCard alliance (Hewlett-Packard/Informix/Gemplus). A single card accommodated the following functions: electronic purse, conference evaluation, logical and physical access, and registration with full customer accessibility and card-owner controlled authentication.

Mondex, an emerging leader in smart cards for financial transactions, is recommending a new standard for a smart card operating system, similar to the one described above, that supports multiple applications. This operating system is called MULTOS. This type of system would allow a single card to have multiple functions. An individual's card could be divided into several logical parts: one for storing digital money, one to store an individual's digital ID, one to store an access key to allow an individual entry into his or her office, one for storing a special code that supplies pre-paid seats at the theatre, one for storing dollar-equivalent values for making long-distance phone calls, and one that may contain key findings of an individual's medical history. Furthermore, the card would be "locked" until activated by the owner's fingerprints or secret code.

Digital Wallet   A digital wallet, the electronic equivalent of a real wallet, stores electronic money, the electronic equivalent of cash or travellers' checks. Residing as software in a desktop or portable PC or on a smart card, the digital wallet has multiple and dynamic stored-value capabilities for adding or subtracting digital cash values as transactions occur.

Today, most digital wallets are proprietary, accepting only currency or tokens minted or specified by the wallet software originators. (This would be like owning a physical wallet that only accepted bills from the country in which it was made.) A true universal digital wallet should offer a variety of features not yet common.

- International currencies.
- Universal payment instruments (credit card, debit card, smart cash card, and electronic checks).
- Versatility (compatible systems at home, at the office, and for banking, shopping, parking, and so on).
- Digital signatures, digital certificates, and private keys (methods for encoding and verifying the validity of electronic messages).
- Compatibility with multiple types of smart card.

Although some wallets—for example, VeriFone's vWallet, the Imagine Card, the CAFÉ initiative (a pan-European project), Mondex, and CyberCash—have demonstrated versions of these features, the very proliferation of schemes indicates that none has yet reached a critical mass of commercial users, let alone consumers.

Just as credit cards created new markets, new modes of selling and buying, new channels of distribution and entirely new international relationships and transactions, at some point digital wallets, cybercurrency, and digital cash will do the same. By late 1997, the market had no clear winner and showed no clear evidence of when and how fast a winner would emerge. For the foreseeable future, the well-established credit card mechanism will almost surely remain the dominant form of electronic payment. Credit card use over the Internet is hampered, however, by widespread consumer fears about safety and privacy. These factors combine to suggest that it may be a decade or more before there is a digital cash bandwagon to climb on. It will almost surely, however, move very, very fast once it gets moving.

Directory Services   Directory services are software that manage intranet directories. (An intranet is a network established by an organization for internal use. Intranets employ Internet technology, including its telecommunications protocol, called TCP/IP, and Web browsers; they may access the full Internet, but often limit outside access to a specific community, generally the establishing firm.) Any network is, in effect, its directory of addresses, just as the telephone system is a directory of telephone numbers; you may have a phone and a working walljack connection, but if the line does not have an active phone number assigned to it and stored by the phone company in their system software, you are not "on" the network.

The Internet has its own massive directory management resources. Intranets, too, need dedicated—intranet-specific—directories to manage information about their users. Typically, a directory server is set up within the intranet to organize and distribute user and group information, giving administrators, applications, and end users access to powerful "white pages" of information, including user names, phone numbers, e-mail addresses, and other data. (The directory server is a special-purpose computer handling only directory functions and storing the directory database.) Netscape's Directory Server, for example, can handle up to one million entries and more than three hundred thousand queries per hour. As an intranet grows, directory servers can be added to distribute directory information automatically.

See also **Intranet.**

DNS   See **Domain Name System.**

Domain Name   A domain name represents the Internet identity of an organization or individual and constitutes a unique identifier, registered with a central agency, that can serve as the base for many transactions. Domain names are registered with the InterNIC (or other registration authority). They are portable and can be moved from server to server. (The server is the physical device that holds a user's Internet-accessible software and data and receives messages for that domain sent via the Internet.) An Internet address is based on a domain name. Many users may share a domain name. An Internet address such as Estarlman@aol.com identifies its holder as an individual using America Online as an Internet Service Provider. Other domain names indicate that the holder has a more direct Internet connection, for example, IBM.com.

Suffixes and prefixes added to a domain name provide additional information about the holder. The standard prefix http://www, for instance, as in the address http://www.megamega.com, indicates a hypertext document suitable for processing as a World Wide Web page. Further additions to the name narrow the site down from the entire domain name to a subset of it; for example, http://www.salesmall.megamega.com provides direct access to the salesmall subset of megamega. The suffix /html carries the information that a Web page is formatted using the HTML (Hypertext Markup Language) software. And so on.

All domain names include a suffix indicating the type of organization holding them. A commercial firm, for example, uses the suffix .com; a school or college uses .edu; and a governmental agency uses .gov. The U.S. conventions for extensions differ from those in other countries. Typically, domain names for non-U.S. holders end with a country code, for example, it. for Italy or .se for Sweden. Even where no country code is used, the extension may be unfamiliar; the United Kingdom, for example, uses .co rather than .com to indicate a commercial firm.

Registration of a Web site domain name costs about fifty dollars payable to the InterNIC organization. Desirable names are in short supply, and often a prospective owner will discover that the name he or she sought to register has already been registered. In that case, either another name can be chosen or the owner can be offered money to sell the name; domain names are widely sold. Such names are independent of the particular Web server, so files can be transferred to a new server without any change in domain name or inconvenience to the Web site users.

See also **Domain Name System;** and **Internet Protocol Address.**

Domain Name System (DNS)   The Domain Name System is the worldwide naming convention that allows every Web site to register its unique identity. Every PC, camera, or other device connected to the Internet has a unique numeric address called its Internet Protocol or IP address. (IP is the core Internet telecommunication protocol binding it to a worldwide database system.) These numeric addresses are like telephone numbers: Dialing them produces direct connections to the servers or other devices they refer to; the database system automatically translates a domain name into an IP address and vice versa. If your firm's domain name is *mycompany.com,* for example, and your company's Web site resides on server 134.34.345.103, customers instructing their browser software to contact the numeric IP address 134.34.345.103 will be directed to *mycompany.com;* for those directing their browsers to *www.mycompany.com,* the browser will look up the equivalent IP address and point the customers to 134.34.345.103, connecting them to that Web site.

The Domain Name System (DNS) is the essential component in the Internet's operational infrastructure. It locates machines on the Internet, not people or organizations. The Internet does not directly access mycompany.com, therefore, but the device whose address is 134.34.345.103; it maps human-friendly names to their transport (IP) addresses.

The system for coordinating and managing the domain name registration process on a worldwide basis is built on the name extensions known as Top Level Domains (TLD); these include the familiar .com, .gov, .net, .org, .edu, and so on. For more than ten years the existing set of TLD registries has been stable and sufficient; but the recent explosive commercialization of the Internet has produced a need for an enlarged pool of TLDs and revamping of assignment procedures. To help solve this problem, the IAHC (International Ad Hoc Committee) was created. This international entity, drawn from the broad Internet community, focused on specifying and implementing policies and procedures relating to international Top Level Domains and worked to satisfy the urgent requirement for enhancements to the Internet's global Domain Name System.

In early 1997, the IAHC proposed an increase in the number of names available to specify Internet locations and a new administrative plan that would allow more firms to act as name registrars. The IAHC developed a list of seven new generic Top Level Domains (gTLDs) to be added to the existing list. The new gTLDs and the intended fields are shown in Table 5.

It is possible that within a few years the TLD .nom may have the largest number of registered names. These names will provide the equivalent of those unique, roaming telephone numbers that follow the subscribers anywhere.

Dynamic Catalogs   Dynamic catalogs are online electronic catalogs that function more like database management systems

Table 5 Proposed New Generic Top Level Domains

New Domain Classification	Scope
.firm	For businesses or firms
.store	For businesses offering goods for purchase
.web	For entities emphasizing activities related to the World Wide Web
.arts	For entities emphasizing cultural activities
.rec	For entities emphasizing recreational activities
.info	For entities providing information services
.nom	For individuals desiring a personal domain name (or nomenclature)

Source: International Ad Hoc Committee (IAHC), 1997.

than printed catalogs, in that they are kept continuously updated rather than being periodically revised. Electronic catalogs that mimic the periodicity of print are known as static catalogs. This pattern, similar to that of a monthly magazine, was typical of many early Web sites.

The unparalleled growth in the number of Internet users and in the amount of Internet usage resulted in the opportunity for businesses to be open worldwide twenty-four hours a day. As a result, many organizations have put their product and service information online. This can be done in one of two ways. First, fastest, and easiest is the static catalog, in which print information is replicated as Web pages. As the volume of information grows and the need for updating becomes more frequent, however, static catalogs become difficult to manage and search.

Dynamic catalogs manage data more efficiently, by storing product information in standard databases instead of in standard Web files created using HTML software (the foundation language of the Web). Dynamic catalog databases are updated continuously; if a firm changes prices in its purchase order system, customers logging onto the Web site get the new price. The need to convert existing paper catalogs into product information databases makes implementing dynamic catalogs more of a challenge than implementing a static catalog. Once a product information database is created, however, it becomes the single source for generating information in numerous forms—a dynamic catalog on the Web, a printed catalog, or a CD-ROM catalog, for example.

In addition to flexibility in format, dynamic catalogs offer two more advantages over static catalogs: They allow the catalog author to manage the information better, and they allow catalog users to find the information faster. In dynamic catalogs, for example, users can select from a list of product features those they are looking for and the system will match their requirements to specific products, displaying them in a table for convenient comparison. Sophisticated search interfaces and techniques guide users during the selection process to avoid "sorry, no match" messages. Some "parametric" search engines—those allowing the user to specify parameters such as cost, size, or features—help users find the products they need by interactively narrowing down their choices and by process of elimination. This method very effectively and quickly locates products that match specifications such as "Price between $100 and $130, dual voltage, and under 3 pounds in weight," while ensuring that all available options have been investigated. Companies such as Hewlett-Packard and AMP use this technique to make their large industrial electronic parts catalogs manageable. (AMP, the world's largest supplier of electronic and electrical connectors, has a catalog widely cited as a model to follow; it displays items in eight languages.) Both HP and AMP have catalogs containing more than one hundred thousand entries; purchasing agents and engineers directly access the catalog and using the parametric interface easily find the components they need.

Business managers in charge of producing catalogs today should work with software vendors of dynamic catalog tools to create a product information database. The conversion of a paper catalog into a product information database involves creating a taxonomy (a product family tree), a product feature matrix (a table showing all the features of each product in a family), and

Website Travel, offering online travel services, learned the following lessons: The customer should be led from general information to specific information to checkout within three or four screens. The process should take no longer than it would take to make the same transaction using an 800 number. Shoppers should not be made to enter a lot of information, and they should never be asked to enter the same information twice. Website Travel's advice is move your customers as quickly as possible to a decision to buy; this is best done by presenting the product quickly. The average shopper will not remain at a site that dilly-dallies.[23]

detailed data sheets including specifications, pictures, drawings, and so on. When product changes are made, only the database needs to be updated. Dynamic catalogs play a key role in disseminating efficient product information and facilitating selection for both business-to-business and business-to-consumer applications.

EC　See **Electronic Commerce.**

Ecash　Ecash stands for electronic cash and refers to the many proposals for creating electronic equivalents of coins and bills to be stored in the user's "wallet" on a hard disk, used in Internet transactions, and converted to "real" funds by the merchant supplying the product or service purchased.

See also **DigiCash;** and **Digital Wallet.**

EDI　See **Electronic Data Interchange.**

Shopping 2000, formed in 1994, was the first true Internet online shopping mall. Shopping 2000 was way ahead of its time, and it failed. Impulse buying was hindered because consumers had to remember stock numbers and then get to a phone. This led to one stop visits, with the consumer visiting only one store before leaving the site to place (or not) an order. Catalog participants (Tower Records,

Electronic Commerce (EC)　*Electronic commerce* is the general term for Internet and non-Internet computer-to-computer processing of a growing variety of transactions, ranging from electronic data interchange—the well-established handling of business-to-business purchase orders, invoicing, remittance notices, and other routine documents—to electronic payment systems, credit cards, and, most recently, consumer sales of goods and services.

Increasingly, however, the term is used to mean Internet commerce for two reasons. First, the Internet's size, growth rate, and ease of access open up immense, though highly unpredictable, market opportunities for large and small firms. Second, the economics of the Net will make it increasingly attractive—under some circumstances—to move today's electronic commerce onto the Net from the many company, industry, and special-purpose value-added networks that are currently the main vehicles for EDI, FEDI (Financial EDI), and other electronic commerce transactions. The Internet can reach out to new customers and reduce both the supplier's and customer's set-up and transaction costs. The advantages of existing EC delivery systems, however, often offset those of the Internet, because the Internet has many weaknesses: It is less reliable, less secure, lacks support (there is no Universal Internet Help Desk), and is slower in delivery.

Electronic commerce has grown at a compounded rate of 15 to 20 percent per year for the past decade, albeit it from a very small base; even today, it is estimated that no more than 150,000 of the more than ten million U.S. businesses use EDI, the simplest form of electronic commerce, whose benefits have been proven again and again to be tremendous. (Several examples of typical, not exceptional improvements under EDI appear in the Introduction; see page 17.)

The main barriers to adoption of EDI have been the challenge of making the necessary organizational changes, rather any technology challenges. Use of the Internet reduces just about all of the technology barriers and can dramatically improve the economics of electronic commerce, but it doesn't alter the organizational demands in terms of business process redesign, skill-building, and management of relationships.

Electronic Data Interchange (EDI) Electronic data interchange is the inter-company, computer-to-computer transmission of business information in a standard format. For EDI purists, "computer-to-computer" means direct transmission from the originating software application program to the receiving, or processing, application program, and the EDI transmission consists only of business data, not any accompanying verbiage or free-form messages. Purists might also contend that a standard format is one that is approved by a national or international standards organization, as opposed to formats developed by industry groups or companies. Pragmatists define EDI as simply electronic messages that automate business-to-business transaction processing.

Any EDI system has four components:

JCPenney, Spiegel, and others) gained no advantage by being part of the mall.[24] The mall was not advertised or promoted, and no real public relations effort was made. The mall lacked a consumer support service and did not respond in a timely way to consumer inquiries. The organizers seemed to think that it was enough to be on the Internet to lure customers. This proved untrue. The experiment clearly showed that just being "on the Internet" is not enough to build a commercial service.

"Since it costs 60 percent to 90 percent less to send EDI traffic over the Internet compared to Value-Added-Networks (VANs), the only question is not whether the estimated $300 billion of EDI traffic shifts to the Internet, but when. Even the VANs, recognizing the powerful

appeal of Internet EDI, are jumping in with Internet offerings of their own, although these are carefully crafted to avoid impacting the bulk of their lucrative VAN traffic. However, it needs to be remembered that the VANs have long prospered because they offered valuable service to hubs and trading partners, including mailboxing, auditing trails, compliance checking, etc. In addition, VANs are extremely knowledgeable about the needs of hubs and trading partners, and can assist with implementation, technical support, and related issues. Although companies are attracted by the tremendous cost-savings promised by Internet EDI, they are understandably loath to abandon the security-blanket services provided by VANs."[25]

- Electronic storage and retrieval facilities, usually in the form of an electronic mailbox to which messages are sent by the party initiating the transaction, whenever and from wherever it wishes, and from which the trading partner picks them up, whenever and wherever it wishes.

- A communications network that transmits and receives messages, provides security and information control, and efficiently routes transactions.

- Translation software that converts, say, a firm's purchase order document into a structured, formatted message that can be interpreted automatically by the supplier's order processing software.

- An applications program interface, that is, software that links the firm's transaction processing software to the EDI translation software.

With the focus in EDI shifting from the technological aspects to the business functions it supports, enables, or adds value to, business managers have an increasing need to understand its impacts and the procedural changes an organization must make to move to EDI, a largely unfamiliar way of doing business. As EDI technology components become commodity products, managing business process change, EDI contracting, and building EDI relationships become the premium element in the transition. Many value-added networks, along with a growing number of consulting firms, provide business process change reviews and management-oriented education in EDI and electronic commerce.

The Internet does not in itself provide for these. Nor is it as secure or reliable as the many EDI network services that have been in place for a decade or more. EDI constitutes both a technology and a set of network infrastructures, support mechanisms, and operations independent of the Internet. But the Internet offers a dramatic increase in the variety of EDI relationships a firm can build; most importantly, it makes it easy to add small suppliers and customers to a company's electronic trading partner base. It also reduces transaction costs in comparison with established EDI value-added networks.

See also **Internet EDI.**

Electronic Mall   Electronic malls or cyber malls offer an assembly of electronic stores collected on a single Web site. By grouping merchants together, they allow users to search a number of stores without having to move from one Web site to another. Electronic malls appeal mostly to business-to-consumer providers.

From the consumer side, electronic malls offer *potential* long-term benefits. These include a shared universal payment and authorization method that allows incoming shoppers to register their payment preferences only once, with the assurance that the chosen mechanism will be accepted by all tenants. In addition, consumers get efficient product comparison shopping, aided by specialized search software, that allows them to sift through all the relevant products in the mall to find the best deals on items they specify in great detail *before* visiting any store. The software matches the item from a particular store to the price, size, feature, and service specifications set by the consumer.

For merchants, the benefits include automatic presence in a high traffic area on the Web. A small merchant may have great difficulty attracting prospective buyers to its Web site, whereas as part of a large mall that generates volume traffic, even small companies gain in visibility and customer traffic. Another benefit to merchants is that, even if they do not want to or cannot set up their own electronic storefronts (due to lack of skills or resources), by using a common infrastructure and service, and paying a fraction of the costs, they can gain quick access to a new electronic marketplace. Some electronic mall landlords will offer integrated shipping logistics, automatically coordinated with product orders, relieving tenants of the need to make shipping

A Girl Scout troop in Connecticut put up a Web site on Open Market and sold more than $300,000 worth of cookies. People online know what to expect when they order Girl Scout cookies; the brand is already established.[26]

arrangements to possibly remote parts of the world. Finally, merchants will gain access to statistics on prospects, navigation habits, demographics, and buying habits that will enable them to offer targeted marketing and personalized service, matching goods to a buyer's profile.

All these benefits are as yet potential, not actual. First-generation electronic malls have had limited success. They have thus far lacked the rich content and sufficient product organization that will give consumers the type of compelling shopping experience that will entice them to come back again. For this reason, controlled electronic shopping environments set up by Internet Service Providers such as America Online and CompuServe, because they present a more cohesive environment, have been much more successful than early Internet-only cybermalls.

Electronic Signature   An electronic signature is a code attached to an electronic message that authenticates the identity of an individual or entity on the Internet, making it the equivalent of a written signature.

See also **Digital Signatures.**

Electronic Wallet   *Electronic Wallet* (also called a *digital wallet*) is one of many terms used to describe the storage of electronic currency, whether that currency is called cybercash, electronic tokens, or digital cash, to cite the most frequently used names. The electronic wallet serves as the electronic equivalent of a physical wallet containing coins and notes with value for buying and selling goods anywhere in the issuing country. To be effective, the currency contained in electronic wallets must gain the same acceptability as coins and bills. The value, stored on the owner's PC or on a smart card, may be transferred by making a credit card transaction or a bank account debit from one of the banks or bank-like institutions that will offer digital cash. As payment for an Internet purchase, funds will be transferred from the buyer's to the seller's wallet.

It's fairly certain that all this is a matter of "will be" not "may be." All that remains uncertain is "by when."

See also **Digital Wallet.**

E-Mail (Electronic Mail)　By far the most widely used application on the Internet, electronic mail, or e-mail, enables holders of unique e-mail addresses to send and receive messages. Before the advent of the Web, e-mail was the Internet's main application, and it still accounts for half of the time users spend on it. With e-mail, simple text messages can be composed and transmitted in seconds to one or more recipients on the Internet anywhere in the world. To contrast it with the speed and convenience of e-mail, many people now call regular post mail *snail mail.*

Electronic mail works in three stages: transmit, store, and forward. *A* composes and sends a message over a telecommunications network to *B* at an address something like somebody@somewhere.com; the network interprets the address and routes the message to *B*'s electronic post-office box or mailbox, where it is stored. When *B* logs on to the system, he or she is informed of the message, which the network then forwards.

An e-mail or Internet address such as *somebody@somewhere.com* identifies the user and the location or affiliation of his or her Internet connection. Each e-mail issuing entity is unique and has direct control over issuing e-mail accounts for its users, making each e-mail address universally unique: It is impossible for two people to have the same e-mail address. It is, of course, possible for the same person to have more than one e-mail account. Furthermore, e-mail accounts can be set up to forward messages automatically to a specified secondary e-mail account, so that the first account acts like an alias for the second.

Before the Internet, only large organizations or academic institutions had e-mail. E-mail software applications were proprietary and worked well only within the limits of the initiating organization: Little or no interoperability existed among the various systems. Furthermore, each company or institution having e-mail had sole responsibility for developing and running their network infrastructure. These factors hindered e-mail for several decades from moving beyond its original academic and scientific communities and the few companies that used it for internal communication. Existing e-mail systems were complex and largely incompatible, to the extent using them was like having to use five different phones, none of which could send or receive calls to or from the others. Other factors hindering the spread of e-mail were widespread fear of using computers and lack of correspondents with whom to communicate.

The Internet has largely eliminated these problems. Internet-based mail has made inroads into proprietary mail systems as organizations grapple with the ever-increasing need to exchange electronic information with external clients and suppliers as easily they do among their own employees. In addition to providing a reliable, standard means of communication between disparate organizations, Internet-based messaging gives managers greater freedom in selecting messaging-system suppliers. The established standards mean that organizations can experiment with different mail servers without changing their client software or choose a different client package without switching their current mail server.

Electronic mail is now the simplest, most popular, and most widespread use of the Internet and online services. Employees who choose not to use their firms' e-mail systems are increasingly locked out of many informal and formal communication networks. All but a few business cards today carry both a fax number and an electronic-mail address. The fax number is a reminder of e-mail's limitations. Electronic mail predates the arrival of low-cost fax machines, which took off because they are so easy to use. E-mail began to catch up only when it, too, became simple, although even now the effort needed to fax a document is still far less than that needed to log on to a PC and the network and then to create and send a message. The tremendous advantage

About 2.6 trillion e-mail messages were expected to move through U.S.-based networks in 1997, up from 1.65 trillion the previous year, according to the Electronic Messaging Association in Arlington, Virginia. The average worker sends about eighteen electronic-mail messages daily and receives thirty-nine. About 20 percent of the messages received have attachments.

of e-mail, however, is its ability to store and forward: The fax message goes to a machine, but the e-mail message goes to a person. If the recipient is not at the fax machine location, he or she doesn't get the message. Electronic mail is delivered to the addressee whether he or she is in Indiana, Italy, or India—that is, wherever the recipient can log on to the relevant network, which, increasingly, means the Internet. Given all the differences across the world in terms of Internet access, wire connections, and the technical requirements for connecting a PC to a telecommunications network, the fax machine is still easier to use and more likely to get a message through. More and more, however, it is becoming possible to log on to the Net almost anywhere in the world and retrieve e-mail messages, if the recipient knows the name of the server where they reside.

Overall traffic on the Internet is almost equally divided between e-mail and Web access. According to MIDS, a market research firm in Austin, Texas (http://www.mids.org), the number of Internet mail users as of January 1997 was 71 million, up from 3.4 million in January 1990. E-mail traffic was reported to be about 200 million messages per day in early 1997.[28] In the United States and most other countries where Internet use is widely established, the daily number of e-mail transmissions surpasses that of daily regular post mail traffic. About two thirds of e-mail traffic originates with corporate intranets.

A wide variety of Internet mail-based services and software exist, ranging from specialized Internet-based messaging systems to LAN-based messaging packages that have been switched over to Internet-based protocols. (LANs are local area networks that link clusters of PCs, printers, and servers, typically within a building, and that connect to other networks, including other LANs, wide area corporate networks, and the Internet.) Most Internet messaging systems offer many features already found in many proprietary mail systems, including message tracking; delivery notification methods, such as receipts; and rich text and multi-

David Frost, IS capability leader at Owens Corning in Toledo, Ohio, notes: "In our company, the pendulum swung too far to where people did everything by e-mail and nobody saw each other anymore."[27]

media options. Just about every proprietary system now includes the ability to send and receive messages to and from any Internet address.

E-mail gave rise, inevitably, to junk e-mail, unsolicited e-mail messages broadcast to hundreds of recipients for commercial purposes, such as advertising. E-mail has thus clearly become a marketing communications medium, similar to the telephone or television.

E-mail watchers note many emerging trends, including the following:

- *Automated receipt of personalized information.* Several information services will regularly e-mail you with information you requested. Amazon.com, for instance, the very successful Internet online book store, automatically sends e-mail to customers about new books on topics or by authors that they requested they be kept informed about.

- *Wireless e-mail.* Several brands of cellular phone and personal communicator are being equipped with Internet e-mail capabilities that allow users to stay in touch while mobile.

- *Multimedia e-mail.* Today, most e-mail transmissions consist of plain text. Emerging multimedia capabilities will, however, enrich basic messages with integrated voice or motion or still images.

- *Secure e-mail.* Most e-mail today is sent "in the cold," leaving it vulnerable to intruders and snooping hackers. Some e-mail messages have even turned up in the results of search engine queries, because they were stored on servers open to public access. As more and more businesses depend on e-mail communications, the sensitive nature of shared information and documents will necessitate a much higher level of security.

Increasingly, companies are encrypting their e-mails to protect them during transit to the intended destination.

- *E-mails as program launching pads.* As "network-centric" software programs proliferate throughout the Internet, e-mail messages will become transport vehicles for launching applications across the Internet, such as a request for information automatically read and responded to by a software, not human, agent.

- *E-mail assisted EDI (Electronic Data Interchange).* As Internet e-mail becomes more secure and robust, it will become a practical means for sending standard EDI transaction messages between computers.

- *Universal inbox.* Users will soon have the option to use a single interface for handling all incoming and outgoing communications. Netscape's announced Mercury product, for example, will provide a true universal inbox, not only for e-mail messages but for faxes, voice mail, and video e-mail.

Encryption Encryption (enciphering) converts data into an unintelligible numerical form to ensure its privacy. Decryption (deciphering) converts the cipher back to its original form, allowing the intended recipient to read the message. Encryption is essential for transmissions of sensitive or confidential information.

Many methods of varying strength are available today for encrypting and decrypting information; some use mathematical procedures, or algorithms, that are so complex and that use and generate such large numbers, or keys, that the chances of their being broken by an intruder with no matter how powerful a computer are minimized. The cost of adding strength and security lies in the cost of the computer power needed to carry out the algorithms, to use the result to encrypt the data, and to use

Table 6   Estimated Cost of and Time Required to Break an Algorithmically-Derived Key.

Cost to crack the code*	40	56	64	80	128
		Length of Key in Bits			
$100,000	2 secs	35 hours	1 year	70,000 years	10^{19} years
$1 million	.2 secs	3.5 hours	37 days	7,000 years	10^{18} years
$100 million	2 milli-seconds (thousandths)	2 minutes	9 hours	70 years	10^{16} years
$1 billion	.2 milli-seconds	13 secs	1 hour	7 years	10^{15} years
$100 billion	2 micro-seconds (millionths)	.1 secs	32 secs	24 days	10^{13} years

Source: Bruce Schneier, *Applied Cryptography*, 2 ed., (Chichester: Wiley, 1996), 6. Reprinted by permission of John Wiley & Sons, Inc.
*Cost here means the amount of computer power and talent the would-be code-cracker is willing to spend. So, for example, $100,000 cracks a 56-bit key in 35 hours, but for $100 million the time is reduced to just two minutes.

the key to decrypt it. Sender and receiver must have in common knowledge of the specific encrypting method used.

Encryption requires two keys, both of which are generated by the algorithm: one for encoding and a second for decoding. The number of possible keys each algorithm can generate depends on its length or, in digital terms, on the number of bits in the key. The difficulty of cracking an encrypted message is, therefore, directly related to the key length. An 8-bit key, for example, allows only 256 possible permutations, that is, 2^8. Substituting a 40-bit key yields 2^{40} possibilities, or 549,755,813,888. A fairly fast computer, however, can check all of these permutations on a trial-by-error basis in about two seconds. By choosing a 128-bit key, however, the number of permutations possible increases to the extent that it would take centuries to crack the key, thus securing the message. The number represented by 2^{128} is so large that it does not exist in nature. Table 6 shows the 1996 costs and estimated times needed to break codes. Exact figures are less relevant than their relative scale; the longer the key, the less likely a hacker with a PC can break it.

The science or art of encrypting data is called cryptography. Two basic methods are used, both of which use the key concept:

secret-key or symmetric encryption and public-key or asymmetric encryption. In secret-key encryption, both the sender and recipient have access to the same key, and they each use it to first encrypt and then decrypt information. The method is appealingly simple, but it has two major drawbacks. First, the users must keep track of a large number of keys, since one must be established for each correspondent with which an organization has private dealings. Second, the identity of the originator of a message cannot be authenticated or proved. Since both the recipient and the sender possess the same key, either one could compose a message, encrypt it, and claim that the other sent it. The process of generating messages the sender of which is uniquely identified is called nonrepudiation; it is necessary for secure electronic transactions, and it is impossible to achieve using secret key cryptography.

Public-key cryptography uses asymmetric encryption algorithms to produce a pair of keys that work together. Each key can encrypt information but in such a way that only the second key can decrypt it. One of the keys, the private key, is known only to the designated owner; the second, public key, is published widely but is still associated with the owner. If Mary wants to send a message to Tom, for example, Mary uses Tom's public key, accessible to anybody wishing to communicate with him, to encrypt the message. Only Tom, using the corresponding private key, which only he knows and can use, can decrypt this message. When Tom receives the message encrypted with his public key, he uses his private key to decrypt it. Usually, public keys are managed by a trusted third party, a Certification Authority, which maintains them and takes responsibility for certifying their authenticity.

Public-key cryptography allows recipients to authenticate the identity of a message's originator. If Tom originates a message encrypted with his private key, and the recipient can decrypt it using his public key, the recipient can be assured that the message came from Tom. Private keys on electronic documents, therefore, serve as the equivalent of a signature on a paper document.

Public-key cryptography is the single most important element in making Internet messages first very, very secure, and, if mathematical theorists are correct, very soon perfectly secure. That possibility has made public-key cryptography a major issue for the U.S. National Security Agency. Since security strength is a function of the key length, not of the type of algorithm used, the U.S. government has become very concerned about the export of long keys from the United States. Cryptography can become a tactic employed against U.S. interests, for example, by terrorists hiding plans and incriminating information.

As encryption techniques grow in strength, it may become impossible for the legal authorities to decrypt information critical to criminal and other investigations. A possible resolution to this dilemma would be to place all keys in escrow, so that, in case of an investigation, they could be made available to the government. Another solution that has been proposed is a "key recovery" mechanism that allows government access only in the case of an emergency. To put it mildly, such proposals are controversial, raising serious issues of privacy versus the national interest.

The U.S. federal government maintains that national security is far more important than privacy in cases where privacy is being used to damage security. For well over a decade, the government has worked very hard to restrict exports of strong cryptography software and hardware and has even prosecuted leading figures in the development of public-key cryptography. It proposed in 1993 that a special Clipper Chip be used in all encryption, whether in personal computers, bank payments systems, hardware devices, or any other context. The communications would still be encrypted with a secure key, but a copy of the key would be kept by an authorized government-controlled escrow agency that would make the key available to law enforcement authorities if and only if the courts issued a warrant requiring that the key be handed over.

The proposal unleashed a flood of protest in the computer-science community. Some of the objections concerned intrusions on privacy, some that the (unpublished and secret) mathematical procedures proposed for encrypting data would not be secure, and some on the economic grounds that, by restricting the development, use, and export of "strong" encryption chips, the government would hamper U.S. business, effectively handing the market over to Japanese competitors.

In 1996, the Clinton Administration started to relax the restrictions on the use and export of cryptographic chips and software, and it looks like the original proposal for the Clipper Chip is dormant, if not dead. However, the issue that gave rise to it has not gone and will not soon go away: privacy versus national security.

See also **Cryptography.**

Extranet   The term *extranet* refers to a new type of intranet (an internal network using Internet technology) that accesses many organizations' intranets to form a network unified by common interests. Extranets seem very likely to become significant tools for business-to-business electronic commerce among large companies that have a long-established and ongoing need to communicate with one another; such extranets will have the capacity to process electronic data interchange transactions for product ordering, invoicing, and many other everyday logistical tasks.

Historically, EDI has relied on special-purpose value-added networks, operated either by telecommunications service providers, telephone companies, or industry groups. The Internet offers companies an alternative platform for relationship management and electronic intercompany business activity. Companies now use the cost-effective, though relatively unreliable and insecure Internet or create their own intranets linked to the Internet. Linking intranets to form extranets is a logical next step. The technology is in place today to extend existing corporate intranets beyond company boundaries to reach a much larger audience, allowing enterprises to reap even greater benefits from their existing investments in networking. Deploying applications based

"Look for increased deployment of private networks based on Internet technology and focused on the needs of vertical markets. So called 'extranets'—secure private networks based on Transmission Control Protocol/Internet Protocol (TCP/IP)."[29]

Although every industry faces challenges in its supply chain, the agricultural chemical industry (especially those connected with crop protection products) is particularly challenged since the majority of

product sales occur during approximately an eight-week window each year and weather conditions can drastically affect the amount of product required. In a paper-based system, product sales information generally reaches companies three to four weeks after the fact. The American Crop Protection Association decided to rectify this problem by "bringing their community into a paperless future." The solution: PowerAG, a subscriber-only secure electronic commerce network, based on Internet technology. The extranet currently serves agricultural chemical manufacturers and will ultimately include other industry divisions, such as seed, feed, fertilizer, and equipment suppliers, as well as universities.[30]

on the open (that is, standardized and universal) Internet communication protocols enables enterprises to simplify and enhance their communications with business partners, suppliers, and customers by connecting the business applications on which companies depend. So Intranets combining to form an extranet have the wider reach provided by the Internet and the greater reliability and security characteristic of intranets. (Extranets themselves pose some security challenges because in joining them companies relinquish strict control of their corporate information systems to new user communities. It's one thing to keep customers up-to-date on the latest product and pricing information, but quite another to give them access to company financial data.)

Extranets integrate not only technology, but also applications, such as placing and processing orders, coordinating shipping logistics, and handling funds transfers, bidding, brokering, and so on. Organizations evolving an intranet integrated with the Internet may well find themselves involved with an extranet. Effective integration depends on treating the Internet and the intranet as one seamless service. Businesses that have accomplished this will find it possible to travel inside the intranet, outside onto the Internet, through the Internet to other intranets, and back into their own intranet. Figure 9 illustrates this process.

Extranets will soon be a dominant means for handling routine but private transactions as well as business transactions. The following example shows how an employee might process a health insurance claim, for instance.

1. The employee completes a health benefit form on the company intranet.
2. The completed form is submitted online, traveling from the company intranet via the Internet to the health insurance company's intranet.
3. An insurance company intranet application captures the form.

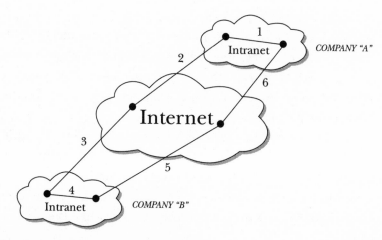

Figure 9   An Example of an Extranet
Source: CYBERManagement Inc., 1996.

4. The form is processed by an insurance company employee.

5. After processing and approval, the form is returned via the Internet to its originator.

6. The originator receives the approved form, which may be a mere confirmation of the claim or a payment or refund, processed through one of several acceptable Internet payment mechanisms.

Extranets are a hot area of development and activity, but companies should obviously have substantial experience with electronic data interchange and with intranets before venturing into extranet territory.

See also **Intranet.**

E-Zine   E-zines, also known simply as zines, are electronic magazines. Maintained entirely online, they can be kept totally up to date, even to the minute. E-zines are accessed over the Internet or automatically downloaded from the Net to a PC.

Despite much recent interest in the phenomenon, E-zine readers must struggle with a number of problems, including slow

Because of copyright fraud, humor writer Dave Barry stopped posting his weekly articles on the Internet. Although clearly marked with

*copyright labels, the
columns were illegally
copied so widely that they
began to lose their value.
Barry subsequently
boycotted the Web,
joining the many writers
concerned about the
ineffectiveness of
copyright protection
online.*[31]

*With the potential threat
of hackers lingering in
the near distance, some
companies have begun to
employ innovative
defense systems. Pilot
Network Services, in
Alameda, California,
connects their corporate
clients to one of the
company's service centers
around the country
rather than connecting
them directly through the
Internet. At each service
center, Pilot provides
supervised Internet access
for about $5,000 per
client per month. Their*

speed and cramped PC screen displays. Zines are an idea whose time will come, but none has had major, sustained success. Even Microsoft's much touted *Slate,* edited by Michael Kingsley, one of the top journalists in the United States, has been a bust, despite an editorial policy aimed at avoiding the mistakes and inadequacies of earlier E-zines.

Obviously, the stakes are huge in the wider game in which E-zines strive to be players. The future of mainstream magazine publishing, totally dependent on advertising, may lie increasingly online. The ads will go where the readers are, and traditional print publishers must be on the Internet when the demand takes off.

Firewall   A firewall is a security device that places a combination of hardware and software between a firm's internal network and systems and the Internet. The term comes from building construction, where it refers to a wall capable of isolating a fire to prevent it from spreading. Network firewalls similarly aim to trap and contain any security threat, such as a hacker or computer virus (intrusive software that works its way into a firm's systems and onto its PCs, propagating itself, and disseminating anything from harmless frivolities to total destruction of information and software).

As organizations move business processes onto the Internet and allow trading partners and customers to enter their intranets, company boundary lines blur. At the same time, as companies make more and more information about themselves available to outsiders, they have the need to protect other information from unwanted intruders. It is thus increasingly essential that companies not take messages directly from the Internet and that they place firewalls around the information technology resources they want to protect from outsiders.

Firewalls consist of a router (hardware) and appropriate software residing on a computer or collection of computers. The router, a hardware box, allows only selected traffic to filter through. (Routers are a key component of all networks; as their name suggests, they handle the routing of traffic across a network, interpreting destination addresses and managing traffic jams among their many other communication, coordination, and management functions.)

Every corporate intranet or Web server must have a firewall. But, because of the intricate physical "topology" of the Internet, the many paths across it and links among devices on it, intruders seeking access to unauthorized information can lurk on the Net and "listen-in" outside a computer, gaining valuable information without venturing to enter it. Firewalls will not solve that problem. In addition, hackers determined to break into a computer with a firewall will find their jobs much more difficult, but not impossible. Firewalls aren't 100 percent proof against intrusion. A house alarm system may do an excellent job of protecting against intruders entering through the windows and doors, but what if an intruder drills a hole in the wall? The standard alarm system would fail to detect it.

Today, the prices of firewall systems range from $7,000 to $12,000 for a single set-up and much more for complex global intranets. As with all standard hardware, prices are decreasing steadily and may reach the $500 per unit level by the year 2000. The firewall market continues to grow rapidly, closely paralleling the increase in the number of computers connected to the Internet and of intranets. The number of computers connected to the Internet is very likely to exceed two hundred million by the year 2000 (up from around thirty million in mid-1997), and most of these will need a firewall to ensure proper protection of their data and software.

See also **Security.**

system consists of a "dynamic" five-layered firewall monitored twenty-four hours every day by a team of human electronic cops who routinely change data pathways to mislead hackers. Says founder and CEO Marketta Silvera, "You're dealing with a challenge that moves. If you buy a static, shrink-wrapped firewall in a box, so can a hacker."[32]

Groupware and Team Collaboration See **Communication and Collaboration.**

Hacker Hackers are computer experts who use their skills either to explore new solutions to tough problems or to illegally break into elaborate computer systems for personal gain or satisfaction. The first construction dates from the early days of computing, when technology use was less straightforward than it is today. During that period, savvy computer users were called "hackers" to indicate the extent of their knowledge and their ability to use the technology backwards and forwards. Often able to see new ways around long-standing problems, they devised many amazing innovations. Much of the Internet's development was due to the efforts of graduate student hackers, especially at the University of California at Berkeley.

Hackers in the second sense direct much of their work toward breaking the security measures established by corporate networks to protect their data and systems from unauthorized or unwanted users. Hackers sometimes do this simply for fun or to show off, without any intent to cause damage. When in the late 1980s a student at Cornell University, the son of a famous old-style (that is, non-damaging) hacker, brought down the Internet, thus destroying many databases containing the results of ongoing scientific experiments, however, it really didn't matter whether his intrusion was well-intentioned "harmless" play, deliberate sabotage, or an effort to steal information. The damage was done.

It is now commonplace to hear in the news that a certain hacker has been arrested for illegal entry into a computer network. Damage created by hackers can cost millions of dollars, especially if they tinker with financial information. Proper, multifaceted security measures are essential. As with burglar alarm systems, the goal in establishing security from hackers is to make a given system more difficult to break into than the next guy's. Various approaches have been developed, including specialized monitoring software that instantly informs network managers that an intruder is attempting to break into the system. Because of hackers' resourcefulness, law enforcement organizations frequently enlist the help of ex-hackers to track and find active hackers.

IBM's development teams routinely perform so-called ethical hacking on the complex secure systems they install. Ethical hacking tests the resilience of these systems; if they are broken, the company is able to correct the flaws detected preventatively. Many companies concerned about security employ their own resident ethical hacker to continuously test the strength of their security systems.

See also **Security.**

That's how you learn. You break into programs, commit piracy, all kinds of wild and crazy things."[33]

History of the Internet

The Internet was born in late 1969 when the first four networked computer sites were set up on the ARPANet. ARPA, which stands for Advanced Research Projects Agency, is a part of the U.S. Department of Defense. To meet DOD's requirement for a decentralized computer network with no single "point of failure," ARPA funded a project to design a hub of interconnected computers that couldn't be collectively disabled in case of a nuclear attack.

Through 1987, ARPANet continued to grow in size and versatility, but its use and evolution remained almost entirely confined to the academic and technical communities. Using ARPANet required technical knowledge, a lot of patience, and computer hardware and software that was largely outside the mainstream of business and personal computers. It relied on workstations using the Unix operating system, which then offered many advantages over other options for both building software and working in a networked environment, primarily speed, power, and interactivity. Unix was about as nonvisual an operating system as could be envisaged, and it lacked the basic security features necessary to all business software. The early ARPANet community was trying to build just that—a *community* that could share information across the Net without impediments, controls, or bureaucracy.

PC evolution ran parallel to, but was entirely independent of, the ARPANet evolution. Bringing the two together created the Internet revolution. PCs used different hardware chips from Unix, which meant that software built for one environment could not run on the other. The two main PC evolutionary paths, that of Apple and that of Microsoft, also had to converge before the Internet revolution could take off.

In 1987, the National Science Foundation added to the ARPANet by creating NSFNet, which connected its supercomputing centers with universities. Shortly after its creation, NSFNet was opened up to the public and to U.S. allies. The combined entity that included ARPANet, NSFNet, and other regional networks spawned by the latter became known as the Internet. In the early 1990s, neither Microsoft nor Apple saw the Internet as even peripheral to their business strategies. They had no need to. The Internet remained a specialized network, the main services of which were electronic mail and file transfers. Between 1987 and 1994, PCs were used either as stand-alones, having no telecommunications links except for dial-up connections via modem to network services, or were attached to corporate local area networks. Apple failed to recognize the essential importance of ensuring that personal computers could link to corporate data bases; PCs were increasingly powerful engines whose fuel was data. That lack of recognition cost it the corporate market. Microsoft seized the corporate market, adapting its primitive and clumsy Windows operating system, built as an extension of DOS, to mimic the Mac GUI (graphical user interface), and pushing Apple into a niche position from which it has struggled to free itself for almost a decade. (Apple's survival remains very uncertain.) Unix became the operating system of choice for building interactive systems requiring efficient processing. The programming language C++ was developed to supplement the established computer programming languages in which most businesses' basic applications had been built.

The breakthrough that moved the Internet from being exclusively for technology-savvy PC and Unix users was the invention of the World Wide Web. Once it was introduced in 1992, followed by the development of the first easy to use browser, Mosaic, the forerunner of Netscape's Navigator, it rapidly gathered a large and growing body of users. Both the Web and Mosaic were developed in scientific research labs, but the computer industry quickly took over. Since 1992, the rise in popularity and development of the Web has been nothing short of meteoric. The period of early preparation for and interest in the Web by pioneers from 1992 to 1995 was followed by the current explosion that the Web is continuing to experience. The year 1995 is viewed as a turning point because this was the first year when traffic on the Web surpassed the traditional traffic on the Internet. From then on, nothing has stopped it. By mid-1997, over one million Web domains, where the main commercial activity takes place, populated the Internet. The period from 1997 to 2000 represents the exploitation of the Web as a major commercial center, with increasing sources of revenues for all participants. There isn't one company today that is not affected, one way or another, by the Internet.

See also **Internet2;** and **Transmission Control Protocol/Internet Protocol.**

Hits   Hits are the most basic measure of popularity of a Web site. Basic doesn't mean accurate or useful, however. A hit means only that a Web page has been accessed; whether by teenagers or qualified customers, by intent or accident, by someone looking at it for several minutes or by a user who immediately moves on to another site remains unknown. It is much more difficult to count the number of people who really "visit" a Web site than it is to count the number of times they "hit" the mouse to request a new Web page. It is an even tougher job to find out who those people are.

A hit is a request to the Web server to send along a file. A page hit may involve several file hits. One hit, for example, may be a request for the text and a second hit for the graphics file. Even though it seems that the number of hits should indicate how many people ask for pages from a Web site, sites with a lot of

Of the thirty thousand systems managers asked about "hits per day" in a 1997 survey conducted by Andromedia, 40 percent claimed to have Web sites that generate 1000 to 25,000 hits per day; 20 percent claimed a Web site volume of 25,000 to 50,000 hits per day; 17 percent claimed 50,000 to 150,000 and 8 percent claimed more than 1 million hits per day.[34]

Netscape, the busiest site on the Internet in late 1996, reported that it was getting about 80 million hits per day.

graphics on a page push counts artificially high. Also, some of the tricks used by computers to speed things up (like saving recently accessed pages on the PC hard disk so that the next time they are requested they can be taken from the disk, thus not recording a new hit) will render counts artificially low. Web owners still talk about how many hits their sites get per week (or per month or per day), however, even though the number can be used only to measure relative activity, not to indicate the quality or quantity of visitors.

HotJava   HotJava refers to software libraries built using the Java programming language, which many see as the emerging mainstream for the increasingly Internet-dominated world of computing and telecommunications. HotJava allows developers to build customized network-centric applications. It is ideal for developing desktop environments that run on devices enabled by the Java operating system (Java OS), a lightweight operating system designed for network computers and consumer devices.

See also **Java.**

HTML   See **HyperText Markup Language.**

HTTP   See **HyperText Transfer Protocol.**

Hypermedia   Hypermedia is an extension of hypertext; both terms refer to blocks of information that can be dynamically linked, as on the World Wide Web, where the blocks are computer data files called pages and the links are represented by highlighted text or icons (small pictures) displayed on the user's PC screen. *Hypertext* refers to linked text files, and *hypermedia* to files that can include text, but also graphics, video, still pictures, sound, and so on.

Hypertext   Hypertext provides a dynamic means to organize and access information (text); the connection is accomplished through a software interface within the text. Hypertext, first proposed in the late 1960s, made possible the World Wide Web. Conceptually, the idea is simple: Set up a file of computer data of any type and size and provide it with a unique identifier; design and employ software (HTTP, or Hypertext Transfer Protocol) that can interpret a user request and directly access any requested file that is in hypertext format. In a text, words highlighted, underlined, or in a distinct color indicate the otherwise hidden links to related documents or to other computer systems. By clicking on a hypertext link, users can move to the page designated by the link.

In addition to being the standard means for displaying information on the World Wide Web, hypertext is also used in Microsoft Windows' help programs and CD encyclopedias to jump to related references elsewhere within the same document. The method has proven to be a productivity enhancement for sifting through quantities of information.

See also **Hypermedia.**

HyperText Markup Language (HTML) HTML is the very foundation of the World Wide Web as we know it today. HTML is the plain text language used to define the elements of a Web page or document. HTML uses a series of commands, called tags, to tell a browser how to display each page, including layout, font size, graphics, and links to other pages and Web sites.

Development and maintenance of HTML standards is coordinated by the World Wide Web Consortium (the W3 Consortium). The latest version of HTML is HTML 3.0. HTML 3.0 offers, over its predecessors, enhanced graphics capabilities that enable Web-page designers to display tables, create multiple frames within a single window, and to flow text around figures. A browser must support HTML 3.0 to be able to read HTML 3.0 documents.

Looking beyond HTML 3.0, an anticipated major enhancement to HTML is dynamic HTML, which is expected to give Web designers the ability to make Web pages come alive graphically and typographically, bypassing the annoying click-and-wait model that characterizes almost all Internet services today. Dynamic HTML gives Web pages the capability to change *after* they are loaded into the browser: The page doesn't have to make the slow trip back to the Web server for an update. Text might shift from one size or color to another, for example, or a figure might move from one location on the page to another, both in response to some specific user action, such as clicking a button. With dynamic HTML, Web designers can load huge quantities of information (for example, complex outlines or tables of product parts and prices) and simply keep the information hidden until the user requests it, piece by piece.

HyperText Transfer Protocol (HTTP)   HTTP, the workhorse of the World Wide Web, is the software running on a Web server (a special-purpose computer) that locates and moves hypertext files across the Internet. This specially developed protocol made the Web, developed within the Internet, possible. Hypertext, a block of computer data or a Web page, can be linked to other hypertext pages on any computer anywhere on the Web. An Internet user's Web browser initiates the request for an HTTP transaction; an HTTP server is needed at the other end to fulfill incoming requests from browsers.

HTTP is by far the most important protocol used on the World Wide Web. Its efficiency and speed are currently being improved and enhanced, yielding a new protocol called HTTP/1.1. The basic tool for designing Web pages and adding hypertext links is HTML, HyperText Markup Language, though other recently developed software helps users design pages with more options for display, multimedia, audio, video, and so, than HTML makes available.

See also **HyperText Markup Language.**

IETF   See **Internet Engineering Task Force.**

IMC See **Internet Mail Consortium.**

Intercasting Intercasting is a recent technology promoted by Intel and the Intercast Industry Group. It makes it possible for home PCs to receive standard Web pages (those using the now venerable HTML Web design software language, but not those written in any of the more recent and exotic languages that include, for instance, virtual reality applications) and video "streaming" of information along with regular television programming. While watching a favorite show, users can also get in-depth articles, links to related sites, or even access to other applications— they could be working on a spreadsheet while watching the Super Bowl.

According to Intel, research indicated that people were excited about the Internet but didn't know what to do when they got there. Seeing that the most popular sites on the Web had to do with television, Intel believed the fun and familiar context of television could draw people into a more interactive experience. Out of this research, Intercast technology was born, exploiting the desire expressed by so many consumers for instant results versus having to "surf" the Web for information.

Intercasting epitomizes the marriage of the television and the Internet that many companies in each of these industries see as a potential goose ready to lay solid gold eggs. Members of the Intercast Group include leading television networks, program providers, cable operators, broadband communications equipment suppliers, computer manufacturers, and computer hardware and software vendors. Earlier goose hunts have included the billions of dollars of investment in interactive TV, which to date has generated minimal revenues.

Intercasting is just one of the new hunts. The hot Internet topic in early 1997 was "push" technology, the automatic feeding of Internet information to PCs—or television sets. Rather than searching and surfing for information—pulling—the user specifies items, names, or topics of interest, and the Web pushes in-

During the 1997 NBA All-star Game, NBC broadcast Intercast content containing a "virtual locker room," a three-dimensional area that simulated an actual NBA team locker room. It was filled with "hot buttons" that, when clicked, gave player statistics and an animated coach's chalkboard with play diagrams. Other interactive areas included an animated quiz on referee hand signals and a sports fan sound effect button that cheered.

formation on those interests to the consumer's designated device on a continuous basis.

Internet   In 1995, *The Economist* ranked the importance of the Internet revolution "ahead of the telephone and television but behind the printing press and the motor car."[35] Every organization must meet the challenge of making the Internet more important to them than the telephone and television have been. But have the telephone and television changed our lives? Or have they just changed the way we communicate and are entertained? Those questions can only be answered individually. Some might liken the Internet to the microwave, for example, the appliance that did not pervasively change our lives but that certainly did change many peoples' eating habits.

The Internet is best described as simultaneously a network, a medium, a market, a transaction platform, and a software development platform. These five identities can be fully taken advantage of only by developing and applying a different strategy for each. The synergistic effect realized by addressing each of the five faces of the Internet's identity will enable organizations to take maximum advantage of the Internet, intranets, extranets, and related and dependent applications, such as electronic commerce and collaborative capabilities.

Below are a few issues of particular concern for each of the five Internet identities.

- *The Internet as a network.* The Internet is actually a network of networks. Large organizations have for several years used the Internet structure and mixed it with their own private networks; only now is it becoming affordable for smaller companies to do the same. With proper security, organizations can use the Internet as a virtual private network linking employees and offices. (The term *private network* is used in the telecommunications field to indicate a network that, while using public transmission links, appears dedicated to a given firm. Previously restricted to larger firms because of the high monthly cost, the Internet opens the opportunity to operate private networks to all firms.) Company-specific intranets can form the basis for valuable intracompany human collaboration as well as corporate information publishing and sharing.

- *The Internet as a medium.* The Internet augments the traditional marketing mix, offering a new channel. A medium for advertising, PR, and marketing departments or agencies, it also serves as a publishing, entertainment, and broadcasting medium. For corporate communications, service information, and product marketing, the Internet offers a communications channel and a medium for creating online "virtual" communities. The Net's very breadth of opportunity, the pace of multimedia innovations, and its newness have all combined to generate a flurry of experimentation—and hype. It will take years before companies learn to use the new Internet media fully.

- *The Internet as a market.* The Internet has been likened to a vast open marketplace where a company's next customer may never know with whom he or she is dealing. For a given business, the Internet is a market only if it directly generates new or additional revenue. If it provides only leads or referrals, it is still just a medium. The allure of the Internet as a market is, of course, immense: It is also immensely uncertain. Estimates of the growth of consumer electronic commerce on the Internet from the 1997 level of around $500 million range so widely and wildly—from $1.5 to $600 billion in 2000—that it is obvious that tapping the Net market remains as much a gamble as a strategy.

- *The Internet as a transaction platform.* This is the Internet's newest and most exciting but also its most challenging face. The Internet offers the opportunity to move more and more business transactions into the Internet marketspace, with all financial transactions and links to suppliers, customers, and financial institutions completed online. Three Internet developments have solved long-standing problems for companies using information technology in their core systems: first, the networking technology (called TCP/IP, the foundation of the Internet) that permits any computer of any type to link to any other; second, browsers and hypertext, which combine information from many sources; and third, an "application programming interface" that links transaction processing systems to Internet-based systems.

- *The Internet as a software applications development platform.* Organizations are running or extending existing client-server applications on the Internet and developing new network-based applications (for example, using Java technology). Java propels organizations into the new Internet-centric computing paradigm, in which the Internet is a vast resource of technical capabilities to be harnessed collectively by applying the technology across organizations and around the globe. The Internet is now the mainstream for innovation in software development tools, the laboratory for new methods, and the target for leading vendors.

Every company will view and treat the Internet differently. Some firms will soon not know what to do without it. Others will find its effects marginal. In reality, almost no organization is immune to the Internet's influence. It must be seen as an opportunity to be exploited. Each firm must determine the areas appropriate for it to target for exploitation in order to meet its business objectives, and it must then develop and execute plans for realizing them, while remaining fully aware of the rapid development occurring in this field.

What is the Internet? Whatever you would like it to be. The degree of business commitment a given company makes will obviously strongly shape selection of the Internet elements—network, medium, market, transaction platform, and development platform—it targets. The range of choices, risks, and uncertainties is immense. Which should carry more weight in managers' minds: the opportunities or the risks? Only individual managers can answer that question, but it is obviously a question that must be asked. The Internet isn't going away.

Internet2   Internet2 is a proposed new mini-Internet dedicated to research organizations needing reliable, very high-speed data communication. The Internet2 Project, a result of President Clinton's Advisory Committee on High-Performance Computing and Communications, Information Technology, and the Next Generation Internet, is being promoted by the U.S. and Canadian academic and research communities, who claim that heavy commercial usage has in many places slowed the Internet to a crawl, damaging its effectiveness as a research tool.

In 1996, a group of U.S. universities realized that the Internet they had known before its entry into the commercial world was overdue for a major overhaul. After its early inception and expansion throughout the late 1980s and into the early 1990s, the Internet remained in use largely among universities. In the mid-1990s, the business community moved onto the Internet in force. The universities, used to having the Internet to themselves, now had to share its capacity with millions of other users. The Internet's burgeoning popularity and the resulting traffic overload has made it unreliable for the kind of dedicated high-speed data transmission on which the universities rely.

Just a decade after they played a major role in creating it,

In June 1996, BT and MCI announced the world's first high-speed, high-reliability global Internet services. Concert InternetPlus expanded the two companies' substantial existing Internet networks to form new regional Internet "hubs." The networked hubs provide alternative routes for data, providing redundancy and responsiveness not found in any other Internet network. The Concert InternetPlus offerings also include the first-ever global Internet service performance guarantees, improved response times, and greater availability.

Ira Fuchs, vice president for computing and information technology at Princeton University, believes it possible that by the time Internet2 is built, researchers will already be clamoring for Internet3. He cites what he calls Fuchs's Law, which states that the time to acquisition is longer than the time to obsolescence. "What that means is that the technology is advancing so rapidly that by the time the computer you originally asked for is finally delivered, you don't want that computer any more. That same problem is going to have an effect on Internet2. We have to worry, Will we have enough time to test, and to think, before everybody is beating down the door to get on this thing?"[36]

Canadian and U.S. university users are fleeing an apparently congested Internet and building their own private networks. They need, they maintain, a new dedicated Net—Internet2. The Internet seems to have come full circle, back to its origins among university and research organizations. In his fiscal-1998 budget, President Clinton asked Congress for $100 million to fund Internet2, but the bulk of the money needed to get the project up and running will come from the participating colleges and universities, each of which has pledged $500,000 to become a part of it. The Internet2 project consists of an upgrade in current Internet connections to universities and research institutions to attain much higher speeds, a guaranteed quality of service, and more reliable uptime than the current Internet offers. At the same time, developers hope to insulate the new network from commercial Internet users. The networks will run at state-of-the-art speeds, using fiber optic links. The project, to be conducted in phases between 1997 and 2002, is expected to number among its initial participants one hundred universities, a number of U.S. and Canadian government agencies, and many of the leading U.S. and Canadian computer and telecommunications companies. During the summer of 1997, the first phase of Internet2, including a connection to its Canadian equivalent, CAnet2, became operational.

Some analysts argue that Internet2 is not needed, or at least not needed for the reasons researchers claim it is needed. The Internet as originally conceived and developed, even if it had stayed within the confines of university campuses, would not have been able to run the kinds of applications that are today being proposed for it, anyway. In addition, private industry is pouring billions of dollars into products and services for improving the Internet, an investment much greater than the initial $150 million or so budgeted for Internet2. The business community requires a resilient, reliable Internet if it is to serve as a commercial platform for the conduct of commerce and to run corporate mission-critical applications demanding service levels that approach, if not surpass, those required for research applications. (Among their proposed improvements is a commercial Internet with IPng, or "next generation Internet Protocol," referring to the telecommunications transmission procedure used by the Internet.)

The types of applications being targeted for Internet2 are next generation multimedia-heavy applications, requiring continuously available high bandwidth, for teaching, learning, collaboration, and research. Among the proposed new applications, considered essential for higher education, distance education, lifelong learning, and national research objectives, are the following:

- *Distance learning:* Real-time multimedia content transmission from one university to another.

- *Scientific research:* Shared resources from national laboratories, computational facilities, and large data repositories, including real-time access to data.

- *Telemedicine:* Remote consultation and diagnoses.

- *Learning:* Digital libraries, with "streamed" (constantly broadcast) media content, very large and detailed bitmap scanned images, and interactive services to manipulate data online.

- *Art and music:* Music instruction via stereo quality audio and high quality video; low latency (transmission delay) to allow remote improvisation and synchronization of audio, video, digitized sheet music, and annotations.

- *General collaboration:* Virtual lab support (remote instrumentation), real-time chat (audio, video, and text), and session record and playback with multiple windows and "whiteboard" features.

- *Tele-immersion:* A common, realistically rendered virtual environment shared by several participants who communicate normally within that virtual environment and who interact with a common application.

Internet Appliance Internet appliances are specially designed hardware devices that exploit the Internet as a software delivery vehicle, as well as for its traditional services, and that perform a targeted range of functions rather than, as personal computers do, operating as general-purpose systems. They are the most controversial element of IT industry competition because network computers (NC), a subset of network appliances, have the potential to erode the dominance of personal computers, effectively ending Microsoft's control of the software market.

The Internet's unique telecommunications protocols (procedures and message formats) support just about any type of hardware and allow messages to pass between completely different types of devices. You can't plug a toaster into the phone system or send an e-mail message from a coffee pot to a camera, but phones, cellular phones, cameras, television sets, coffeepots, cars, traffic lights—all these can be made into Internet devices.

The term *Internet appliance* refers to a device specifically designed to operate via the Internet. As special-purpose devices, unlike the far more general-purpose multimedia personal computer, Internet appliances will nonetheless be more than just hardware: They will be smart toasters or cameras, containing software "applets" that send and receive instructions and information. A car's microprocessor may send location data via the Internet to, say, a cellular phone, which will interpret and display it via a Web browser, or images captured by a digital camera will be uploaded to a Web site—the possibilities are literally endless. They are also very practical. The Internet really does host coffeepots and toasters. The ever decreasing cost of microchips will guarantee a non-stop flood of innovative network appliances. Whereas today around thirty million computers have Internet access, the future will see thirty billion special-purpose Internet devices within a very few years, each with its own Internet address.

Businesses will use many of these. Some of the immediate

business opportunities lie in diagnosis and fault monitoring of remote equipment, data collection on traffic flows, security systems, and telemetry.

Internet Commerce   See **Electronic Commerce.**

Internet Directory   Internet directories are the electronic equivalent of indexes and library catalogs. They classify information spread across the entire Internet, including the Web, USENET discussion groups, and computer databases. Given the enormous amount of information available on the Internet, users must be able to locate what they need without knowing the Internet address at which the information resides. Web directories, each specializing in a certain specific interest area, have mushroomed. Some directories cover the full Internet, but most confine their indexing and searches to the Web, since that is the main information resource on the Net.

Internet directories are not to be confused with Internet search engines. Search engines (such as Alta Vista or InfoSeek) search the entire Internet in response to a given query. In contrast, Internet directories categorize information by specific categories and enable users to search only within those categories. Information received from Internet directories tends to be of higher quality than that retrieved with search engines because it has already been filtered and organized.

The following are some of the most popular Internet directories:

- *Yahoo!* The Internet's most popular search tool, this software service indexes information by topic and builds and accesses abstracts about it.

- *ABC to the XYZ Mall.* This large directory points users directly to shopping locations for just about anything available on the Internet.

- *Buy It Online.* This index advises users, before they buy, to check Buy It Online first. Whatever a Net consumer might be looking for, it is probably available online.

- *Internet Directory of Directories.* This index uses pointers to indicate resources, products, and services accessible through the Internet.

- *The Internet Yellow Pages.* This very popular directory provides direct links to selected Web pages, rather like a Yellow Pages phone directory that dials the number for you, and "posts" (adds information about) new sites within twenty-four hours of their appearance on the Net.

Internet EDI   Electronic Data Interchange (EDI) is a set of data and message formats that facilitate interorganizational exchanges of information and execution of business transactions such as product ordering, or payment transfers. EDI was synonymous with electronic commerce (EC) when, in the early 1980s, it became a growing component of customer-supplier relationships among large automakers, retailers, and petrochemical and other manufacturers. Since then, electronic commerce has evolved to include many other mechanisms for commerce, such as electronic payments, security infrastructures, and the Web and other online catalogs. EDI remains the core of business-to-business EC.

To facilitate EDI, firms typically draw on specialized organizations that operate as "hub-and-spoke" systems, sitting between trading partners (the spokes). These organizations, known as VANs (value-added networks), facilitate the transfer and management of electronic messages between trading partners, thus acting as public data networks. VANS also provide services to assist trading partners in managing their data and handling message transfers. A large component of the "value-added" services provided by EDI VANs is the assurance that EDI transactions handled via the VAN are not compromised in any way. VANs operate their own private networks, enabling them to protect against unauthorized access. When the Internet came along, companies began investigating its usefulness as a possible replacement for the often expensive VANs. Measures must, however, be taken to defend against security threats when an EDI interchange is in transit across an "open" network such as the Internet. Internet EDI promises to become a more cost effective way to conduct EDI, once security is fully adequate. As it becomes more affordable, Internet EDI is likely to reach a larger number of small- to medium-size firms that previously couldn't justify the costs of implementing traditional EDI.

One emerging philosophy for Internet EDI is to treat the Internet as the transport medium and to preserve the format of EDI transactions by sending them as secure Internet e-mail messages. The most rapidly emerging trend is the development of EDI "gateways," with easy-to-use forms-based EDI questionnaires that are automatically formatted into EDI transactions messages and then routed to the appropriate business partner. This system allows organizations to switch almost immediately to EDI, without spending time and money on data formatting and structuring software.

Internet-based EDI offers advantages from both the consumer and the business perspectives. Bell Atlantic, for example, is providing a secure way for large customers to receive and pay their phone bills via EDI procedures and message formats, without their having to sign up with a VAN. Diamond Shamrock sends secure financial EDI transactions over the Internet to Chase Manhattan, a system it began with about 25 percent of its three hundred trading partners, mainly utility and freight handling companies. Shamrock's EDI files sent via the Internet reach their destination in real-time.

Internet Engineering Task Force (IETF) The Internet Engineering Task Force (IETF) is a large international community of network designers, operators, vendors, and researchers concerned with the evolution of Internet architecture and the Internet's smooth operation. Open to any interested individual, the actual technical work of the IETF is done in its working groups, which are organized into several topic areas (for example, routing, transport, security, and so on).

The IETF has no legal standing and no formal governance mechanism vis a vis the Internet. None of the many telecommunications service providers operating parts of the physical Internet telecommunications network, the organization managing the assignment of Internet addresses, or the U.S. or any other government, is involved in the management of the Net. One analogy for the Internet as an organizational phenomenon is food services in New York City. In that bustling, even chaotic, metropolis, people get fed. At lunchtime, a stream of bodies moves in and out of restaurants and delis and delivery service employees move in and out of offices. This complex, self-adaptive system has no central management or scheduler and relatively few direct rules and regulations, such as licensing or health and safety checks. But people still get their lunch every day: Chaos works. It is arguable that if an official city lunch supervision plan were to be introduced to control the system, the results would be worse in comparison with the innovation, flexibility, and constant change of the non-controlled, non-managed marvel of today.

The Internet operates in the same way, and most experts want to see it stay unsupervised and minimally controlled; they argue persuasively that the floods of innovation that have marked the Internet's development depended on this freedom. Opposing experts, however, point to the Internet's potential problems, such as a possible collapse resulting from traffic growth outstripping capacity; the need to police the Net to prevent or curtail fraud and crime, especially pornography involving minors and pedophiles exploiting the Net's anonymity to ensnare children; and uncertainty over issues such as copyright, taxation and tax jurisdiction, and consumer protection.

The IETF does not constitute a basis for such a central oversight and governance mechanism, but it does bring together the very best technical experts for whom the Internet is as much a mission as part of their everyday jobs. Because of this strength of expertise, the IETF has influence without authority.

Two of the IETF's working groups, the Internet Architecture Board and the Internet Engineering Steering Group, were chartered by the Internet Society (ISOC). Another working group, the Internet Assigned Numbers Authority (IANA), chartered by the Internet Society (ISOC) and the U.S. Federal Network Council (FNC), is the central coordinator for the assignment of unique parameter values (equivalent to part numbers or social security numbers) for Internet communication protocols.

The IETF's impact on the advancement of Internet technologies has been tremendous. IETF has focused on making the Internet a more robust and trusted platform. Some of the areas in which it has proposed or implemented standards to this end include access, directory searching and indexing, calendaring and scheduling, electronic data interchange-Internet integration, Internet fax, HyperText Transfer Protocol, Internet protocols on the Cable Data Network, IPng, the Internet printing protocol, the Internet security protocol, public-key infrastructure (X.509), simple public-key infrastructure, and Web transaction security.

Internet Law The field of Internet law is growing rapidly due to the need to adapt existing policies and regulations to the Internet, as well as to create new policies and regulations responsive to the specific characteristics of the electronic marketplace. The legal field usually lags behind technology in this regard and changes are largely reactive. This is the current situation with regard to the regulatory and legal aspects of Internet commerce. From electronic copyright issues to electronic cash policies (governing digital offers and receipts enforcement), the Internet remains as yet largely unregulated. Two necessary forms of regulation will soon emerge, however: first, self-regulation, and second, imposed regulation. Whereas Canada and the United States tend

In late 1996, two French organizations brought a suit against a small Georgia Tech campus located in France, because its Internet site is in English, which they claim to be a violation of a 1994 French law forbidding the sale of goods and services in France to take place in

any language other than French. (Sony renamed its Walkman "Balladeur" for this reason.) Courses at the French Georgia Tech campus are taught by American professors in English, and most of the students are American. The lawsuit reflects a widespread French obsession that the country will be "economically and culturally marginalized" (in French President Jacques Chirac's phrase) by the dominance of the English language in entertainment, technology, and retailing.[37] The French postal service was sued for naming its courier service Skypack. The suit against Georgia Tech raises important legal issues. Is its Web site a forum for private discussion or a public place? Where is it located? Does French national law apply to organizations the site of which is (or may be) physically outside

to favor self-regulation, other parts of the world, such as Europe, largely favor imposed regulation. Starting in 1998, for example, the European Union will prohibit the export of data to countries that don't adhere to specified standards of data safeguarding and usage.

The following aspects of the Internet give rise to the need for regulation in the near future, if not now.

- *The Internet is global.* Because the Internet has no territorial limits, questions arise about how, where, and when individual countries' rules will be applied to it.

- *The Internet lacks a central location or head office.* Regulations become more difficult to enforce when the entity on which they are to be enforced is both pervasive and protean.

- *The Internet is electronic.* Internet transactions do not generate the paper trails that have developed over the years as legally binding. What legal standing will electronic documents have?

- *The Internet is digital.* Perfect copies of images, documents, software, and so on can be made almost instantaneously in limitless numbers, at little or no cost. How can copyrights be protected?

Internet law analysts Debora Spar and Jeffrey Bussgang have stated that "commerce will migrate to areas where rules will prevail and responsibility can be assigned."[38] Several necessary rules must be put in place for and by specific electronic commerce communities. The most likely scenario for this will be that users will choose rather than legislators impose.

In October 1996, two consortiums were formed to help address the Internet's "no rules" state: the Internet Law and Policy Forum and TRUSTe. The Internet Law and Policy Forum (ILPF), composed of a number of international companies involved in Internet development, proposes to help resolve the challenging legal issues and policy questions arising with the increase of business activity on the global electronic network. The ILPF will endeavor, through analytical reports and recommendations for best business practices, to produce the building blocks for more predictable and enforceable agreements, uniform contracting tools for electronic commerce, and model codes of conduct. Two important areas of focus have been isolated by the ILPF's sponsors as the site of initial efforts: first, business and legal aspects of the emerging functions of certification authorities, and second, the challenges of blocking access to unacceptable materials.

The TRUSTe initiative strives to increase the level of trust in electronic communications, especially on the Internet, held by merchants and consumers. The TRUSTe was founded on the belief that "the greater the level of trust among the participants in a transaction, the lower the transaction costs."

The key principles governing the TRUSTe program include the following:

- *Informed consent.* Consumers have the right to be informed about the privacy and security consequences of an online transaction *before* entering into it.

- *No privacy without appropriate security.* An inextricable link exists between the privacy and security of an online transaction. Privacy is impossible without appropriate security.

- *Privacy standards vary according to use context.* No single privacy standard is adequate for all situations. Three levels of privacy for commercial transactions have been delineated, each of which is, in its context, considered a "best business practice."

The TRUSTe consortium has joined its efforts to those of CommerceNet, thus commercializing the project and reaching many companies already involved in developing electronic commerce best practices. A pilot launched in November 1996 focused solely on privacy issues: creating a reasonable, effective, and enforceable system for ensuring protection of personally identifiable information. It included a contractual agreement that details the

France? The answers to these questions will affect the development and application of laws about pornography, consumer protection, freedom of expression, and libel, in all nations.

rights and responsibilities of a site, specifies the guidelines a site must follow, and licenses TRUSTe servicemarks for use on pilot member sites.

See also **CommerceNet.**

Internet Mail Consortium (IMC) The Internet Mail Consortium (IMC) is an industry organization whose members are mostly vendors of Internet electronic mail software. Other members include hardware vendors who sell Internet mail servers (specially-configured computers that manage the flow of e-mail traffic, including security, accounting, and conversion from one standard message format to another), online services with Internet mail gateways, and other similar companies in the Internet mail market.

The IMC pursues cooperative promotion and enhancement of electronic mail and messaging on the Internet. It represents general mail industry needs and activities, advances new Internet mail technologies, seeks to expand the use of Internet mail in commerce and entertainment, and encourages development of the global mass market for Internet mail. The IMC believes that Internet mail has become an industry requiring a consistent, coherent voice.

The need for such a consortium demonstrates how fragmented the industry has become and how many difficulties remain to be resolved in what is the longest-established and simplest use of both the Internet and corporate networks. Messaging capabilities are critical to a wide range of Internet applications, making it vital that industry players and users develop a common understanding of how to apply the technology. An industry association such as the IMC can help organizations to more quickly gain the required knowledge, while helping to influence technology vendors to reach consensus on standards.

IMC's accomplishments have included influencing the Internet Engineering Task Force (IETF) to develop mail standards, such as the very important MIME standard. MIME (Multimedia

Internet Mail Extension) forms the basis of the interoperability of Internet e-mail systems, allowing communication regardless of the type of computer or software used by sender or receiver. More recently, the IMC has spearheaded initiatives on the vCard and the vCalendar. The vCard is a standardized electronic business card that allows exchange of personal information among various entities such as computers, e-mail applications, or Web browsers. The vCalendar allows correspondents to coordinate their business schedules and other events over the Internet, even if they are using different software applications.

Internet Payment Mechanisms Full-scale electronic commerce on the Internet will require the same range of payment instruments as is available in today's everyday, physical commerce environment. Without the equivalent of coins, small purchases will be too expensive to process. Without security, consumers will remain reluctant to use credit cards for purchases over the Internet.

Despite the flood of efforts to define, pilot, and market Internet payment mechanisms over the past few years, none has moved much beyond the experimental stage and none has, as yet, built a critical mass of consumers, merchants, or financial service providers. The mature electronic commerce market will likely support only a limited number of systems, reducing the potential successes of today's innovations. Firms seeking to establish business connections on the Internet face the problem of predicting who the winners will be and why. Among the current leading contenders with pilot projects and publicity building public name recognition, are Mondex, CyberCash, First Virtual Holdings, and Digicash. Around a dozen other players in the field have less prominent profiles. Figure 10 demonstrates their role in the existing pattern of financial relationships.

The figure simplifies what is in actuality a more complex relationship involving transactional intermediaries and combining manual and electronic processes. Perhaps the Internet has a chance to simplify what should be seamless transactions. Un-

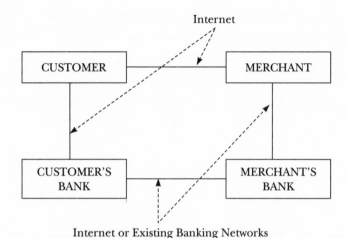

Figure 10   The Internet's Place in Major Financial Relationships
Source: CYBERManagement Inc. ©1996.

doubtedly, the current confusion won't last forever. Three organizations have combined to attack the issue of Internet payments interoperability by providing a forum for collaboration among organizations. This joint alliance, the Electronic Payments Forum (EPF), includes the Financial Services Technology Consortium (FSTC), the Cross Industry Working Team (XIWT), and CommerceNet.

The EPF describes the components of the new world of payments as follows:

> [A] variety of devices, both hardware and software, and digital representations of both paper and plastic instruments that will have to interoperate safely, reliably, and globally. They also include enabling technologies such as payment protocols and public key encryption. A legal and regulatory framework, a reference architecture, and standards for external interfaces must all be defined for this environment.[39]

The world of physical commerce offers a number of payment options: cash, checks, credit cards, traveler's checks, prepaid cards, debit cards, physical tokens, bank notes, secure wire transfers, money orders, letters of credit, and so on. None of these mechanisms is directly transferable to the Internet in unmodified form, however, mainly because each assumes a physical presence or equivalent and a delay in the processing of funds that allows detection of fraud.

The new Internet payment instruments must, of necessity, take other forms.[40] Following are some examples:

- *Digital Cash.* Also referred to as electronic cash, digital cash is a "token-based" currency that is the direct equivalent of real currency units guaranteed by a bank. A trusted authority allows users to conduct and pay for transactions after establishing an identity and relationship. Interoperability standards are not yet in place for digital cash, which remains a protean concept with several forms.

- *Smart Cards.* Smart cards look like credit cards but contain computer chips that can store information, including a value representing money available for transactions. The stored value increases or decreases as deposits and purchases are made. Cardholders can use the Internet or other electronic connections to replenish the card with new money from remote locations. Some cards, rather than store a currency value, contain a private encryption key, a digital signature or electronic token that can be used to initiate an authentication process during a payment transaction, exactly like using a credit card to authorize a payment. A new generation of smart cards, referred to as relationship cards, store considerably more information and link to databases for updates. Useful for multiple applications, a single relationship card, such as the one recently demonstrated by the ImagineCard alliance (Hewlett-Packard/Informix/Gemplus), can accommodate functions such as an electronic purse, conference evaluation, logical and physical access, and registration with full customer accessibility and card-owner controlled authentication. Summarized below are the various types of smart cards and their emerging uses. Reusable smart cards can have either single or multiple functions.

Segmentation of Smart Cards

Consumables (Use once, throw away)	Reusables (Use, reload, reuse)
• Vending machines	• Identification
• Telephone calls	• Electronic access
• Retailer specific	• Device control
	• Physical access
	• Ticketing
	• Loyalty programs
	• Health records
	• Cash value

Source: CYBERManagement Inc. ©1996

The Mondex smart wallet is one of the leading smart card mechanisms for Internet commerce. Other innovations are:

• *Encrypted Credit Cards.* Various methods have emerged to encrypt Internet credit card transactions, with SET (Secure Electronic Transactions) holding the most promise. Internet transactions require, at a minimum, confidentiality of information, payment integrity, and authenticated identities for both the merchant and the cardholder. Digital signatures may augment the transaction, both to ensure nonrepudiation and to further establish the authenticity of the originator. CyberCash leads this field and is likely to establish itself in the mainstream of Internet commerce.

• *Electronic Checks.* Electronic checks are the equivalent of paper checks, but they are written during onscreen dialogues that result in a payment. Authentication and verification are usually achieved instantaneously using digital signatures and time-stamping controls, CheckFree is the main player here.

- *Internet Financial EDI.* Internet Financial EDI will be used by businesses that were already doing financial EDI via VANs (value-added networks). One of the first large organizations to demonstrate the validity of this method and fully embrace it was the Lawrence Livermore National Laboratories, in cooperation with Bank of America. Lawrence Livermore is reported to have processed $300 million in 1996 using this method. Chase Manhattan Bank and Diamond Shamrock have also engaged in large financial EDI transactions via the Internet.

All of the above possibilities (except financial EDI) dictate several systems and implementation methods not universally supported. Each is trying to secure a beachhead or to carve its own niche, without regard for interoperability with other instruments. Several of these systems have their own proprietary application program interfaces to allow integration with the merchant and banking systems. Acknowledging that this new era of electronic payments needs some order, the U.S. Treasury formed a task force in 1997 to study and guide the government in supporting and regulating the electronic money revolution. This task force also seeks the participation of other industrialized nations, since these changes affect the financial industry across borders.

Many obvious and not yet obvious criteria exist for choosing Internet instruments. Organizations need to view the payments issue as an infrastructure module of electronic commerce, not as an add-on, and they must offer their customers several alternatives. Understanding the inner workings of each of today's existing payment instruments is unimportant. It is important, however, to understand the implementation requirements and costs of any payment mechanism under consideration for integration into a firm's electronic storefront or back office.

Managers facing the choice of an Internet payment mechanism should consider the following questions:

- Will the system need to handle microtransactions (small purchases of a few cents or even a fraction of a cent)?

- Is a real-time cash, a debit, or a credit option best?

- Who will process the financial charges? The firm itself or, for a fee, a third party?

- Which is preferable? A smart card system or a token-based, software-only set-up?

- Should any smart card used be simply a digital signature enabler (for credit or debit) or should it store real cash value?

- Should the system require preregistration from sellers and buyers?

- Should the system charge fees to the buyer, seller, or transaction processor?

- Is the firm comfortable enough with financial EDI transactions to move on to Internet financial EDI?

Among current vendors of payment systems are NetChex, NetBill, NetCash, CheckFree, CyberCash, DigiCash, First Virtual Holdings, Mondex, Europay, VeriFone, Millicent, PayWord, MicroMint, KLEline, GCTech, and Blue Money.

Today, most Internet payment mechanisms require a prior arrangement with an issuing entity and participation is limited to an established pool of banks or financial institutions. In the near future, more interoperability will prevail, with organizations such as CheckFree incorporating CyberCash in its CheckFree Wallet or the establishment of joint standards, such as Visa and Master-Card's SET. But the field is only beginning to develop, and a specific storefront should avoid being limited to a particular cash or encryption solution that may serve only a segment of its potential customers or to a list of only a few potential financial partners. A standard is reached when a critical mass of users is online and committed to using a specific mechanism. For back-end transactions, emerging practices may well rely on extending the existing financial networks.

Internet Protocol (IP) Address The IP (Internet Protocol) address is the four-part numeric address for any device connected to the Internet, used for purposes of directing information to and from that device. The main benefit of IP is that it turns physically dissimilar networks into a single, apparently homogeneous network. Called internetworking, the resulting "meta-network" is called an Internet. An IP address is usually written as four decimal numbers, separated by dots, for example, 129.41.23.38.

The number of possible permutations of IP address numbers is close to a billion, thus allowing every device on the Internet to have its unique code number. Some numbers are fixed to denote a permanent connection to the Internet, while other numbers are assigned dynamically, indicating that they are assigned only for the current connection and are likely to change for the next connection. The Domain Name System translates the IP address into a unique domain name. The billion permutations available are not considered sufficient for the Net's expected growth over the coming years; and because of inefficiency in allocating addresses, many are, in effect, wasted. By late 1998, the next generation of IP, called IPng, will be deployed, with the capacity to accommodate a trillion Internet addresses.

See also **Domain Name;** and **Domain Name System.**

Internet Service Provider (ISP) An Internet Service Provider, or ISP, specializes in providing end-users and businesses with network access to the Internet. Before connecting to the Internet, users must first establish an account with an Internet Service Provider (ISP), which offers various speeds and costs suitable to various budget and bandwidth requirements. At the low-end, for example, home users or small businesses can connect at 28,800 bits per second, or bps, roughly a page of printed text per second, using a modem connection. At the mid-range, businesses or homes can connect using an ISDN connection that ranges in speed from 64,000 bps to 256,000 bps. Finally, at the high-end, speeds of 1.5 million bps, called T1, or 45 million bps (T3) are available. Large traffic sites with millions of daily hits may have multiple T3 lines connected simultaneously to multiple Web servers. If you imagine the Internet as a series of interconnected highways, each with several on- and off-ramps, ISPs function to direct users to the on-ramps. Some ISPs resell onramp access available from larger operators of the main highway arteries.

For the home user, an important criterion when choosing an ISP is the geographic distribution of its local access numbers; users should avoid as much as possible having to dial long-distance numbers to connect. Some ISPs have attractive flat-rate, unlimited access rates. Would-be subscribers should check an ISP's history of "up-time" and how often users get a busy signal.

For the business marketplace, ISPs are entering into value-added services, which may include running virtual private (firm-specific) networks, servicing electronic transactions, establishing service-level agreements for corporate customers, and other Internet commerce capabilities.

A few thousand ISPs exist worldwide, whereas none existed only a few years ago. In a recent trend, major telephone companies are becoming ISPs, using their assets of the major traffic paths of the information highway. Some prominent ISPs include UUNET, BBN, PSINet, Netcom, AT&T, MCI, iStar, France Telecom, and Deutsche Telekom.

Internet Society (ISOC) The Internet Society is a nongovernmental international organization for global cooperation and coordination of the Internet and its internetworking technologies and applications. The Society's individual and organizational members are bound together by a common stake in maintaining the viability and global scaling of the Internet to allow businesses and professionals to more effectively collaborate, cooperate, and innovate in their respective fields and areas of interests. It comprises the companies, government agencies, and foundations that have created the Internet and its technologies, as well as innovative new entrepreneurial organizations contributing to maintain that dynamic.

The Internet Society, announced in June 1991 and brought into existence in January 1992, has little real influence other than as a forum for expressing views and reaching consensus.

See also **Internet Engineering Task Force;** and **World Wide Web Consortium.**

Internet Taxes   The subject of Internet taxation is a hot one, due to governments' interests in all parts of the world. The main issue applies to taxing information-based goods and services that are downloadable via the Internet instantaneously. "Physical presence," usually the main factor in determining tax compliance, does not apply to Internet goods and services. A company's Web site can be physically located in a jurisdiction other than their corporate headquarters, raising the question of which tax rate should apply? Further confusion arises if a user living in the United States decides to make an Internet purchase while traveling in France. Which taxes should this purchaser pay—those of France or the United States? Also, can it be proven that the user is in either one of these countries during the purchase? Some countries see flourishing Internet commerce as a tax opportunity and have started to impose new Internet taxes, while other countries are studying the situation carefully, not rushing in with policies that might slow the growth of electronic commerce in their region. It is tempting to apply existing tax rules and systems to the Internet-based goods and services, but these rules and systems will not serve the needs of this marketplace. The United States has sounded the alarm bell on this issue in its "Framework

"With over 6500 state and local sales tax jurisdictions in the US and Canada alone, complying with existing rules is already a major administrative task. And with new technologies and borderless and 'real time' transactions associated with electronic commerce, these tax compliance responsibilities will undoubtedly become even more onerous."[41]

for Global Electronic Commerce" ("no new Internet-taxes"), and the world seems to be listening.

The issue of customs or tariffs is an easier one to tackle. The worldwide trend has been to remove tariff barriers on information technology-related products. In November 1996, the World Trade Organization adopted a Ministerial Declaration on Trade in Information Technology Products (ITA) that commits the European Union and 13 other countries, who comprise over 80 percent of the world trade in information technology, to immediately begin to eliminate all tariffs on these products, with a goal of total elimination by the year 2000. Internet trade tariffs should follow the same trend.

An important part of resolving the issue of taxing Internet commerce is to maintain universal tax policies. Anything else will confuse buyers and sellers, will become impossible to manage, and will lead to a low degree of overall tax compliance. For a small taste of this potential global anarchy, consider that as of 1997, about half of the states in the United States were imposing a sales tax on soft goods downloaded via the Internet, and the other half was not. If this situation is played out globally, the negative effects of such differences on Internet world trade are apparent. Governments also need to focus on growing global commerce that originates from within their own countries. As companies increase their revenues from these new sales avenues, governments can reap the benefits of collecting further corporate taxes. The tax issue can be addressed by answering these five questions about the Internet environment: 1) what gets taxed? 2) what doesn't get taxed? 3) who taxes? 4) who gets taxed? and 5) how are taxes levied?

Internet Telephony   Aside from the obvious fact that users talk into a PC instead of a handset, Internet telephony differs from standard telephones in two important ways. First, rather than using the telecommunications network provided by a long-distance telephone company, Internet phones use the network or combination of networks that constitute the user's Internet connection. Second, the transmission consists of digital data that describes a voice, rather than transmitting an analog signal that electronically reproduces a sound wave.

To make a Web phone call to your friend Jim, involves, first, launching your Web phone program and then dialing Jim's PC, either by entering Jim's IP or e-mail address or by browsing a server maintained by the Web phone vendor and selecting Jim's address from there. If Jim is logged on with the same Web phone software you are (no agreed-upon set of Web phone standards exists as yet), his Web phone rings. Jim completes the connection when he "picks up the phone" by clicking an icon. As you talk, your voice is digitized and converted into packets of data by the Web phone software, which sends those bits onto the Net via your modem or ISDN connection. With most Web phones, you have to speak loudly, clearly, and consistently, or the digitizing process fails and you may get dropouts, irritating audio gaps in the conversation.

Although digitized sound can theoretically match or exceed the fidelity of analog sound (think of CDs vs. LPs), it doesn't do so in a Web phone application yet, because of limitations on the amount of data that can be pumped across the Internet. To achieve telephone-quality sound would require about three times the amount of data "bits" per second that the standard modem can transmit. To compensate, all Web phones use some sort of audio compression software, called a codec (for compression/decompression), which is also responsible for both encoding (converting the analog sound information received by the microphone into digital form) and decoding (converting the encoded sound back into analog form and sending it to the sound board in the target PC). Codecs come in all shapes and sizes, and the best one for you is entirely dependent on your connection and your software and how you plan to use it. A European codec standard for cellular phones, called Global Standard for Mobile Communications (GSM), for example, is the most popular compression scheme. An ISDN link can provide telephone-like quality if the Web phone software is up to the task, but because of line noise and other factors, it is unlikely that a pure connection will be established on a given PC, through the Internet, to another PC.

Your digitized voice may have to traverse a number of servers before it reaches the other party, so you can expect voice transmission delays ranging from a fraction of a second to several seconds, depending on which Web phone you're using. Since there is no echo, the effect isn't quite as annoying as a bad long-distance connection, but it is hardly conducive to warm and chatty conversation.

Finally, another factor is the PC sound card. Most of them are half-duplex, which means that only one person at a time can talk via a Web phone—you're either sending or receiving, almost like CB radio in the old days. A few vendors are beginning to offer full-duplex sound cards that enable simultaneous two-way conversations.

Recently, telephone companies have become more serious about Internet telephony and are embracing it as opposed to seeing it as a threat. Lucent Technologies, for example, is marketing a special switching device that allows local telephone exchanges to connect to the Internet infrastructure, which takes care of carrying the voice signal. This enables a customer with an ordinary phone or fax machine to place or receive calls over the Internet or other data network without really knowing it. According to Lucent Technologies, with this technology's "hop-on/hop-off" capability, a call from New Jersey to San Francisco works like this: A call originating from a standard phone is routed over the public network to the caller's local central office in New Jersey (incurring only a local charge, if any). From there it's handed off to an Internet Telephony Server in New Jersey. The server then sends the call over the Internet (or another data network) to the server in San Francisco, which routes the call to its destination, once again over the local public network and to a standard phone.

Already, Internet telephony is having a profound impact on the telephone industry, despite its limited use and largely primitive quality. *The Economist* magazine calls this the Death of Distance. Phone companies charge by distance: Users pay more to call Boston from Los Angeles than from New York. Modern telecommunications make this payment structure increasingly anachronistic. The Internet has killed it. The cost of a call is not distance-related, nor should the price be. Thus, in 1996 and 1997, providers such as Sprint and AT&T started offering a fixed price per minute, at first charging 20 cents and later going as low as 6 cents.

Intranet Intranets are networks built on Internet-based technology that limit access to people within the originating organization and that may or may not link to the external Internet. They use the Net's core telecommunications protocol, TCP/IP, which supports links among all types of computers; Web sites, protected by firewalls (hardware and software that stands between the Web site's server computer and the Internet connection) from access by outsiders; and Web browsers, such as Netscape Navigator and Microsoft Explorer, for access to and display of information. Intranet Web sites can be linked to the firm's departmental local area networks (LANs) and its long-distance wide area networks (WANs).

This combination of tools enables companies to develop applications that previously were either infeasible or too expensive to be practical. Intranets provide a pragmatic if at times inefficient solution to long-standing problems in the information systems field. Even though the Internet evolved completely outside the mainstream of business technology and predates personal computers and even though its developers were little interested in or even opposed to commercial uses of the Net, the Internet has nonetheless rapidly become one of the key new tools for corporate computing. The reasons for this have to do with the intranet's basic toolchest: TCP/IP, hypertext, and browsers. TCP/IP, offer-

Vicky Pafk, director of systems development at Talent Tree Staffing Services, a temporary staffing service in Houston, comments on intranets. "Sustaining a Web site takes a lot of time and effort. . . . Users might not be aware of how much." When a group in Talent Tree got permission to establish an internal Web page Pafk says, "they were real gung-ho—at first. But after just three months, they lost interest." She says in the future she will emphasize that "content owners" need to maintain the same level of motivation and resources to "sustain what they start."[42]

ing data communications via computer rather than by voice over telephone lines, evolved as an extension of computers, with each major vendor (IBM, Digital Equipment, Apple, and so on) developing its own proprietary protocols. Bandwidth, the main measure of information carrying capacity on a telecommunications link, was limited and expensive, so these various protocols were designed for efficient use of this scarce and slow resource. Security and error-checking added to the systems' complexity and relative slowness. Local area networks, however, were not so constrained; over short distances, bandwidth is basically free. LANs used different protocols than did WANs. International public data networks, provided by national phone service monopolies, had their own protocols. As a result, by the early 1990s, businesses had a plethora of protocols in use. The computer systems that used them required special-purpose devices (called routers, gateways, and smart hubs) to link to networks and computers using other protocols. TCP/IP evolved along a very different path. Its developers made very inefficient use of bandwidth, ignored error-checking and security, and focused on how to link any computer to any computer. Today, bandwidth is plentiful; the low cost of hardware makes it simple to add security; and telecommunications transmission quality has improved so much that error-checking as messages move across the network is not required. In this new context, TCP/IP has become, literally, a liberation. It still has limitations: It is not practical for high-volume online transactions requiring precise synchronization, such as airline reservations, for instance. But TCP/IP makes it simple to define new networks of users and to link them together.

Hypertext linkage among personal computers is a trivial technology in comparison with the major payoff from intranets: faking data integration. Data integration means that information in previously separate databases can be cross-linked and cross-referenced so that it looks to the user as if it's a single database. Integration is a horrendously difficult task, due to many technical, organizational, semantic, and political factors. In the 1980s, several banks each spent $50 to $100 million trying—and failing—to build an integrated customer relationship database. Hypertext doesn't solve the problem of large-scale data integration, but it finesses it. Items of data defined as Web pages can be cross-linked. Human resource departments have rapidly taken advantage of this to pull together information on, say, benefits, job openings, employee records, and training programs. Merck, one of the world's largest pharmaceutical firms, used this simple new trick of the software trade to combine all of its data on clinical trials of new drugs, even though the various databases involved were built on entirely different hardware, software, and telecommunication systems around the world and despite studies that had concluded that such integration was totally impractical; the time needed had been estimated in years and the costs in the range of $100 million. Using hypertext, Merck took only a few months and no capital budget to produce an integrated database. TCP/IP moved the data, and the World Wide Web hypertext created links to access and combine it.

The Netscape browser displayed Merck's clinical trials data *with no user training required.* From an organizational viewpoint, this is perhaps the single most valuable feature of Net browsers. For decades, the software industry has made "user-friendly" software a goal, hype, and claim, but in most instances the term meant something just a little less user-hostile than last year's offering. Browsers such as Netscape Navigator, Microsoft Explorer, and America OnLine's software really are easy to use, so easy that not only don't they require expensive training but they offer a simple and single access tool for a vast range of information and services. Together, TCP/IP, hypertext, and browsers have liberated business use of information technology, creating an intranet revolution that in many ways has had more impact on business than has the Internet itself.

The continuing evolution of intranet technology falls in two main areas. First, developers are looking for new ways to enhance the gathering, sharing, locating, processing, and publishing of information. This will include applications such as knowledge sharing, full-text retrieval, directories, online catalogs, and audio-visual broadcasting. Second, features encouraging and enabling new methods of collaboration, communication, and education for and among people, computers, and entities, including e-mail, discussion forums, and calendaring and scheduling will constitute an important avenue for intranet growth.

IP Address See **Internet Protocol Address.**

IPng Internet Protocol-next generation, abbreviated IPng and pronounced *I-ping*, is a key technical element in the evolution of the Internet. Primarily designed to prevent the Internet from running out of addresses, IPng is an extension of the Internet Protocol, the very foundation of the Internet as a telecommunications transmission system.

IP was a highly pragmatic approach to dealing with the many data communication problems that in the 1970s restricted networks to expensive and slow transmission between a limited number of computer types. Twenty years after its conception, IP is showing its age. It was defined with the simple goal of interconnecting any number of computers, regardless of type and location, to enable them to send and receive flows of digital bits—that is, the Internet was planned as a giant phone system for a million or so computers. Issues of security, reliability, and guaranteed delivery were secondary to just getting the bits through the Net. Now, however, the need is to interconnect the world's *billions* of people and many millions or even hundreds of millions of computers and other devices. When cars, coffeepots, cameras, or digital cellular phones can all be Internet devices, more Internet addresses are needed than IP can provide.

In response to this recent explosion in the number of devices on the Net and the number of types of computer network applications, the Internet Engineering Task Force conceived the next generation of the Internet Protocol, IPng. (The IETF is an informal organization of no legal force that supervises the evolution of the Internet's core technology infrastructures.) IPng, the technical name for which is Ipv6, or IP version 6, is scheduled for implementation in 1998.

IPng will offer much needed enhancements over the current IP (also known as IPv4, or IP version 4), assuring the Internet's growth in size and providing new capabilities critical to its worldwide commercialization. In addition to an expanded addressing scheme, it will add security enhancements (essential for commerce and intra-organizational applications) and features such as multicasting (the ability to direct messages simultaneously to multiple locations without having to send a copy to every address).

The current IPv4 addressing scheme limits the address number of an Internet device to a length of 32 digital bits, which mathematically should allow it to handle more than four billion different addresses (2^{32}). This may appear to be a large enough number to handle the next few years' growth, given that in mid-1997 around forty million devices were connected to the Net. As noted above, however, the addressing IPv4 was wasteful of its numbers, frequently leaving large gaps of unused ones; a large company needing only a few thousand unique IP addresses might automatically tie up about sixteen million. A recent stop-gap solution allowed reassignment of unclaimed addresses, giving the system some breathing room.

How much time does IPv4 have left? With the current addressing schemes, it is estimated that it will probably collapse somewhere between the years 2000 and 2018. The Internet world is, therefore, waiting for IPng, if not with bated breath, then at least with fingers crossed. The transition from IPv4 to IPv6 should be fairly routine, although the very scale of the venture is sure to result in glitches somewhere. IPng is designed to provide a natural evolution from IPv4 and can be installed as a normal software upgrade in Internet devices. It is "interoperable" with IPv4 and can coexist with it for many years. It is also designed to run more efficiently on high performance networks while remaining efficient on low speed ones.

With the new addressing capabilities, IPv6 will increase IP addresses from 32 bits to 128 bits, allowing it to support a trillion device connections by 2020. Given that the world's population in 2020 will be eight billion, this will produce a ratio of 125 connections per human. When you count all the telephone systems, toasters, televisions, gas pumps, air conditioning units, vending machines, and other devices likely to be connected to the Internet, 125 connections per person may not be a farfetched number twenty years from now.[43]

See also **Internet Appliance;** and **Transmission Control Protocol/Internet Protocol.**

ISOC   See **Internet Society.**

ISP   See **Internet Service Provider.**

A CIO of a large transportation firm whose staff spent $1 million developing a major corporate application programmed in Java claims that the same application if traditionally developed and deployed on PCs would have cost $7 million.

Java   Java is the first Internet-centered general purpose software development tool. Java was born as a programming language but has since grown into a multipurpose platform that could possibly challenge Microsoft's Windows as the standard vehicle on which to run business programs. It has come further, faster than any other platform in the history of computing. Since its introduction by Sun Microsystems in mid-1995, the Java language has almost turned the information technology world on its head. Java has sparked a true software and hardware revolution with promises ranging from the drastic simplification of programmers' lives to the transformation of telephones into computers to the development of smarter toasters. Java alone has the promise to do what IBM, Netscape, and Apple couldn't—break the Microsoft PC monopoly.

Java was developed as a response to the problems of programming in C++, one of the main languages for online interactive applications. It is intended to be a simple, object-oriented, distributed, interpreted, robust, secure, architecture-neutral, portable, high-performance, multithreaded, dynamic programming language. The advantage of this stripped-down version of the C++ programming language is that it reduces common programming errors. The Java source code is compiled into a format called byte-code, which can then be executed by a Java interpreter. Compiled Java code can run on most computers because Java interpreters exist for most operating systems, including UNIX, Macintosh OS, and Windows. Even Microsoft has stated that it intends to include a Java interpreter in future versions of Windows, which will enable users to execute Java applets directly from the Windows operating system. So, Java is a platform-independent, easy-to-use, object-oriented language. According to a 1997 survey of Fortune 1000 companies performed by Forrester Research, 62 percent already use Java for some development and 42 percent expect Java to play a strategic role in their company within the year.

Sun has created the term "Java Computing" to encapsulate the entire computing paradigm driven by its Java technology. Equally important, Java Computing can be adopted incrementally at far lower cost than older technologies. Owing to its platform independence, Java can build on an established infrastructure, leveraging existing systems such as legacy mainframes and PCs. According to Sun, today, nearly all of the software industry has licensed Java, has committed to using it, or is performing extensive Java evaluations. Forrester Research reports that "by year-end 1997, Java will have been used to create at least 60 percent of Internet Computing applications—an astonishing ramp for any new language."[44]

Many large corporations are now designing large-scale Java applications to serve thousands of users. More than simple applets for enhancing Web pages, these applications are full-fledged, mission-critical processes that adopters believe will change the way business is done in their industries and bring

International Data Corp. estimates that between 300,000 and 400,000 programmers use Java, and that Sun's Java Developer's Kit has been downloaded 350,000 times since its posting in February 1996. Sun claims that more books are available about Java programming—150 and growing—than on C++. About 160 universities offer Java programming classes.

In late 1997, Sun Microsystems brought a suit against Microsoft, accusing it of violating the license agreement for Microsoft's use of Java in its own products. Microsoft is "modifying" Java, which Sun sees as meaning Microsoft wants to develop a form of Java that requires Microsoft software and thus that strengthens Microsoft's effective monopoly. The case demonstrates both how key Java has already become to the entire future of the software and Internet market and how Sun and Microsoft each knows exactly what the other's strategy has to be.

significant competitive advantages. National Semiconductor, for example, is using Java to keep the entire company and its partners up-to-date—online—about the company's latest parts inventory.

Java's platform independence means that software developers can create one version of an application and deploy it on a wide array of systems. This "write once/run anywhere" ability saves companies the problems in and time needed to master many different programming environments and tools, and it frees them from having to port software to multiple platforms. Although it can be used to write stand-alone applications, the concept of applets, or little programs, to be included with standard Web HTML documents and distributed over the Internet, has caught on and led to the development of HotJava, Sun's Java-capable browser. Most browsers today are Java-enabled, that is, capable of interpreting Java features.

Another tenet of the Java strategy is to spread it on noncomputer devices. To do so, Sun is making available three different versions of the Java Development Kit (JDK): a Personal Edition for PCs and network computers, television set-top boxes and telephones; an Embedded Edition for networked printers and appliances such as air conditioners; and a Card Edition, for smart cards. By splitting the JDK into different pieces, programmers have better tools with which to program a wide variety of devices.

Java has its critics, of course, and it faces many teething problems, but it really does seem to be the missing building block in information technology: a development infrastructure for building systems quickly that allows reuse of components and ensures data security.

Micropayments   See **Microtransactions.**

Microsoft ActiveX   ActiveX is a set of software technologies developed by Microsoft as a base on which organizations can build Internet and intranet systems that go beyond simple displays of information on World Wide Web sites. ActiveX constitutes a collection of products and services that can transform a firm's Internet use from a series of Web pages to a comprehensive base for business processes and commerce over the Net. It is central to Microsoft's business strategy, and Microsoft is aggressively trying to establish it as the standard "platform" for Internet developments and to head off the other main contenders, most notably the recently developed programming language called Java and Netscape's software products. Microsoft already "owns the desktop" (the phrase commonly used in the IT trade to describe the dominance of the firm's Windows operating system), and now it is aiming at the Internet.

ActiveX has no direct relevance for business managers, but the choice of a firm's development platform is a major policy issue for its information services planners and managers, affecting skill base, software development productivity, and the long-term evolution, maintenance, and integration of applications. The software tools used to build standard business applications, such as customer billing and financial reporting, cannot handle the multimedia features now essential for Internet Web sites, and a number of new languages have emerged to address that problem. The early tools for building Internet Web pages were specialized and limited. (The main one was HTML, HyperText Markup Language, which is simple to use but does not accommodate the rapidly emerging new multimedia tools nor does it easily crosslink to processing systems, data resources, and non-Internet internal networks.) Application developers using one of the more than one thousand ActiveX components can render any existing PC-based application compatible with the Internet, thus seamlessly blending corporate information systems, standard PC word processing, spreadsheet software, and so on, into the Net.

Microtransactions Microtransactions are very, very small electronic payments. In a world in which more and more intellectual capital resides in the hard drive of personal computers, information proprietors and consumers have a continually increasing need to protect, sell, and buy it. Snippets of information—a photograph for example, or a small piece of software—are economic goods for the Internet, but only if they can be paid for. The question for purveyors is how to efficiently and economically conduct transactions worth just a few cents. If the cost of processing the payment exceeds the value transacted, the economic model has failed.

Daniel Lynch, founder and chairman of CyberCash, claims that microtransactions will be the energy pill for a new world order and that they will radically affect the "soft" goods world of information in the same way that bar coding has changed retail and manufacturing in the hard goods world. Lynch maintains, further, that "microtransactions is bar coding at the financial level."[45] He could be right, but little evidence as yet indicates that microtransactions have a practical near-term future. It is worth keeping in mind, however, that credit cards took a decade to reach critical mass. The business logic in favor of microtransactions is so compelling that they are likely to be the Internet equivalent of credit cards; not in 1998, perhaps, but surely by 2008.

Among merchants currently accepting CyberCash's Cyber-Coins for micropayments for products and services are the following:

- American Sightseeing, Inc., a global tour operator, in payment for low-cost discount coupons.
- BrainTainment Center, specializing in IQ tests, in payment for brain-tuning tests.
- ESPNet Sportszone, in payment for a one-dollar Day Pass, granting access for twenty-four hours to its premium sports news online.
- Game Socket, in payment for its multi-player Internet games.
- Intouch U.S.A., in payment for instant, prepaid cellular service, worldwide long distance, and international

origination long distance, avoiding charges to a regular phone service.

- Lombre Books, publishers of virtual books, in payment for reading material to be placed in a secure environment and immediately downloaded to a PC and read either onscreen or printed out.
- Nordic Entertainment Worldwide, in payment for music of CD quality, available song by song.

Microtransaction infrastructures, users, and uses are not yet widespread, but they are gaining momentum and will likely be ubiquitous within the next ten years.

MIME See **Multipurpose Internet Mail Extensions.**

Mondex Mondex is the proprietary name for a type and brand of smart card used for holding and dispensing cash, developed by a start-up European firm acquired in 1997 by the National Westminster Bank in England. Mondex is based on stored value, a concept initially popularized by prepaid telephone cards. The general principle of a stored value card is that a sum of money value is loaded onto the card and can be drawn on electronically by inserting the card in a reader that deducts an amount from the card to cover purchased goods or services. The recipient of the value later redeems the amount from its issuer. Mondex and similar schemes use extremely sophisticated cryptographic techniques to prevent forgery and fraud. It is conceptually possible that the code of a smart card could be broken and replicated, but this is currently seen as practically impossible.

Stored-value cards have been around for many years, but the Mondex card is a more generic, cross-service money card than were any of the earlier cards; it can interact with a large and diverse number of vendors and individuals, and the money value it stores can be transferred person to person, using a special device, and even over the phone. These capabilities allow Mondex to

"For someone used to credit-card transactions or even debit-card transactions, using Mondex is unbelievably fast. I bought about [$40] worth of stuff. The clerk puts the card in the reader and that's it; the transaction is over. You begin to focus on the speed with which the clerk can put your goods in the bag. Clerks can't bag fast enough to keep up with Mondex. I guess

it's because everything is on the card; the till doesn't need to go anywhere else to get the data."[46]

bypass both the banking and the taxation systems, raising business and regulatory concerns. Mondex was intended, however, to handle mainly low-value transactions unsuitable for credit card or even debit-card transactions. Mondex might be considered as electronic pocket change.

Mondex has potential applications on the Internet and in other electronic media, where value must be transferred electronically. With a home card reader and an established procedure, a Mondex card could become the basic exchange mechanism for Internet purchases. The several international trials of Mondex, however, have had only inconclusive results.

Multipurpose Internet Mail Extensions (MIME)   The Multipurpose Internet Mail Extensions standard is a specification for formatting messages so that they can be successfully sent over the Internet and received in good form at the other end. Used for electronic mail applications, it enables many different e-mail software systems to interoperate seamlessly with each other.

See also **E-Mail; Internet Mail Consortium.**

NC   See **Network Computer.**

Netcasting   See **Web Casting.**

Network Appliance   See **Network Computer.**

Opinions on the viability and likely impacts of the network computer range from "Yeah!!!" to "Never!!!" So it's a definite maybe, perhaps. If it's a yeah, the NC will change the direction of IT as profoundly as the

Network Computer (NC)   The term *network computer,* or NC, was first coined in 1995 by Larry Allison, chairman of Oracle Corporation, who envisioned a "thin" PC aware for its operation only of the network of which it was part and independent of a hard drive or Windows operating system. Soon after, Oracle received overwhelming support for this concept from Sun, IBM, Apple, and many other hardware, software, and consumer electronic firms. Whether the concept makes sense or not is still debated, as the first few full-production units became available only in mid-1997. IT professionals often take very strong positions for or against the NC.

Following the NC approach, the mainstream of Internet and corporate users can become less dependent on Microsoft Windows, but become rather more dependent on the Web as an operating system. NCs will run applications written for and residing on the network, mostly in the form of applets that are downloaded to do a job and then returned to the network. Most NCs are based on the NC Reference Profile, which consists of a set of open standards and guidelines. A number of different types of network computers will be developed, some priced as low as $500, but others as high as a few thousand. Microsoft and Intel plan to introduce their own version, more like a "light" PC, called NetPC.

See also **Internet Appliance.**

PC did, with Microsoft Windows relegated to the same status now held by IBM mainframes. (But note: The death of the mainframe pronounced so frequently in the press never happened.) Whatever happens with the network computer, PCs are here to stay. But let's hear a quiet "Yeah!"

Newbie Newbie is a semi-affectionate term used for a new Internet user, a new Web site, or a new, highlighted feature on a Web site. In the rapidly growing Internet world, be prepared to encounter a lot of newbies.

PGP See **Pretty Good Privacy.**

PKI See **Public-Key Infrastructure.**

Plug-In The term *plug-in* refers to a hardware or software component or another product that adds specific features and services to a PC or application. In the world of open systems—that is, nonproprietary or nonvendor specific—functionality can be added by merely "plugging" a new element into a main module. A number of plug-ins on the Netscape browser, for example, allow third parties to extend or enhance its features, mostly multimedia capabilities. For the user, plug-ins are almost indistinguishable from baseline features.

Pointcasting See **Push Technology.**

Pretty Good Privacy (PGP) Pretty Good Privacy is a method for encrypting data that allows Internet communication with minimal fear of privacy violations by hackers. (In theory, PGP can be cracked; it is pretty good, but it doesn't claim to be APP—absolutely perfect privacy.) PGP and other methods like it are beginning to be used for transmitting data to protect transactions from being stolen, impersonated, or tampered with. PGP allows fairly secure transmission of credit card information online, for example. While the technique is still in its infancy on the Web, it is rapidly becoming an important issue of online commerce.

PGP was developed by Philip Zimmerman. Zimmerman has been a pioneer of cryptographic theory and practice and an active opponent of the United States government's efforts to restrict information on and export of "strong" cryptography. PGP has become one of the most widespread means of protecting Internet messages because it is effective, easy to use, and free. PGP is based on the public-key method, which uses two keys, one a public key disseminated to anyone from whom the holder wants to receive a message and the other a private key known only to the holder and used to decrypt messages received. A simple message, for example, such as "Hello John. This is Tracy. Please call me tomorrow at 10," encrypted using John's public key, becomes gibberish on the lines of "eGr4#galP_r5flV4%1ghaU19Ld$lam=Cxk$q4y-Wv*mm" until it is received and decrypted by John, using his private key.

PGP users must exchange keys and establish trust in each other. This informal "web of trust" works well for small workgroups but can become unmanageable for large numbers of users. PGP is a very effective encryption tool. The U.S. government actually initiated a lawsuit against Zimmerman for making it available in the public domain and hence for making it possible for enemies of the United States or terrorists to use it. After public outrage and debate, the lawsuit was dropped, but PGP is still illegal in several other countries. It really is pretty good.

Proxy Server   A proxy server is a hardware device that duplicates features of a central server. Its main reason for existence is to speed up Internet access for a large number of intranet users. Typically, a corporate intranet would include a number of proxy servers strategically located in various physical locations in proximity to groups of users. To serve its 110,000 employees on a worldwide basis, for example, Hewlett-Packard has about 3,000 proxies, also distributed worldwide, as part of its intranet.

Typically, a proxy server is very powerful computer with lots of memory and disk space that can handle thousands of requests per second. Because of this high level of performance, the delay of requests between a user and a remote server are greatly reduced. Proxy servers can also do caching, storing recently used files on a local disk so they do not need to be transferred across the world for each person requesting them. If a company makes available a new version of a given software needed by three thousand users, for example, caching proxy servers can keep copies locally so that, as it is requested, it can be served to the three thousand potential users from local storage. The users need not know and would not care about this, but their request will be processed much more efficiently.

Public-Key Cryptography   See **Digital Certificates.**

Public-Key Infrastructure (PKI)   The term *public key infrastructure* (or PKI) refers to the coordination and protection of the "keys" that encode and decode messages to ensure security and privacy. It is commonly agreed that a full deployment of successful Internet-driven electronic commerce will not be possible without an effective, reliable PKI in place. Public and private keys are needed to properly engage in remote secure transactions, and PKI provides a framework for managing this process that will be especially important for Internet transactions.

A secure and trustworthy PKI requires the following features:

- *Authentication.* Authentication establishes the identity of the parties to a transaction.

- *Privacy.* Internet transactions must be kept private, with only authorized people and systems having access to information, which involves protection during transport on the network and against unauthorized insiders.

- *Nonrepudiation.* Nonrepudiation prevents participants in a transaction from denying that they authorized it.

- *Transaction integrity.* Transaction integrity ensures that transactions are not tampered with. This aspect is intended to avoid a situation in which a buyer receives two hundred pounds of chocolate after ordering only two.

- *Nonrefutability.* Nonrefutability ensures the possibility of verifying the transaction by providing a digital receipt or similar proof of payment.

- *Time-stamping.* Time-stamping is especially important where transactions involve bids or proposals with competing bidders or submission deadlines.

These six requirements represent technical goals. In terms of business goals, they could be expressed as confidence, trust, efficiency, effectiveness, and cost containment.

Public-key management is an important (but cumbersome) factor in the growth of digitally secure transaction environments.[47] In a multi-user environment, distribution and management of secure keys becomes very complex. Public-key cryptography was developed to address this issue in relation to digital certificates, which, in effect, provide electronic notarization of a user and his or her public key. Certificates, issued by trusted Certification Authorities (CAs), can be revoked by them if they are mismanaged. The challenge for business today is to use and support this concept widely.

A second challenge is educational: Businesses are not yet

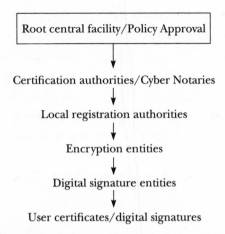

Figure 11 PKI Hierarchical Structure
Source: CYBERManagement Inc. ©1997.

accustomed to the certification process and its management requirements. Possibly, better education will lead to better adoption, but equally possibly, businesses may be awaiting simpler solutions with transparent processes, invisible to users, for generating and distributing keys.[48] Figure 11 shows how a public-key infrastructure might be organized.

An effective PKI would require authorities at each of the various levels of guarantee involved—user certificates, digital signatures, encryption, and registration—all linked to a root facility, probably a government agency, which would have information about all the other entities. This infrastructure, however, far from being ready for the large number of transactions expected when electronic commerce takes off, is nearly nonexistent.

New players are needed for each of the levels, and new roles are emerging for established authorities that can set up secure environments for buyers and sellers to use to meet one another and conduct business safely. PKI represents a business opportunity: Organizations collect fees for generating certificates and maintaining public keys. Some of the businesses that are now beginning to fill this role include banks, postal agencies, licensing agencies, large corporations, financial processing brokers, tele-communications companies, cable companies, universities, large retailers, and publishers. As applications for public-key cryptography increase, a specialty field will emerge to handle—and collect the fees for—these services. But because these service providers are not yet in place, the next phase of public-key cryptography will likely see the emergence of a number of competing management schemes and CAs.

See also **Certification Authority; Digital Certificate;** and **Digital Signatures.**

Push Technology   Push technology feeds information to users automatically, without their having to pull it down from the Internet. Currently, most people access Internet content by browsing, in effect "pulling" from the Net the information they desire. With push technology, the Web server doesn't wait for users to request a page: The user signs up for a specific content segment, which is then delivered—"pushed"—automatically to the user's PC whenever requested.

A number of "push providers" are emerging, offering information delivery that is similar to a television or radio broadcast, to which viewers or listeners subscribe or tune in on a specific channel. The Web model offers even more powerful features than does the traditional broadcast model. Web push technology users can select any number of channels from which to receive content, and they can "fine-tune" them to provide exactly the segments they want to receive on the schedule and at the frequency with which they want to receive them. Furthermore, the user can automatically store the pushed content for later review—like having an unlimited video tape always available in the VCR. Some prefer to label push technology as "programmed pull." Either way, companies conducting commerce on the Internet should think of various push strategies as a new way to augment the frequency and quality of customer interactions. When devising a push strategy, it is important to remember that perhaps only a given percentage of information may be suited to the push method, so knowing what to push and what not to push is critical. Pushed information can also lead an individual to purchase a product or service, but in broad terms could be equated to sending "junk-mail" unless it is sent to pre-registered users. Push technology can be used in delivering personalized news and information, one-to-one marketing efforts, and customer support-related applications. An overwhelming array of vendors and technologies has rapidly emerged since early 1997. Some of these include: Marimba's Castanet, BackWeb, PointCast Network, Lanacom Head-Liner, and NETdelivery, to name a few. Push content at its most trivial level means around the world, around the clock sports scores. At a more sophisticated level, it can offer a complex system providing news, information, and alerts.

See also **Web Casting.**

RSA RSA Data Security, Inc., is a company in the cryptography business the name of which has become almost synonymous with the product. RSA claims to have more than seventy-five million copies of its encryption and authentication software installed and in use worldwide. RSA technologies are part of existing and proposed standards for the Internet and World Wide Web, through which they are gaining even more popularity and widespread usage. The initials RSA stand for the three inventors of the RSA public-key cryptosystem; Rivest, Shamir, and Adelman, the mathematicians who created the industry.

Secure Electronic Transaction (SET) The SET protocol provides the full set of message formats and security procedures required for Internet-based transactions among consumers, merchants, and banks, including authentication and assurance of the integrity and privacy of the payment information transmitted. Jointly spearheaded by Visa and MasterCard, SET is intended to solve the problem of consumers' continuing reluctance to use their credit cards on the Internet to purchase goods and services spontaneously from previously unknown providers.

Credit card companies, early on in the Internet revolution, shared and exacerbated consumers' fears about security and liability. Visa, for example, in the days before SET, made the following explicit statement on its Web site:

> PLEASE NOTE: Until now there has been no readily available, secure way to prevent fraud or theft when giving out a Visa card number or other sensitive information over an open network, such as the Internet. For this reason, we strongly encourage consumers, merchants, and financial institutions to avoid using Visa card accounts over open networks until there is a secure transaction system in place.[49]

The first end-to-end credit-card purchase using the Secure Electronic Transaction (SET) protocol was a thriller. In December 1996, under a pilot program, Carl Christian Aegidius, IBM's Nordic Director, purchased the Stephen King novel Rose Madder, *a story about a woman on the run from her husband.*

Translated from cautious officialese to plain language, this statement reads "Don't even think about using your credit card over the Internet—when *we're* ready, we'll let you know."

Today, the SET protocol is being incorporated into several payment options, including digital cash, smart cards, credit cards, debit cards, electronic checks, and more, and Visa now lets consumers know that using a credit card on the Internet is safe. A number of technology vendors offer SET tool-kits that allow companies to incorporate the SET protocol into their own applications.

Visa and MasterCard have jointly issued a statement describing SET's goals and parameters:

> SET is a payment protocol designed to protect consumers' bankcard information when they choose to use bankcards to pay for goods and services on the Internet and other open networks. SET does not go beyond that scope or explore areas that are being addressed by the computer industry; specifically, it does not define the shopping or ordering process; it does not

define payment method selection such as credit card, check or mail device or operating system.[50]

For consumer shopping, SET works like this:

1. The cardholder fills out a registration form online on the PC screen, responding to requests for basic information such as name, card account number, card expiration date, billing address, and whatever is deemed necessary for authenticating the respondent's identity. Once transmitted, this information is encrypted and securely sent to the computers of the card-issuing financial institution. The issuer verifies that the account is valid and then issues an electronic certificate by adding its digital signature to the applicant's. This certificate will henceforth authenticate the consumer's credit card and can be stored on the consumer's PC for future use.

2. Merchants similarly register to participate in secure shopping. They simply fill out basic information, including their merchant ID numbers, on a PC screen. The merchant's bank then issues them a digital certificate for the conduct of electronic commerce.

3. Once consumers have registered and received their digital certificates, they can begin shopping. To verify their identities to customers, merchants present their SET certificates, either by sending a copy to the cardholder by electronic mail or by publishing a copy on the Internet that anyone can easily inspect. After confirming that a merchant has a valid digital certificate, consumers can make their purchases. First, an order is sent electronically to the merchant, who then seeks authorization for the dollar amount of the purchase. After receiving approval, the merchant processes and confirms the order. The whole

transaction can take just a few seconds, and after shipping of the product, whether physically or electronically, the purchase is soon in the purchaser's hands.

Uncertainty remains in the marketplace over how SET will co-exist with current credit card company business practices. These companies have been accused by some industry analysts and merchants as being slow to adjust to the rapid release cycle of Web-based products. "The security was easy," said a source close to the development. "It's the business problems that have proven to be difficult."[51]

Security   Security on the Internet has always been a hot topic, and it only gets hotter. Because the Internet was originally a private network for military and later for educational use, it was not designed as a public network. Its security, therefore, lay in its exclusivity: Only insiders used it. The ethos of research empha-sizes open communication, with a free flow of information and a minimum of controls, "policing," and bureaucracy. Most early Internet designers and users never envisaged its use as a commer-cial medium: Many, in fact, have fervently opposed the growing presence and influence of business on the Net. With business, however, came an imperative need for security, which has become a multifaceted Internet industry in itself.

See also **Certification Authority; Cryptography;** and **Pretty Good Privacy.**

SET   See **Secure Electronic Transaction.**

Simple Mail Transfer Protocol (SMTP)   The Simple Mail Transfer Protocol (SMTP) was designed for reliable and efficient mail transfer and is today the standard protocol used on the In-ternet for this purpose.

See also **Multipurpose Internet Mail Extension.**

SMTP   See **Simple Mail Transfer Protocol.**

TCP/IP   See **Transmission Control Protocol/Internet Protocol.**

Thin Client   *Thin client* is politicized jargon for a device designed as a client for services provided over a network and accessed through or delivered by a server. A thin client is a network computer with minimal storage and a stripped down operating system; a fat client is a personal computer with ever insufficient disk storage, regardless of how high its memory is boosted. The network computer is the main weapon launched by Microsoft's enemies to break its stranglehold over ever widening areas of computing. Microsoft and Intel initially belittled the idea and then accepted it, substituting the term *thin client* for *network PC* to show that, as far as they are concerned, it is still a PC world and Microsoft still controls it.

According to the Gartner Group, the annual cost to large corporations of running a standard PC fat client is approximately $11,900 per "seat."[52] Savings as high as 90 percent of a network access budget have been posited as the likely result of a move from fat-client to thin-client architecture, a savings, that is, of approximately $84 million annually for an enterprise with 10,000 clients.

See also **Internet Appliance;** and **Network Computer.**

Transmission Control Protocol/Internet Protocol (TCP/IP)   Transmission Control Protocol/Internet Protocol, the procedures and formats that create, transmit, and receive messages on the Net, is the Internet's core. TCP/IP allows *any* computer anywhere to talk to any other computer anywhere, even if they are completely dissimilar in hardware, operating system, and applications software. TCP/IP makes the Internet what it is today: a network of networks.

The TCP/IP protocol traces its origins to the Internet's earliest incarnation as a research project funded in 1969 by the United

States DARPA (Defense Advanced Research Projects Agency). In 1975, the project became operational as the ARPANet, and in 1983, the new protocol suite TCP/IP was adopted as a standard that all hosts were then required to use. TCP/IP is the only protocol not in any way specific to a type of computer, operating system, or telecommunications environment.

From its early days, TCP/IP has continued to evolve in trustworthiness and security, to the extent that corporations rely on it for mission-critical applications. Applications running over a TCP/IP network give the illusion that the network is really a single system. TCP/IP makes the network nearly transparent, encouraging many companies to use it on their own networks.

Several recent TCP/IP enhancements contribute to its increasing security, robustness, and ability to manage the ongoing growth in Internet traffic and applications. Some of these initiatives include IP security, IP printing, IP over-cable, next generation IP (IPng), and IP for wireless and mobile devices.

TCP/IP combines IP (Internet Protocol), which establishes unique, four-part numeric addresses for each device connected to the Internet, used for routing information, and TCP (Transmission Control Protocol), the software communication protocol that facilitates network communication over the Internet. The process of connecting various networks that share the TCP/IP protocol is called internetworking.

TCP takes the information to be transmitted and breaks it into pieces. Each piece is numbered, so that receipt can be verified and the data returned to its proper order. After numbering, the information is placed in a TCP envelope, which, in turn, is placed in an IP (Internet Protocol) packet. On the receiving end, the local TCP software collects the TCP envelopes, extracts the information, and organizes it correctly. If data is missing or any other problem arises, TCP automatically asks the sender to retransmit the information.

TCP builds a reliable service on top of IP. But its essential property is that it handles IP addresses in such a way as to give network users the illusion that a simple connection exists between a sender and a recipient of information. Users need not care about how and along what route their data travelled to reach them. A TCP connection functions as a two-way conduit, connecting whatever lies at either end without any effort by either communicating partner.

See also **Internet Protocol Address;** and **IPng.**

TRUSTEe   See **Internet Law.**

Trusted Authority   See **Certification Authority.**

Universal Resource Locator (URL)   URL stands for Universal Resource Locator and refers to a unique resource on any computer connected to the Web, whether the beginning of a Web-site home page, a specific file, a command query, or a secondary page within a site. The format of a URL consists of two main parts, as shown here: *protocoltype://resourcename.*

The protocol may be one of several types. HyperText Transfer Protocol, abbreviated http, is the protocol used by most web browsers most of the time. The File Transfer Protocol, or ftp, is mostly used to transfer files between various computers and from PCs connected via the Internet to other Web servers. Telnet allows access to a remote server from a PC emulating a non PC terminal and is used, mostly by programmers, but almost never by casual users, for direct access to Web server software. The gopher protocol type refers to a predecessor of the Web; gopher pages could have hypertext linkages but not graphics or multimedia. Finally, the protocol type labelled news indicates a newsgroup, which is an online discussion forum focused on a specific interest. The resource name in a URL may be a computer name (as in www.mycompanyname.com), a numeric IP address (as in 34.178.39.56), or a file name (as in www.mycompanyname.com/aboutus.html).

All Web sites have several URLs, with the main URL pointing

to a Web site's home page. A URL is a like a family's telephone number or street address; either one can be used to get in touch with the occupants. Because Web-site URLs can be long and difficult to remember, most browsers provide a bookmark feature that allows users to save the URL of favorite Web sites to which they want to return often.

See also **Internet Protocol Address.**

Virtual Reality Modeling Language (VRML)   Virtual Reality Modeling Language or VRML (pronounced *vermel*), is an industry-wide standard description language for building 3-D scenes, or worlds, on the Internet. With VRML and other software tools, designers can create and view interactive 3-D worlds that are rich with text, images, animation, sound, music, and even video, and which can then be distributed over the Internet. VRML 1.0 supported simple animations, but VRML 2.0 supports complex 3-D animations, simulations, and behaviors.

The goal of VRML is to create the infrastructure and conventions of cyberspace, a multi-user space of many virtual worlds coexisting on the Net, and it is becoming the Web language of choice for modeling and creating 3-D environments. For merchants, these enhancements can be powerful draws and inducements for buyers, bringing the quality of their experience of an image of a product close to that of a physical encounter with the real products. This will become increasingly important for consumers, who will want to be entertained as they shop for products and services.

The current Internet implementation of VRML 2.0 is called Moving Worlds, and more than fifty vendors have taken it for a standard. Moving Worlds maintains VRML's conformance to open standards and leverages Java and JavaScript to create behaviors, motion, and interactions. It also enables unmodified third-party plug-ins, adding useful 3-D capabilities to Web-based database, design, and other real-world applications.

Moving Worlds represents a major step forward in the evolution of the 3-D open standard for the Internet. Support for the proposal came from throughout the Internet community, expressed via Web-based polling booths and mailing lists. To make the benefits of 3-D technology available to all Internet users, Moving Worlds emphasizes practical applicability and relies on standard desktop computing power. Its sophisticated software architecture allows 3-D data sets to be scaleable for viewing on a variety of computer systems, ranging from low-cost Internet PCs to powerful 3-D graphics workstations. VRML can enhance existing browsers by allowing users to enter new virtual worlds, gaining a new level of Internet experience. Ideally, for the user, a transparent transition can be established between the 2-D and 3-D worlds. The Moving World consortium sees the following possibilities for the technology:

- Powerful 3-D enhancements that let users visualize database information in real-time.
- True 3-D graphics derived from complex spreadsheet data.
- Walk-through virtual product showrooms connected to other online shopping services.
- Multiplayer virtual reality games.
- Multimedia chat rooms.
- Photorealistic 3-D models.
- Collaborative design teams with members located at centers around the world.

As one commentator noted, this technology puts "the *space* in cyberspace." The writer goes on to ask, "The world isn't flat, so why should the World Wide Web be?"[53]

W3C See **World Wide Web Consortium.**

Web Advertising As the Internet grows it becomes a more and more attractive medium for advertising. But as shown in following

Table 7 Advertising Expenditures in Various Media (1995)

Advertising Medium	Total U.S. Expenditures (billions of dollars U.S.)
Direct Response—Mail	31.2
Direct Response—Phone (telemarketing)	82.7
Outdoor—Traditional (Billboards)	1.83
Outdoor—Out of home (transit, bus, airport, etc.)	3.00
Print—Magazine	12.5
Print—Newspaper	37.7
Radio	11.1
Television	38.1
Web	0.3

Source: Compiled from data supplied in 1996 by the Direct Marketing Association.

Winston Advertising specializes in promoting high tech companies and grosses $25 million annually. Its revenues from Web advertising grew from zero to $50,000 per month in the first six months it targeted this new market. The agency makes another $50,000 per month creating and maintaining Web sites for its clients. Winston's president believes that the Web affects how his

Table 7, Web advertising expenditures represent a medium in its infancy.

The most popular format for Web advertising is the banner. Banners today come in a number of sizes, but the industry is seeking to standardize by agreeing on a few common sizes in order to streamline the design process. Charges for Web advertising can be assessed in various ways including raw click-through rate, per thousand impressions, per keyword linked, or a flat rate for a given timespan or a given section on the Web.

Following is a glossary of useful Web ad terms, from CyberAtlas, a prominent Web site that compiles Web data from many Internet research firms.

- *Ad Clicks:* The number of times users click on an ad banner.
- *Ad-Click Rate:* Sometimes also called "click-through," the percentage of ad views that result in an ad click; the average click-through rate is about 2 to 3 percent.
- *Ad Views (Impressions):* The number of times an ad banner

is downloaded and presumably seen by visitors. Because of browser caching, this statistic may understate ad impressions if the same ad appears on multiple pages simultaneously. This rate corresponds to net impressions in traditional media. Currently, it is not possible to ascertain whether an ad was actually loaded. Most servers record an ad as served even if it was not.

- *Banner:* An ad on a Web page that is usually "hot-linked" to the advertiser's site.

- *CPM:* Cost per thousand for an ad on a particular site. A Web site that charges $15,000 per banner and guarantees 600,000 impressions has a CPM of $25 ($15,000 divided by 600).

- *Page Views:* Number of times a user requests a page containing a particular ad. This indicates how many times an ad was, potentially, seen, that is, the number of "gross impressions." Page views may overstate ad impressions if users choose to turn off graphics, which is often done to speed browsing.

- *Unique Users:* The number of different individuals who visit a site within a specific time period. To identify unique users, Web sites rely on some form of user registration or identification system.

- *Visits:* A sequence of requests made by one user at one site. If a visitor does not request any new information for a period of time, known as the "time-out" period, the next request by that visitor is considered a new visit.[55]

A recent report in CyberAtlas[56] examined the relative effectiveness of key parameters on the click-through exposure level. Some of its findings were as follows:

- *Animation.* Adding animation to banners boosts response rates by 25 percent.

company does business: "We get more time-to-market pressure. After all, for a banner ad that runs one month, if we can get it up to two days earlier, that's 10 percent more selling time. . . . We want to create forums in which customers can communicate with us and with each other."[54]

- *Cryptic message.* Messages that include the phrase "Click here," unaccompanied by any other text, registered 18 percent higher response rates than the average.

- *Question.* Banners that pose a question, such as "Too many passwords to remember?" elicited a 16 percent higher click-through.

- *Call to action.* Asking prospects to "See us now" improves response rates by 15 percent.

- *Free!* The effectiveness of free offers depends on the quality of the offer. Hardware or software offers raised response levels by 35 percent. Travel offers, on the other hand, produced a 10 percent *lower* transfer rate, while money offers performed 6 percent below average.

- *Colors.* The use of bright colors, such as blue, green, or yellow, enhanced ad performance. Red, white, and black were found less effective.

- *Urgency.* Prospects don't want to be rushed. Ads including phrases such as "Limited time only," "Last week," and so on, generally performed below average.

Organizations that invest in Web advertising need to keep in mind the issues discussed here in order to create truly effective advertising and maximize their results.

Web Browser See **Browser.**

Web Casting Web casting is an emerging method for replicating TV-style broadcasting on the Internet. The Web is a medium with multiple continuous channels, and Web casting allows users to tune into one of them, sit back, and enjoy the multimedia program the channel "pushes" at them. At least a dozen companies offer specialized software that enables a PC to become a "receiver" as opposed to a browser of information.

See also **Push Technology.**

Web Master   One of the many new jobs created by the Web is Web master. Responsibilities of a Web master may include anything from HTML programming to content management to content architecting or to managing other Web masters. The following condensed, but real job descriptions for several levels and types of Web master illustrate the variety of requirements for this increasingly important job.[58] Many other related job titles exist— Internal Web master, Corporate Web master, Assistant Web master, IT Engineer Web master—but here is a sample.

Web master (I). Your responsibility will be to write, design, and keep updated our External and Internal intranet. You will work closely with marketing, engineering, and network administration to keep our Web current, secure, and informational. Ideally you have managed a Web for 2+ years, have an eye for design, and understand technically all Web-related technologies, especially implementing Java applets.

Web master (II). We are in need of a creative, enthusiastic, and energetic Web master to take our site to the next level of professionalism and interactivity, with just the right amount of hype and glitz. The right individual for this position will have a thorough understanding of Netscape Server software, CGI, HTML, Adobe Acrobat, graphics editing tools, and page layout programs. Forays into Java programming and C++ literacy are definite pluses. Experience? Two years, please, though this requirement may be waived for the right combination of education and chemistry. Education? Yes, a BA or BS is a must; BSCC is preferred.

Internal Web master. Business areas will include: Sales, Finance, Operations, Marketing, Communications, Legal, CEIS, Engineering, and other services. Candidate will provide business and technology guidance on target internal Web uses and develop appropriate Web end-user applications. One to two years + Web applications development experience. Familiarity with HTML, Perl, CGI, and other development tools/environments required. Strong end-user support experience required. Pro-

Strangest Internet Job Titles: Web Technical Guru, Cyberdog Engineer, Internet Guru, Cyberjournalist, Web Spinner/Web Weaver, Internet Content Evangelist, Java Beans Engineer, Web Advertising Traffic Cop, Internet Concierge.[57]

cess re-engineering and workflow experience required. Ideally have 3+ years end-user support in re-engineering and workflow analysis desired. Java knowledge and other "t"-oriented tools preferred. Network and Operations familiarity with managing Web sites a plus.

I.T. Engineer II: Web Master. Requires BSCS and 6 to 10 years software development/engineering experience. Must have ability to program in Oracle Pro C, PL/SQL, Triggers, and packages; C and C++; Unix Shell scripting and socket programming; CGI-bin and HTML. Also requires database design and tuning experience. Must be a team player with excellent communications skills. Effective time management skills are essential. Prefer experience with Java programming and Netscape Commerce Server. Familiarity with new WWW security standards and key commercial WWW tools, including: HTTP server management, electronic commerce, text indexing/search, and sockets is helpful. Also prefer software development on Macintosh, Windows, and Windows NT. Develop shared WWW applications with open API's for use by development groups. Develop core Web infrastructure applications and tools in Unix, C, C++, Perl, PL/SQL and Oracle RDBMS. Support the definition of technical architectures in support of WWW applications.

Cisco's Micro Webserver—the first Web server appliance? "For $1,000 and a foot-print equivalent to the book you are holding, you can have a 'plug-and-play' Web server appliance that allows organizations to get an Internet presence quickly and

Web Server   A Web server is the hardware on which a Web site resides. Web servers are really the gateway to any company's presence on the Internet. When a user points to a company's Web site address, this request to visit that site is routed throughout the Internet to the physical location of the company's Web server, a computer whose task it is to fulfill this request. Large companies that generally experience heavy traffic usually have several Web servers that function in parallel, possibly answering millions of hits per day. As the level of sophistication in multiple applications increases, it has become common to use several specialized servers, each focusing on a specific function. For example, one com-

Table 8 Most Frequently Used Web Server Software, August 1997.

	Number of Sites	Frequency of Use
Apache	548,990	42.23%
Microsoft	209,102	16.47%
Netscape	134,752	10.61%
NCSA*	63,338	5.30%

*Free software
Source: Adapted from NetCraft Survey, 1997 (www.netcraft.com)

pany might have a commerce server, a transaction server, a publishing server, an EDI server, and a security access server. Another common strategy to handle heavy traffic is to locate several Web servers around the globe, in close proximity to large groups of users. This increases the responsiveness and speed of interaction for users, since the computing load is distributed not only across several servers, but also across locations. According to NetCraft, a company that regularly checks the status of Web servers being utilized at a variety of sites around the world, the table above indicates the types of software being run on Web servers as of August 1997.

See also **Commerce Server.**

WebTV A WebTV is a device combining the features of a television set with Internet access capabilities; WebTVs are one element in the technology that aims to create Web-TV. Today, a television set is the most widely deployed communications medium, with more than 1.2 billion in use throughout the world. Television has better penetration in poorer countries and low-income homes than does the telephone, making it a target of opportunity for the addition of Internet capabilities. In addition to the installed base advantage it offers, TV doesn't need time to warm-up (as in the PC boot-up), and the Internet connection made need not be done deliberately or even consciously. Many

cost-effectively. It is ready to be installed out-of-the-box within minutes, and is ideally suited for kiosk-types of applications. For example, once you have designed your Web commerce application, you transfer it to the Micro Webserver, and install it as a kiosk in a mall or other public locations. The appliance weighs 2.5 pounds."[59]

reports predict the percentage of penetration expected for TV/Internet appliances in homes. Although the numbers vary, a reasonable estimate for penetration in certain developed countries may be up to about 20 percent of all households by 2002.

Internet capabilities can be added to the TV in three ways: by connecting existing TVs to a set-top box, also known as a cable modem, that will transport the Internet signal using the current cable infrastructure; by connecting TVs to a digital receiver, thus creating a black-box PC that enhances the television as a viewing screen and connects to the Internet using a phone line; and by developing new classes of TVs with built-in television and Internet capabilities that allow users to choose one or the other function. By the year 2000, it is possible that most TVs will be manufactured with a built-in Internet access capability.

WebTV is a complete Internet solution, and early models are inexpensive and user-friendly. Vendors in this area include Sony and Philips Magnavox; each offers a 33.6Kb modem and help in configuring and setting up an Internet account.

See also **Internet Appliance.**

World Wide Web   The World Wide Web is a space within the Internet that employs a standard method of organizing and displaying any type of information—pictures, words, video, and sound—and links that information to any other resource that adheres to Web conventions anywhere on the Internet. It was developed by Tim Berners-Lee, a British scientist working at the Geneva European Particle Physics Laboratory in Switzerland.

The Web is only one of many services that can be found on the Internet. What makes the Web increasingly the most popular Internet community tool is that, unlike other tools on the Internet, its use—including the creation, maintenance, or use of Web pages—requires service and information providers, as well as users, to have minimal computer expertise. This lack of a need for programming skills has liberated information systems. Complex Web sites do need specialized development, but because very simple scripting conventions of the Hypertext Markup Language (HTML)—which anyone familiar with word processing or spreadsheet software can learn—are used to develop and maintain standard Web pages, working on the Web requires minimal computer expertise. Further, the flexibility of the many software tools available for designing sites makes maintenance easy as well—a far cry from the time and specialized skills required when making a change in a computer program written in languages like C++ or COBOL.

Berners-Lee is one of the very few Internet innovators not interested in making money from his work. He is an advocate of the Internet as an open, noncommercial community and social force. He created the Web to make it easy for researchers to share data files. The ease with which individuals could use the Web increased Internet use; hitherto, using the Net required learning some very complex routines and typing in a lot of arcane commands. The innovation—also developed at a scientific research institute—that seemed to increasingly make the Web the equivalent of the Internet for many users was the first browser, Mosaic. Developed by a team at the University of Illinois, Mosaic—after some academic politics and falling out among team members—evolved to become Netscape. It was Netscape that moved the Web out of the research and professional world and into that of the general public. The Web then truly became worldwide.

See also **Hypertext, HyperText Markup Language.**

World Wide Web Consortium (W3C) The W3C was founded in 1994 to develop common technical standards to guide the evolution of the World Wide Web. It is a vendor-neutral, international industry consortium, jointly hosted by the Massachusetts Institute of Technology Laboratory for Computer Science (MIT/LCS) in the United States; the Institut National de Recherche en Informatique et en Automatique (INRIA) in Europe; and the Keio University Shonan Fujisawa Campus in Asia. Initially, the W3C was established in collaboration with CERN (European Center for

Particle Physics), where the Web originated, with support from DARPA (the U.S. government Defense Advanced Research Project Agency) and the European Commission.

The Consortium, currently led by Tim Berners-Lee, director of W3C and creator of the World Wide Web, is funded by its approximately 150 commercial members. W3C works with the global community to produce specifications and reference software that is then made freely available throughout the world. According to the W3 Consortium, its goal is to find common Web specifications so that while the Web goes through its dramatic and rapid evolution, numerous organizations can work independently but cooperatively in their own fields to exploit and build on top of the Web's global information space.

Services provided by the Consortium include a repository of information about the Web for developers and users; reference code implementations to embody and promote standards; and various prototype and sample applications to demonstrate uses of new technology. The three major areas of research and discussion activities are user interface, architecture, and technology and society.

W3C activity signposts the Web's future, indicating, for example, what Internet technologies are likely to be commercialized and pointing the way to as yet undreamed of (at least by the general user) new Web capabilities.

See also **Internet Engineering Task Force; Internet Society.**

Zine Another name for an E-zine, a *zine* is an online electronic magazine usually appearing on the Internet. Every update becomes instantly available to millions of potential readers. E-zines can also be sent via e-mail to subscribers, thus providing delivery direct to their mail boxes, just as printed magazines can be delivered by mail to subscribers' homes and businesses.

See also **E-Zine.**

Notes

Introduction

1. Jim Sterne, *Customer Service on the Internet* (New York: John Wiley and Sons, 1996), 57.
2. Amy Cortez, "Business Week/Harris Poll: A Census in Cyberspace," *Business Week*, 5 May 1997, 84.
3. Mary Meeker and Chris Depuy, *Morgan Stanley: The Internet Report* (New York: Harper Business, 1996), 1–23.
4. Daniel Burstein and David Kline, *Road Warriors: Dreams and Nightmares Along the Information Highway* (New York: Dutton, 1995), 105.
5. CyberAtlas, www.cyberatlas.com.

Business Internet Vignettes

1. Thomas Anderson, "Millipore: Marketing Products to the Global Desktop," in *The Internet Strategy Handbook: Lessons from the New Frontier of Business,* ed. Mary J. Cronin (Boston: Harvard Business School Press, 1996), 133.
2. Ibid., 133.
3. Ibid., 120.
4. Ibid., 134.
5. Ibid., 135.

6. Bill Rusconi, RealTime Press Conference, www.millipore.com, 30 May 1992.

7. Ibid.

8. Steve L. Swenson, "Lockheed Martin: Integrating Information Resources," in *The Internet Strategy Handbook,* 90.

9. Lawrence M. Fisher, "The Wired Enterprise: Here Come the Intranets," *First Quarter* 6, 84–90.

10. Swenson, 110.

11. Elaine Hinsdale, "Lockheed Martin Honored as Top IT Performer," Lockheed Martin Press Release, www.lmco.com, August 8, 1996.

12. Jim Sterne, *Customer Service on the Internet: Building Relationships, Increasing Loyalty and Staying Competitive* (New York: John Wiley and Sons, 1996), 229.

13. Eric Matson, "Two Billion Reasons Cisco's Sold on the Net," *Fast Company,* February/March 1997, 34–36.

14. Sterne, *Customer Service on the Internet,* 245.

15. Ibid., 246.

16. Ibid., 247.

17. Matson, "Two Billion Reasons Cisco's Sold on the Net," 34.

18. Clinton Wilder, "Know How to Make Real Money on the Web? Think business-to-business," *Information Week,* 17 March 1997, 42.

19. Sterne, *Customer Service on the Internet,* 232–237.

20. Matson, "Two Billion Reasons Cisco's Sold on the Net," 34.

21. Clinton Wilder, "Cisco: A Wider World Web Site," *Information Week,* 24 March 1997, 32.

22. "Third Annual Tenagra Award for Internet Marketing Excellence Announced Today," www.cisco.com.

23. Sterne, *Customer Service on the Internet,* 234.

24. Ibid., 238.

25. Ibid., 252.

26. Wilder, "Cisco: A Wider World Web Site," 32

27. Chuck Martin, *The Digital Estate: Strategies for Competing, Surviving and Thriving in an Internetworked World* (New York: McGraw Hill, 1997), 76.

28. "American Airlines AACCESS via the Web Sees Dramatic Increase in Usage During Fare Sale," www.amrcorp.com, 25 February 1996.

29. Magdelena Yesil, *Creating the Virtual Store* (New York: John Wiley and Sons, 1997), 45.

30. Bill Roberts, "Airlines Hope Web Ticketing Will Fly," *Web Week*, 22 July 1996, 23.

31. Yesil, *Creating the Virtual Store*, 45.

32. Ibid., 47.

33. Alain Pinel, Press Release, www.apr.com, 1996.

34. Fisher, "The Wired Enterprise: Here Come the Intranets," 84.

35. Yesil, *Creating the Virtual Store*, 49.

36. Ibid.

37. Ibid., 52.

38. Eugene Marlow, *Web Visions: An Inside Look at Successful Business Strategies on the Net* (New York: Van Nostrand Reinhold, 1997), 45.

39. Ibid., 46.

40. Marlow, *Web Visions*, 50.

41. Yesil, *Creating the Virtual Store*, 137.

42. Ibid.

43. Daniel C. Lynch and Leslie Lundquist, *Digital Money: The New Era of Internet Commerce* (New York: John Wiley and Sons, 1996), 137.

44. *Netguide*, February 1997, 18.

45. Daniel Bubbeo, NetGuide Press Release, www.virtualvin.com, February 1997.

46. Elizabeth Gardiner, *Web Week*, November 1996.

47. Rosalind Resnick and Jim Sterne, *Home Office Computing*, April 1996.

48. Joe Kilsheimer, *Orlando Sentinel*, December 1995.

49. Lynch and Lundquist, *Digital Money*, 135–136.

50. Ibid., 136.

51. Walid Mougayar, *Opening Digital Markets: Advanced Strategies for Internet-based Commerce*, 1st ed. (Toronto: CYBERManagement, 1996), 184.

52. "Amazon.com Announces Financial Results for Second Quarter 1997," www.amazon.com, July 10, 1997.

53. Ibid.

54. Deborah Claymon, "Storming the Amazon," *Hits* 3 (1997), 8.

55. *Information Week*, 3 March 1997, 63.

56. Michael Cranzt, "Amazonian Challenge," *Time*, 14 April 1997, 71.

57. Martin, *The Digital Estate,* 138.
58. Tom Field, "Getting in Touch with Your Inner Web," *CIO Magazine,* 15 January 1997, 42.
59. Ibid., 43.
60. Ibid., 45.
61. Marlow, *Web Visions,* 69.
62. Ibid., 71.
63. Clinton Wilder and Marianne Kolbasuk McGee, "GE—The Net Pays Off," *Information Week,* 27 January 1997, 14.
64. "Suited, shopping and surfing," *The Economist,* 25 January 1997, 59.
65. Marlow, *Web Visions,* 66.
66. Ibid., 64.
67. *HotWired*'s homepage, www.hotwired.com.
68. Marlow, *Web Visions,* 64.
69. Ibid.
70. Ibid., 132.
71. Ibid., 144.
72. Hoover Company Profiles (Austin, Texas: Hoover Inc., 1997).
73. Marlow, *Web Visions,* 193.
74. Ibid., 189
75. Mary J. Cronin, *Global Advantage on the Internet: From Corporate Connectivity to International Competitiveness* (New York: Van Nostrand Reinhold, 1996), 39.
76. William Golden, "Electronic Commerce at Work: Kenny's Bookshop and Art Galleries, Galway, Ireland," in *Ninth International Conference on EDI - IOS,* eds. Paula M. C. Swatman, Joze Gricar, and Jozica Novak (Bled, Slovenia: Zalozba Moderna Organizacija, 1996), 294–301.
77. Ibid., 297.
78. Ibid., 296.
79. Hoover Company Profiles (Austin, Texas: Hoover Inc., 1997).
80. Mary J. Cronin, *Doing More Business on the Internet: How the Electronic Highway Is Transforming American Companies* (New York: Van Nostrand Reinhold, 1995), 78.
81. E. B. Baatz, "Net Results," *CIO Magazine,* 1 February 1997, 77–82.
82. Ibid.

83. Cronin, *Doing More Business on the Internet,* 75–82.

84. Baatz, "Net Results," 79.

85. Ibid.

86. Ibid.

87. Ibid., 80.

88. Ibid.

89. Cronin, *Doing More Business on the Internet,* 195.

90. Ibid., 198.

91. Ibid., 210.

92. Ibid., 203.

93. Ibid.

94. Ibid.

95. "What Is Uncover?" www.uncweb.carl.org.

96. Ibid.

97. Fisher, "The Wired Enterprise," 86.

98. Joanne Huang, "Application Brief," IBM Press Release, 18 February 1997.

99. Ibid.

Glossary of Terms

1. Janis L. Gogan, "The Web's Impact on Selling Techniques: Historical Perspective and Early Observations," *International Journal of Electronic Commerce,* (Winter 1996–1997): 103.

2. "Internet Explorer Gains on Netscape," *Byte,* April 1997, 34.

3. *Rolling Stone,* 1 May 1997, 45.

4. Michael J. Miller, "Desktop Wars Revisited," *PC Magazine,* 6 May 1997, 4.

5. "BXA Issues Encryption Rules: Congress, Courts Threaten Challenge," *ec/edi Insider,* 20 January 1997, 5.

6. CommerceNet Research Note, "Business Applications of Digital Authentication—Nine Business Strategies in Action," 10 February 1997; Note 97-01.

7. Ibid.

8. Walid Mougayar, *Opening Digital Markets: Advanced Strategies for Internet-based Commerce,* 1st ed. (Toronto: CYBERManagement, 1996), 78–79.

8A. Ibid.

9. Gary H. Anthes, "In Web E-Trust," *ComputerWorld,* 18 November 1996, 21.

10. Eugene Marlow, *Web Visions: An Inside Look at Successful Business Strategies on the Net* (New York: Van Nostrand Reinhold, 1997), 68.

11. Ibid., 176.

12. "Leonsis Forecasts Web Winter for Competitors," *Washington Technology* (8 May 1997): 1, 36.

13. *Internet and Java Advisor,* March 1997, 22.

14. Ibid.

15. Magdelena Yesil, *Creating the Virtual Store* (New York: John Wiley and Sons, 1996), 16.

16. Eugene Marlow, *Web Visions: An Inside Look at Successful Business Strategies on the Net* (New York: Van Nostrand Reinhold, 1997), 193.

17. Yesil, *Creating the Virtual Store,* 141.

18. Ibid., 138.

19. Chuck Martin, *The Digital Estate: Strategies for Competing, Surviving and Thriving in an Internetworked World* (New York: McGraw Hill, 1997), 78.

20. *Internet Shoppers,* Spring 1997, 45.

21. Walid Mougayar, *Opening Digital Markets: Battle Plans and Business Strategies for Internet Commerce,* 2nd ed. (New York: McGraw-Hill, 1998).

22. Mougayar, *Opening Digital Markets,* 1st ed., 199.

23. Yesil, *Creating the Virtual Store,* 28.

24. Ibid., 30.

25. Brent Laminack, "S/MIME vs. FTP: Which Is Better for Internet EDI?" *EC World,* April 1997, 4.

26. Yesil, *Creating the Virtual Store,* 141.

27. David Frost, IS Capability Leader at Owens Corning: Toledo, Ohio.

28. *Fortune Magazine,* January 1997, 51.

29. "Insider's Predictions for 1997," *ec/edi Insider,* 7 March 1997, 4.

30. "A Paperless Future," *ec/edi Insider,* 3 February 1997, 6.

31. Kim S. Nash, "Online Legal Issues," *Computer World,* 1 June 1997, 1.

32. "The Hacker Threat," *Fortune Magazine,* 3 February 1997, 70.

33. Ibid., 64.

34. www.andromedia.com

35. Christopher Anderson, "A Survey of the Internet: The Accidental Superhighway," *The Economist,* 1 July 1995.

36. Ira Fuchs, *Chronicle of Higher Education,* 28 March 1997, 5.

37. Nicholas Negroponte, "Where Do New Ideas Come From?" *Wired* March 1996.

38. Debora Spar and Jeffrey J. Bussgang, "Ruling the Net," *Harvard Business Review* 74, no. 3 (1996):125–133.

39. International Engineering Task Force Homepage, www.IEFT.com, 1997.

40. Mougayar, *Opening Digital Markets,* 1st ed., 70.

41. Karl A. Frieden and Michael Porter, The Arthur Andersen Report, The Taxation of Cyberspace.

42. Alice Laplante, "Grow Your Own Intranets," *ComputerWorld,* 17 March 1997, 96.

43. Mougayar, *Opening Digital Markets,* 1st ed., 178.

44. CyberAtlas, www.cyberatlas.com.

45. Daniel C. Lynch and Leslie Lundquist, *Digital Money: The New Era of Internet Commerce* (New York: John Wiley and Sons, 1996), 45.

46. Eric K. Clemons, David C. Cronson, and Bruce W. Weber, "Reengineering money: the Mondex stored value card and beyond," *International Journal of Electronic Commerce,* (Winter 1996–1997): 22.

47. Mougayar, *Opening Digital Markets,* 1st ed., 76.

48. Ibid., 77.

49. VISA Website, www.visa.com.

50. Ibid.

51. Ibid.

52. Gartner Group, "Strategic Planning Research Note SPA–140–22," 26 April 1996.

53. Udo Flohr, "Create and Explore 3-D Web Worlds Within the Virtual Reality Mark-up Language,"*Byte Magazine,* March 1996, 82.

54. Yesil, *Creating the Virtual Store,* 146.

55. CyberAtlas, www.cyberatlas.com.

56. Ibid.

57. Mougayar, *Opening Digital Markets,* 1st ed., 77.

58. Ibid.

59. Walid Mougayar, *Opening Digital Markets: Battle Plans and Business Strategies for Internet Commerce,* 2nd ed. (New York: McGraw-Hill, 1998).

Index

About the Authors

Peter G.W. Keen is the author of seventeen books on the link between information technology and business strategy, an international adviser to top managers, named by *Information Week* as one of the top ten consultants in the world, and a professor who has held positions at leading U.S. and European universities, including Harvard, Stanford, MIT, and Stockholm University. Companies with which Keen has worked on an on-going, long-term basis include British Airways, Citibank, MCI Communications, Sweden Post, Cemex (Mexico), The Royal Bank of Canada, CTC (Chile), Unilever, and many others. All of his work focuses on bridging the worlds, cultures, and language of business and information technology. He is the chairman of Keen Innovations.

Walid Mougayar is president of CYBERManagement Inc., a management education and consulting firm, focused on Internet commerce business models and electronic markets competitive strategies. He is the best-selling author of *Opening Digital Markets: Battle Plans and Business Strategies for Internet Commerce* (1997), in which he explains breakthrough thinking for creating, competing in, and dominating electronic marketplaces. Walid is an internationally recognized consultant, educator, thinker, writer, and speaker on exploiting Internet commerce for business purposes.

He is the creator of a one-day MBA executive seminar on Internet commerce business strategies, and the publisher of *CYBER Review*, a widely read electronic newsletter on business thinking for Internet commerce. Walid is the founding chairman of CommerceNet Canada. Prior to founding CYBERManagement Inc. in 1995, he spent 14 years at Hewlett-Packard in a variety of sales, marketing and consulting management positions, including HP's Internet initiatives. He can be reached at walid@ cyberm.com, or at www.cyberm.com.

Tracy Torregrossa is the research director for Keen Innovations, where she supervises the firm's studies and publications on electronic commerce and analyzes case studies for the effective business use of the Internet and intranets. Ms. Torregrossa has an extensive background in business, academic, and social research. As research associate at the Margaret Chase Smith Center for Public Policy, she authored over 10 public research reports and prepared evidence for the presentation of a class action suit to the Supreme Court of Pennsylvania. Her other projects include an economic study of the historical shift in jobs in the U.S. Virgin Islands and work in the area of ISO 9000/9001 standards.

traffic is imperative to the success of its Web site and that hyperlinks (dynamic pointers among Web pages) help to establish the "right" traffic; the distinguishing feature of the Web is that its users gain access to a wide range of information resources rather than being limited to the information in a single database. The potential for information interaction makes a site a success; Millipore's Web-page design made its customers need and want to use it.[4]

- *The Internet facilitates internal communication.* Easy to use electronic mail and "live chat" capabilities encouraged more pointed and beneficial internal dialogues.[5]

In addition to these benefits, the Internet allowed Millipore to more closely observe its competition. That may, however, be one of the Internet's downsides. Companies can more easily reach out to their customers and provide them with information, but competitors, too, can reach in and grab that same information as well.

Millipore's Internet organization-wide resource developed over seven years from inception to full operation. The following stages and milestones marked this course.

- *1987:* Internet access is made available for internal use in the then prevailing traditional, academic mode: links to university research centers, e-mail, and file transfers.

- *1994:* Millipore builds an early version of a powerful database of all Millipore products, accessible via the Internet. This phase shifts the company's use of the Internet from an academic to an information supply mode.

- *February 1994:* Millipore initiates active Internet marketing, constituting a customer-contact mode.

- *March 1994:* Millipore provides access to its product catalog via the Mosaic browser, forerunner to Netscape's